The Pilot's Guide to
Air Traffic Control

Who's Really in Control...
Real Life ATC Stories

ANDY WATSON

10 9 8 7 6 5 4 3 2 1

Library of Congress Control Number: 2022905306
ISBN (Hardcover): 979-8-9857358-0-2
ISBN (Paperback): 979-8-9857358-1-9
ISBN (eBook): 979-8-9857358-2-6

For

Laura, Emma, James, Ethan, Alex, Lilly, Mom, Dad,

Katie, Eric, Aspen & Colson

CONTENTS

FOREWORD BY JEFF GUZZETTI

Andy Watson is one of those people that you first meet in passing, and then look forward to meeting again and again. When he asked me to write a forward for this book, I was flattered.

As a seasoned air traffic controller and instrument-rated pilot, Andy entered my world when he first attended my daily "Round Up" meetings each morning at the Federal Aviation Administration (FAA) Headquarters in Washington, D.C. As the Director of FAA's Accident Investigation Division, my job was to lead the office that represented the agency in all civil aircraft accident investigations. Our small staff of senior inspectors and accident investigators were the primary liaison to the National Transportation Safety Board (NTSB), and the one-stop-shop for anyone at FAA regarding the agency's role and actions in the aftermath of significant accidents and incidents.

Each morning, my staff would gather all of the reports that came into each of the FAA's Regional Operations Centers during the previous 24-hour period - or 72-hour period on weekends. We would then brief the FAA brass at 7:30 a.m., and then I would host the "Round Up" at 8:30 a.m. The Round Up was open to any FAA employee who wanted situational awareness about all of the aircraft accidents and incidents that occurred the day before. It was an effective method to keep the FAA on point with its primary mission of aviation safety.

Andy worked one floor above me in the Office of Air Traffic Safety Oversight at FAA headquarters, and he never missed a meeting. Having worked in numerous and varied air traffic control facilities, Andy's double-barreled experience as a Certified Professional Controller (CPC) and an instrument-rated pilot always benefited our Round Up discussions.

Andy is genuinely gifted with explaining arcane FAA rules and complex air traffic procedures to the layperson. He does so with great ease and a folksy presentation that sticks with the audience… even if the audience is one. My staff and I quickly learned that Andy added value to any conversations related to aviation safety, especially when it involved potential air traffic control involvement. He was well-versed with the history of accident investigations and the improvements to safety that came from them.

It's no wonder, then, that this book, "The Pilot's Guide to Air Traffic Control," is so rewarding to read. It contains a wealth of easily digestible, fascinating, and informative information. I can't think of another publication for pilots - or aviation enthusiasts of any type - that provides more clear and memorable lessons about how ATC works in our country, and how pilots can become safer by understanding these lessons. This book contains hundreds of unique bits of knowledge and anecdotes and accident trivia – just a tiny portion of what Andy has to offer.

I spent 18 years with the NTSB as an air safety investigator and seven years with the FAA as a safety engineer and manager. I now teach accident investigation at the University of Southern California and other places, and provide consulting for aviation safety. Having said that, I still have so much more to learn about aviation in general, and air traffic control specifically. I think I am a good judge of character and quality when it comes to people who share their knowledge of aviation safety.

In my book, Andy is top shelf. He is truly a safety professional, and you will be a better person after reading this fascinating book.

Jeff Guzzetti
FAA Supervisory Air Safety Investigator (retired)

ACKNOWLEDGMENTS

I started writing this book four years ago, and I kept adding stories along the way. Writing a book takes a lot of time and I couldn't have done it without everybody who supported me along the way, and there have been many!

My wife, Laura, has been one of my biggest supporters. She has worked harder on this book than I have as she has single handedly taken care of our four young children not only during the time I spent on the book, but also while I work full time as a controller. Most of this book has been written during the COVID-19 pandemic, which has severely limited different options. It truly amazes me how she pulls it off. Every day we spend together, she becomes more beautiful. She is the love of my life and best friend.

My kids have given up a lot of time with their Daddy, especially these last few months. They are young and probably won't remember this time later in life, but I will always know. I am excited to finish this project to get my time back with them as they are all growing so quickly.

Emma is in Kindergarten, learning how to read and write. For more than a year, she has loved the Disney "Frozen" movies and decided to grow her hair long to be like the princesses. No matter what, she will always be Daddy's little princess.

James is my little red head. He loves being around and playing with his Daddy. He likes airplanes but he loves big trucks of all kinds with his current favorites being Cement Mixers, Trash Trucks, and "Big Rigs"- which can be many different types depending on the day.

Ethan is our little jester. Out of the blue, he will start giggling loudly for no reason, making everybody in the room start to laugh. He is the one who loves airplanes almost as much as his Daddy, but also loves big trucks like his big brother.

Alex is our youngest who has been walking for several months now. He is a super smiley kid who always seems to be happy, but is able to get his point across very effectively when needed!

My parents have supported me throughout the years for all of my entrepreneurial ventures, and I wouldn't have come as far as I have without them.

My Dad grew up a farmer, and has a great business mind because of it. I remember my Dad encouraging me to think about things from the business owner's point of view ever since I started my first job at fourteen years old at Donatos Pizza. Dad is a "numbers guy" and thus taught me how to think about profit and loss. But most importantly, he taught me how to work hard for whatever I'm after. I've never met anybody that has worked harder than him!

My Mom has always been willing to try anything. I have a saying: "What's the worst that could happen?" I relate that to Mom's can-do attitude. Even though it is simply a statement, it has helped me think critically about scenarios to determine the risk. This mindset has given me the confidence to try many things that I probably would have never attempted.

My sister, Katie, and her husband Eric, have always been supporters and willing to help. Katie has always been good at writing and spent many hours reviewing this book. I can't thank her enough!

My niece, Aspen, is an incredible young woman. She is very smart and builds competition robots. Aspen is also a great athlete - practicing hard and competing with the best. No matter which direction in life she chooses, I know she will excel!

My nephew, Colson, loves airplanes and specifically the "Memphis Belle", a Boeing B-17 "Flying Fortress" that gained fame during World War II, as much as I do. He is also a very smart young man, and has said for several years that he wants to be an air traffic controller. If he does, I'm sure he will do well.

I have several close friends who have helped tremendously throughout the years for both my public speaking and this book. Tom Henery, Troy Pakiz, James Crawley, Matt Berg, Linda Morgan, Chris Declama, Matt Hory and Gary Bartleson have all helped in so many ways!

My business coach, Kevin Hogan, is simply the best! He has provided guidance which had me dig deep and create something so much better than I would have done on my own. He is single-handedly responsible for the idea of interviewing people for their stories and making sure there was enough content for this book. Thank you, Kevin, for your friendship and support.

I first met Christopher Freeze about a year and a half ago. He is a certified flight instructor who, like me, also volunteers with Civil Air Patrol. By trade, he is a professional technical writer and freelance journalist, making him the perfect person to edit this book. His advice on where to add more or to delete portions of the stories were invaluable, and has improved this book significantly.

Also, Laura, Mom, Katie, Chris Declama, and Josh Shields edited and provided notes to me in the final rounds of editing the book. Thank you!

I truly would like to thank everybody I interviewed, as they enhanced the stories meaningfully. They are Steve Collision, Bob Hendrickson, Jay McCombs, Robert Ochs, and Bill Salazar, M.D.

There are several people I want to thank for discussing topics, helping coordinate interviews and giving me ideas to write about: Jeff Guzzetti, Tom Henery, Chris Declama, Eric West, Ken Dech, Scott Gilson, Rodney Watcher, Julia Pounds, Brian White, Rod Ott, Gary Bartelson, Troy Pakiz and Matt Hory.

I would like to thank my flight instructors throughout the years starting with Mark Houser, Troy Pakiz, Matt Hory, Mark Marian and many more!

I would like to thank Kyle Schoeneberg for the idea on how to incorporate my Operating Initials "XI" – two letters assigned to a controller in each ATC facility so they can be identified on landline recordings – into the book. I originally chose these initials as they were both easy to say and write. In true controller fashion, my colleagues at Washington ARTCC refer to me as "Eleven".

Of course, I'd like to thank all of my co-workers who have helped throughout the years.

Getting pictures in the Washington ARTCC took a lot of help to ensure the simulation was setup properly and reflected the correct data blocks. Thank you to Mike Christine, ZDC NATCA President, Scott Davis, Brad Starkey, Chase Denhoff, Adelyn Laing, William Laing, Christine Dole, Jeffrey Johnson and the controller who gave me the idea for using a silhouette on the cover, you know who you are. In addition, thank you to Leslie Swann and Stephanie Faison for approving my requests to take pictures inside the facilities.

I would like to thank Carrie Merlin and her team who helped make videos of the radar with radio replays which I use for seminars.

Thank you to Lisa Baccus, Phillip Edwards and the legal team within the FAA's Chief Council's Office for the expeditious ethics review and to the Air Traffic Organization for the security review.

I'd like to thank my colleagues at Air Traffic Safety Oversight (AOV). They helped me on many fronts including reviewing and providing advice for the Safety Recommendations I submitted.

A special thank you goes to the FAA's Accident Investigation and Prevention (AVP-100) group including Jeff Guzzetti, Scott Hubbard, Pat Hempon, Eric West, Bob Hendrickson, Matt Rigsby, Dave Keenan, Dave Gerlack, Patrick Lusch, Anne Torgerson and Matt Cabak. As I was leaving AOV, they presented me with a Certificate of Appreciation, along with one of their challenge coins - which they normally only give to foreign dignitaries - an honor I still cherish to this day.

In addition, I would like to thank all of the controllers who have taken the time to train me at my various facilities. I have done my best to make you all proud!

There have been many more people throughout the years who have helped me in different ways, thank you!

I would like to thank the National Air Traffic Controller's Association (NATCA), including all of the Reps I've worked with up to the top leadership:

- Rich Santa, President
- Andrew LeBovidge, Executive Vice President
- Brian Shallenberger, Eastern Regional Vice President
- Drew MacQueen, Great Lakes Regional Vice President
- Mike Christine, ZDC Local President
- Brian White, ZOB President

I would like to thank people and groups in the aviation industry who have made a difference:

- Civil Air Patrol
- Aircraft Owners and Pilots Association (AOPA)
- Experimental Aircraft Association, Inc. (EAA)
- John & Martha King of King Schools, Inc.
- Sporty's Pilot Shop
- Tailwinds.com
- The National Museum of the U.S. Air Force
- Smithsonian National Air and Space Museum
- Women in Aviation International
- National Business Aviation Association (NBAA)
- AvWeb
- Aviation Week
- Aero-News.net
- AINOnline.com
- Avgeekery.com
- GeneralAviationNews.com
- Simple Flying
- LiveATC.net
- Air Care Alliance
- Angel Flight
- Pilots N Paws
- Special Olympics Airlift
- King Air Nation
- Citation Jet Pilots
- Cirrus Owners and Pilots Association (COPA)
- Pilatus Owners and Pilots Association

- TBM Owners and Pilots Association
- Piper Owner Society
- American Bonanza Society
- Cessna Pilots Association
- Cessna Owner Organization
- Cessna Flyer Association
- National Association of Flight Instructors
- Boldmethod

I'd like to thank the following YouTube channels:
- Captain Joe
- DutchPilotGirl
- Flight Chops
- Aviation101
- Swayne Martin
- FLY8MA.com Flight Training
- Baron Pilot

In addition, I would like to thank the following Podcasts:
- The Fighter Pilot Podcast
- AvTalk – Aviation Podcast
- Opposing Bases: Air Traffic Talk
- Fast Five from Sporty's – aviation podcast for pilots, by pilots
- Aviation News Talk podcast
- F-14 Tomcast
- Private Pilot Podcast by MzeroA.com
- "There I was…" An Aviation Podcast
- The Afterburn Podcast
- Pilot to Pilot – Aviation Podcast
- The Finer Points – Aviation Podcast
- I Learned About Flying From That
- Flight Safety Detectives
- Airplane Geeks Podcast
- FAR AIM – Aviation Reg's – Aeronautical Info - FARAIM
- Airline Pilot Guy – Aviation Podcast
- The Merge
- Flying Midwest Podcast
- 21.FIVE – Professional Pilots Podcast
- AviatorCast: Flight Training & Aviation Podcast

- The Aerospace Advantage
- 10 Percent True – Tales from the Cockpit
- Lovefly fear of flying
- On the Step with thatmallardguy
- Between Two Wings
- The Low Level Hell Podcast
- Exit Point
- Midlife Pilot Podcast
- Hard Landings
- Cirrus Aircraft Flight Fix
- Fly Cool Shit – An Aviation Podcast About Flying Cool Shit
- Stuck Mic AvCast – An Aviation Podcast About Learning to Fly, Living to Fly, & Loving to Fly
- AIN's Tales from the Flight Deck

Again, thank you all, and keep on flying safe!

Andy Watson
March 2022

INTRODUCTION

When I was seven years old, my parents took my sister and I on a family vacation to Washington D.C. Being from Marysville, Ohio, we flew out of the Port Columbus Airport (KCMH), and I remember being excited and scared as I walked down the jet bridge to board the TWA Boeing 727. I sat in the window seat. As the aircraft started down the runway and rotated, the fear faded away and my excitement grew. As the 727 climbed, I was mesmerized.

Every day while we were on vacation, I asked my parents how much longer before we got to fly again. I was hooked! And, even though most people are not ready for vacation to end, I couldn't wait to get on an airplane again.

As we boarded the Boeing 737 (I can't remember which airline) for our return trip, my parents told the flight attendants about my excitement and I was allowed to visit the flight deck. As we found our assigned seats, I sat in the window seat again - able to see the left wing and engine.

As we were approaching the runway to land at KCMH, my eyes were glued outside. Shortly after we touched down, I saw something. I yelled "MOM, THE ENGINE JUST FELL OFF!" I was so loud the whole aircraft heard me! Everybody started to look out the left side of the aircraft very concerned, as did the flight attendant, who then scrambled to make an announcement to the cabin, saying the engine did not fall off, and everything was fine.

In hindsight, it must have been the reverse-thruster being used to help the plane slow down. Either way, that family vacation sparked a passion inside me that has shaped my life. From that point forward, aviation became my sole focus.

Several months later, my Mom saw an advertisement on the paper placemats at our local Pizza Hut for a 30-minute introductory flight lesson at the Union County Airport (now KMRT) and chose to surprise me with a flight for my 8th birthday. I remember waiting in the airport lobby for the flight instructor and airplane to return from their previous flight. For some reason, I was getting more nervous the longer I waited because it was a small airplane. However, once we started our takeoff roll, the excitement took over and I was no longer scared. My flight in that white Cessna with blue stripes made me want to be a pilot even more.

After graduating high school, I attended the University of North Dakota, majoring in Commercial Aviation and earning my Private Pilot Certificate. But during my sophomore year, several key events happened for me – namely, the terror attacks of 9/11 happened and all of the flying jobs were going away.

I also took a required class for my major called "Introduction to Air Traffic Control." The class was set up using complex simulators to control aircraft in approach airspace and I quite enjoyed it. There, I realized that, as a controller, I would get to go home every night! So I changed majors.

I am very proud of my accomplishments as a controller, and I hope the stories I share in this book reflect that.

Since I became a Certified Professional Controller (CPC) at Cleveland Air Route Traffic Control Center (ARTCC), my career has taken me places I never thought I would have gone. I was a Front-Line Manager at Chicago ARTCC and then became an Air Traffic Safety Inspector at FAA Headquarters for the Office of Air Traffic Safety Oversight. I spent a year in Charleston, South Carolina and I am currently working at Washington ARTCC in Leesburg, Virginia.

I have several great stories about my time at Charleston (CHS) Terminal Radar Approach Control (TRACON) even though we were only there a short time. Only a couple months after I started at CHS, my wife delivered our second child. Then, two weeks later, we had to evacuate from our house due to Hurricane Florence. The typical 11-hour drive back home to Ohio with our 2-year-old, 2-week-old and our yellow Labrador Lilly took almost 26 hours!

Then, a couple months later, we were surprised to find out we were being blessed with another child. That is when we realized we were too far away from our families in Ohio. Switching facilities as a certified controller can be a process that can take 3 or more years since the FAA determines the controller's release date to leave their current facility. Since I was not certified yet, I withdrew from training and took a transfer back to the busy traffic of Washington ARTCC. While in Charleston, I learned a lot about terminal controlling and I know these stories can benefit pilots.

Controllers are trained using live traffic with an On-the-Job Training Instructor (OJTI). The equipment is setup so the OJTI can override the trainee's microphone by simply keying up their own headset, which ensures safety as the OJTI always has full control of the radio. The stories from Charleston TRACON are of when I was working with an OJTI.

There are several stories in this book that include fatal accidents. I tell these stories with a heavy heart, as I am always aware there were actual people involved whose lives were cut short. My hope is the family and friends of the deceased can find comfort that their loved one's story can help others learn to hopefully avoid the same outcome.

There are a few stories where I have changed the locations or aircraft call signs to "protect the innocent." However, the substance of the stories remains the same.

I use abbreviations throughout the book for call signs. Airlines use two letter codes which are used by the pilot side of the industry, but since this is an ATC book, and it is what I know and use on a daily basis, I use the three letter ATC codes (i.e., AAL- American Airlines, DAL- Delta, UAL- United and SWA- Southwest). I also use the ICAO aircraft type designators (i.e., B739 is a Boeing 737-900, A332 is Airbus A330-200, etc.).

The stories in this book are experiences I've had first-hand, been briefed upon, or had discussions with the controllers involved throughout my air traffic career. To ensure accuracy, I have referenced official reports for some chapters but other stories are simply my best recollection. They are accurate to the best of my memory. I sincerely hope you enjoy them all and are able to take away insights that will aid your flying adventures.

PROLOGUE: BASIC DESCRIPTION OF THE ATC SYSTEM

For any readers who are not instrument-rated pilots, or who are curious about some ATC information not described in the stories, below is fundamental information about air traffic control facilities, positions, airspace, and phrases used.

There are three basic forms of air traffic control, which pilots call the tower, approach control, and center. These facilities have technical names, which is how controllers refer to them other than when talking to pilots on frequency.

Air Traffic Control Towers (ATCT) are located at the airports and are positioned so controllers can see the airport surface. They control the taxiways and runways. Essentially, they clear aircraft to taxi from the gate to the runway and clear aircraft to take off or land on the runway. In addition, they control the "traffic pattern," but it all leads to getting a clearance to land on the runway. There are "non-movement areas" which are not controlled, such as the ramp where aircraft park. As of August 2020, there are 264 Federal ATCTs and 256 Federal Contract ATCTs totaling 520 ATCTs.[1]

Approach Controls - FAA facilities are a Terminal Radar Approach Control (TRACON), and military facilities are called Radar Approach Control (RAPCON). Every piece of airspace is different, but in general, they are approximately a 30 nautical mile radius around the main airport and "own" from the ground up to between 8,000-14,000 feet above ground level (agl), depending on the size of the main airport. Some large TRACONs own up to Flight Level 230. There are 25 Stand-Alone TRA-CONs, 122 TRACONs which are combined with ATCTs totaling 147 TRACONs.

The Centers, called Air Route Traffic Control Center (ARTCC), technically own all the airspace across the National Airspace System (NAS) and delegates portions of it to the TRACONs/RAPCONs and ATCTs. The ARTCCs control aircraft between TRACONs and at high altitudes.

There are 21 ARTCCs and 3 Combined Control Facilities (CCFs) in the United States, including Anchorage, Guam, Honolulu and San Juan. There are some locations where the ARTCC owns airspace down to the ground. In addition, many TRACONs close at night and the ARTCC assumes their airspace during those hours.

At the end of Fiscal Year 2019, there were 10,419 fully certified controllers working for the FAA. Trainees brought the total number up to 14,375 controllers.

Small airports which have no ATCT, are called "Uncontrolled Airports". At these airports, pilots are responsible for separation between aircraft. They have Common Traffic Advisory Frequencies (CTAF), which is a frequency so pilots can talk to each other to announce their positions. Pilots use basic flying procedures to assist in maintaining separation. Even though there is no tower, a TRACON or ARTCC normally provides approach clearances and departure releases for IFR aircraft flying into controlled airspace, which at non-towered airports normally starts at 700 feet above ground level.

★ ★ ★

The ARTCCs - and some TRACONs - have such a large area of airspace, they are broken down into "Areas." Most ARTCCs have between 4-8 Areas. Individual controllers are assigned to an Area, which are named by either a number, letters, or cardinal direction. For example, in Cleveland, I was assigned to Area 8; in Chicago, to the West Area; and in Washington to Bay (Area) 5.

Each Area usually has between 5-7 sectors. Sectors are a piece of airspace with a lateral boundary line - think a line drawn on a map - and has a base and top altitude. ATC controls airspace from ground level up to the top of Class Alpha airspace of Flight Level 600 (60,000 feet), and higher if an aircraft can make it up that high.

Most low altitude sectors start at either ground level or above the TRACON airspace and extend up to and including Flight Level 230. The high sectors are broken down depending on how busy that chunk of airspace is. Some are FL240 and above, while others have two or even three more altitude stratums divided up.

Radar sectors have between one to three controllers working in each position. The Radar Controller, commonly called the R-Side, is the controller sitting in front of the radar scope, talking on the radio frequency to the pilots.

When it gets busy, a second controller is added to the team called a Radar Associate (RA). The name of this position was changed a while back, but controllers still commonly refer to this position by the former name as the D-Side (Data Controller). The D-Side reviews the flight plan information and coordinates with other sectors via landlines.

The D-Side uses the En Route Decision Support Tool (EDST), which I mainly refer to throughout this book as the D-Side computer. The EDST is an electronic version of the flight progress strips. Further, it can make amendments to the flight plans within the system. A few functions must be performed on the EDST, but most can also be performed by the R-Side through the radar scope.

When it gets crazy busy, a third controller is added called a Tracker (sometimes called an L-Side). When a tracker is added to the team, the controllers can work it a few different ways, but typically the Tracker stands behind the radar controller and acts as an additional set of eyes. I have only seen a tracker be used a few times throughout my career.

In reverse, when it is slow, we combine multiple sectors into the same position. Depending on the ARTCC, during the midnight shifts, all the sectors (normally 5-7) in an Area may get combined up into 1 or 2 positions.

When I discuss Visual Flight Rules (VFR) and Instrument Flight Rules (IFR), this means the type of regulations the pilots are flying under and the type of service ATC provides. At its basics, VFR is when a pilot is flying visually- looking out the window as they go. They reference landmarks such as roads, rivers, cities, towers, etc., to navigate.

When flying IFR, they still look out the window when they can, but they are issued clearances to fly using only their instruments (exact headings, altitudes, routes, etc.) and will fly through clouds. They must be on an IFR flight plan to fly into the flight levels (18,000-60,000 feet msl).

There are different types of airspace in the United States, broken down into "classes". Class A (Alpha) airspace, referred to as flight levels, are every thousand-foot altitudes between 18,000 and 60,000 feet msl (i.e., FL240 is 24,000 feet or FL250 is 25,000 feet).

Class B (Bravo) airspace is the airspace around busy airports such as Washington Dulles (KIAD), Washington National (DCA), and Minneapolis/St. Paul (KMSP) – the Class Bravos I've personally flown through.

Class C (Charlie) airspace is used at medium-sized airports such as Columbus International (KCMH) or Charleston Itn'l/AFB (KCHS).

There are a few other types of airspaces, but they are not relevant for this book.

To avoid confusion over the radio frequencies, both pilots and controllers use the Phonic Alphabet when saying letters. (A - Alpha, B - Bravo, C - Charlie, D - Delta, etc.). Pilots and controllers tend to use those terms in other aspects too. Therefore, when it is referenced in the book, it's stated as Class Bravo airspace.

The air traffic system uses two different types of radar systems simultaneously. Primary radar is the system from the World War II-era which sees the metal - and other things - in the sky.

The Secondary Radar system can interpret beacon codes, which is a four-digit code the pilot selects in the aircraft's transponder.

A few beacon codes are only used for certain things, such as 1200 for a VFR aircraft not talking to ATC or 7700 for emergencies. ATC assigns each aircraft they are talking to a different code, which is how the computer knows which radar target is for each aircraft.

Each airport has a three-letter code assigned to it. In addition, there is a prefix added to specify the general location. For example, "K" signifies the continental United States. Therefore, my hometown airport of Marysville, Ohio, is "KMRT."

ATC facilities also use three letter codes. The facilities which are located at airports use the airport code. The ARTCCs all start with "Z" since it is not used for airport codes. Some ARTCC codes use the name of the larger city they are called and others use letters from the name of the town/city they are located. For example, Cleveland ARTCC is located in Oberlin, Ohio, approximately 45 minutes west of Cleveland. Their code is "ZOB".

Aircraft call signs are either the aircraft registration number painted on the side of the aircraft (i.e., N1585M on the front cover of this book) or an approved three-letter identifiers and telephony designators (name verbally said on frequency) listed in the FAA JO 7340.2L. The call signs are the first line of the data block on the radar scope (see book cover). Approved call signs have a three-letter identifier and a verbal telephony, and they include "AAL - American," "DAL - Delta," "SWA - Southwest," "UAL - United," and hundreds more.

For IFR traffic, a controller has to take a "handoff" before an aircraft can enter that controller's sector. This is typically done electronically through the computer system but can be done verbally via landlines. When accepting a handoff verbally, the receiving controller says, "Radar Contact." If a controller refuses a handoff for any reason, the prior controller must keep that aircraft clear of the next sector's airspace – usually having them turn out to avoid.

If an aircraft is going to fly through a small portion of another sector and that controller does not need to talk to that aircraft, we do a "Point Out" to the other sector. This allows aircraft to enter their airspace and avoid changing frequencies more than what is truly needed.

Whenever a controller needs to get permission from another controller for something non-standard (like flying IAFDOF – Inappropriate Altitude for Direction of Flight), they use the landlines and say "APREQ," which means "Approval Request."

Aircraft use altitudes referencing mean sea level (msl). This is so all aircraft will be spaced using the same system since ground level changes. Above ground level (agl) is an altitude pilots are concerned about as they want to make sure they are flying high enough to clear the ground and obstacles. However, when ATC assigns an altitude, it is always referencing mean sea level.

NORDO- meaning "no radio" - is used to describe an aircraft that should be talking to ATC but isn't. When used in this context, the aircraft does have a physical radio on board.

DataComm – Data Communications is a different term for Controller Pilot Data Link Communications – CPDLC, but it means the same thing.

"Go-around" is when an aircraft is on its final approach and decides to abandon the approach by "going around" to try again. Either the pilot or controller can initiate a go-around.

An Electronic Flight Bag (EFB) is a pilot term for a software program on tablets which provides charts (maps), chart supplements (information about individual airports), and flight plan filing capability among others.

If you are a pilot, Appendix A is some phraseology you can use to practice your radio calls.

If you curious about an aviation word definition, Appendix C is a list of definitions from the Pilot/Controller Glossary which are relevant to the stories throughout the book.

CHAPTER 1

AIR FORCE ONE

On July 13th, 2006, I anxiously stood with my right hand raised with a large video camera rolling. The day had finally arrived! After a two-year hiring freeze, it felt surreal to finally be at the Federal Aviation Administration (FAA) Academy in Oklahoma City and starting my career. I proudly repeated the oath to defend the United States Constitution, and started training as an Air Traffic Control Specialist!

As I sat down, I felt lucky knowing that, once I finished initial training, I was headed to Cleveland Air Route Traffic Control Center (ARTCC). It is a Level 12 facility, which is the highest category based upon the number of aircraft operations the facility works. Cleveland ARTCC had hub airports and also worked overflight traffic going to and from New England, Philadelphia and Washington D.C.

Being originally from Marysville, Ohio, I was working for the FAA only 2 ½ hours away, which is as close to being assigned "home" as it gets.

I completed training at Cleveland ARTCC in April 2008, becoming a Certified Professional Controller (CPC). Shortly after that, I was working the Sandusky Sector, which "owns" airspace over the northwest corner of Ohio.

The ARTCC airspace is broken down into sectors, each owning a large chunk of airspace. Sectors have boundary lines drawn on a map and then assigned a set of altitudes for which they are responsible.

As I reviewed flight plans for aircraft headed my way, I had one with the call sign "AF1," which stands for "Air Force One."

Contrary to popular belief, the AF1 call sign is automatically assigned to any United States Air Force aircraft in which the President of the United States is on board.[2] The President could be on a small executive jet or a giant cargo aircraft and, if it is a United States Air Force plane, its callsign is AF1.

That afternoon, the aircraft was the widely recognized modified Boeing 747-200B used for special air missions. The President was flying back to Andrews Air Force Base near Washington D.C. after a day trip to the Midwest. This particular day, AF1 was flying eastbound and passing through my sector at Flight Level ***.

I let the Supervisor know AF1 was headed my way. He rapidly acknowledged my advisory, as he already had an early notification from the Traffic Management Unit (TMU). The administrative orders that govern air traffic control center require supervisors to monitor the presidential aircraft as it moves through the facility.[3]

The sector west of mine initiated the handoff by flashing me the data block for AF1.

The data block is the tag of information on the radar scope showing the aircraft call sign, altitude, speed and other information. Only one sector can have control of the data block at a time, therefore showing who has the handoff.

I waited for my supervisor to pull up a chair and plug in his headset at my sector station, and I took the handoff.

AF1 checked onto my frequency at Flight Level ***. Having worked with presidential aircraft crews several times throughout my career, they have always been very professional, courteous, and seem just plain nice. I guess that happens when you are responsible for flying the leader of the free world.

A few minutes later, the sector owning the airspace under Sandusky initiated a handoff for a Learjet departing from Detroit and climbing south. I scanned for traffic that could be an issue for the Learjet, and the only aircraft with a potential conflict was AF1. Slightly concerned, I decided on a plan to level the Learjet and I took the handoff.

The Learjet's pilot, a chipper-sounding young man, checked onto my frequency as they were approximately 5,000 feet below my altitude stratum, climbing. I responded, "Learjet 12345, Cleveland Center, climb and maintain Flight Level ***," which was a mere one thousand feet under AF1.

The pilot's voice tone immediately shifted as he read back the clearance and, in the same breath, he asked for a higher altitude!

Luckily, Learjets climb very well - sometimes 6,000 to 8,000 feet per minute. And just like most pilots, they prefer to climb straight through to their cruise altitude without being leveled off. Thankfully, since they climb so well, they often can make it to their cruise altitude without leveling.

I told the Learjet, "Unable higher. Traffic, two o'clock, three-zero miles eastbound, a thousand feet above your assigned altitude, is a heavy Boeing 747."

With a tone of disdain and annoyance for the level-off instruction, the Learjet pilot responded, "we can top them."

Ready for the challenge, I rapidly responded: "Unable, maintain Flight Level ***." He read back the clearance clearly upset!

I would have gladly climbed the Learjet any other day and time, allowing his plane to overfly the B742. However, I was not going to take any chances, as I did not want to have a loss of separation, called a "deal" amongst controllers, especially with AF1!

Mindfully of the verbal exchange, I watched the Learjet like a hawk to make sure it leveled at its assigned altitude. Once I was positive it was going to remain level, I keyed up my frequency and said, "Air Force One, traffic, ten o'clock, two-zero miles, southbound, a thousand feet below you is a Learjet."

AF1's flight crew responded, "looking for traffic."

"Learjet 12345, traffic two o'clock, two-zero miles, a thousand feet above is a heavy Boeing 747," I explained.

This time, the Learjet pilot's voice buzzed with excitement as he said, "Lear 12345, looking!"

Shortly after that, the Learjet reported the traffic in sight, as did AF1.

All in a day's work...

I firmly believe the Learjet was suddenly thrilled to level off and get a rare air-to-air glimpse of AF1 in flight. I know I would love to see it! Still to this day, I have not heard that level of excitement over a radio frequency.

Perhaps someday I will see AF1 midflight... and hopefully soon.

CHAPTER 2

COMMON DEPARTURE MISTAKES (EVEN BY PROFESSIONAL PILOTS)

To most Americans, the day after Thanksgiving is called "Black Friday," a nod to retailers whose shops, open year-round, transition from the accountant's red ink that denotes a financial loss to the black ink of profit. This shift is possible thanks to the healthy influx of retail sales made possible by the de facto holiday and the upcoming gift-giving holidays in December.

It also marks one of our busiest workdays for controllers!

On "Black Friday" in 2018, I was training on the West Radar Sector at the Charleston Terminal Radar Approach Control (CHS TRACON). Each year, the warm weather of South Carolina results in a significant influx of aircraft bound there as the winter holidays approach, so it was pretty busy.

Not only is there an increase in General Aviation (GA) traffic, but there is a large increase in business jets operating to and from the area. A sizable percentage of those jets land at Charleston Executive Airport (KJZI), an uncontrolled airfield located 12 miles south of the main airport of Charleston International Airport / Air Force Base (KCHS) – a medium size, joint-use civilian/military airport. As the smaller executive airfield can get very busy at times, the FAA installed a Remote Communications Outlet (RCO) for aircraft flying under Instrument Flight Rules (IFR) to communicate with us. The RCO is a separate frequency with the antenna located at the other airport allowing us to talk to aircraft while still on the ground when we otherwise wouldn't have radio reception.

On this particular day, I had the pilot of a Cessna Citation call over the RCO requesting their IFR clearance from KJZI. After I found their flight progress strip, I issued their clearance, stating: "N12345, cleared from the Charleston Executive Airport to the Dulles Airport as filed. Climb and maintain 2,000, expect Flight Level 410 one zero minutes after departure, departure frequency 119.3. Squawk 4301. Hold for release..."

After the pilot read the clearance back correctly, I instructed her to call me back when they were number one for departure.

Once the Citation taxied to the runway and was ready for departure, its flight crew called back over the RCO as instructed.

At that point, I was vectoring a Dassault Falcon onto the ILS Runway 9 for KJZI. I directed the Citation to standby due to inbound traffic.

After the Falcon was established inbound on the localizer, its crew reported having the airfield as in sight and requested to cancel their IFR clearance.[4] In response, I said, "N56789, IFR cancellation received. Squawk VFR, change to advisory frequency approved - Good day."

The Falcon acknowledged my instructions, so I promptly told the Citation "N12345, traffic on the ILS Runway Niner, two-mile final is a Falcon. Enter controlled airspace heading 090, clearance void in 5 minutes. If not off in 5 minutes, advise no later than 8 minutes of intentions. Released for departure."[5]

Every controller uses different methods. When I speak directly to the pilot through the telephone or RCO – which is not relayed through Flight Service or Flight Data - I usually issue clearance void times of two minutes. I add that, if they are not off in two minutes, to advise no later than 5 minutes of their intentions. The reason for this is, since there is no control tower, we – the air traffic controllers - have no idea as to if you made it off the ground, if you are late on your departure, or if something unthinkable happened. Effectively, the airport is shut off to additional IFR traffic for at least 30 minutes after the clearance void time - or the expected time of arrival for aircraft flying an approach.[6]

If we don't hear from the pilot within 30 minutes, we have an obligation to start looking for the aircraft.[7] Our first call, during business hours, is typically to any Fixed Base Operators (FBOs) at the airport. They generally look out their windows and let us know if they see the aircraft. If that doesn't resolve the situation, or we can't contact them, our next call is usually to either the Airport Manager or the local Police/Sheriff and have them investigate.

Still holding short of the runway, the Citation came back and said they were unable to accept the takeoff clearance with the inbound Falcon so close. I responded by explaining I cannot issue a takeoff clearance, as only a tower can do that.[8]

I reminded them of the 5-minute clearance void time I issued them so they could depart at their discretion. At that point, I re-read the clearance and, now better informed of their situation, they accepted and read back the instructions correctly.

Sadly, this seemed to be a recurring event, happening multiple times a week! I have seen many pilots - professional and recreational alike – read back a "released for departure" as a "cleared for takeoff."

Realistically, this could just be a slip of the tongue for some of them. However, it doesn't usually sound that way when they say it over the RCO or telephone.

Remember that, both practically, morally, and per regulation, the pilot-in-command is ultimately responsible[9] for safely getting themselves into or out of uncontrolled airfields, as only a tower controller can issue a takeoff clearance. Stay vigilant when operating in those environments!

Also being an airplane pilot gives me a unique insight into my "day job" as a controller. Having earned an instrument rating, it is a skill that requires maintenance, or else you lose skills that could result in dire consequences!

In May 2019, it had been a long time since I had flown any instrument approaches to maintain my proficiency, so I decided to take a flight to practice. I planned my flight from the Mount Pleasant Airport (KLRO), a satellite airport east of KCHS, to KJZI to shoot a couple of ILSs and then a RNAV back to KLRO. Knowing the airspace in that area, I filed for 2,000 feet above mean sea level (msl). That altitude is above the Minimum Vectoring Altitude (MVA - established for use by ATC when radar ATC is exercised) but remains clear of the KCHS arrivals, which controllers typically descend to 3,000 feet.

I got into the airplane with a certificated flight instructor for instruments (CFII). Having started up the plane's engine and taxied to the runway, we conducted our routine safety checks and run-up. My instructor and I were just about ready for takeoff, I pulled out my cell phone as I could finally use my new Bose A20 headset – with Bluetooth - that I recently upgraded to!

Technology has come far in a short time. Using Bluetooth through your aviation headset makes it extremely easy to get a clearance on the ground. It used to be you would have to use the FBO's payphone to get your clearance before you even started your engine. Now, you can call the controlling facility directly from the aircraft as the phone numbers are published in Chart Supplement - formally called the Airport/Facility Directory (A/FD).

There is only one downside to this method: controller staffing is very poor – almost everywhere. Therefore, especially at the smaller facilities such as Charleston TRACON, the radar controller working live traffic is also who clicks a button on the radio and answers the phone call through their headset!

At times, it may ring for longer than the pilot would like, or would have to be placed on hold for several minutes. Either way, I think this new system is much better than the pilot calling from the FBO before even getting into their airplane. It is not only easier, but it is much more efficient for the National Airspace System (NAS) as a whole, and many other pilots agree.

Delighted to be putting this new time-saving device to work, I called the TRACON for my IFR clearance. As fate would have it, one of the supervisors happened to be working the position getting currency. All controllers, including supervisors, must get at least 16 hours a month working traffic.[10]

Similar to pilot currency, 16 hours a month for controllers is nowhere close to enough time to stay proficient with busy traffic. Now, I have been both a controller and a supervisor at large facilities and, in my experience, I can tell you that smart supervisors only get currency when it is slow.

Apparently, this supervisor did things differently, as I found out he was very busy when I called for my clearance!

With a rushed tone, he asked which runway I would be departing, and I told him Runway 17. Class E (also called "Echo") airspace starts at 700 feet above ground level (agl) at both KLRO and KJZI. Therefore, technically, the pilot doesn't have to tell controllers which runway they will be using or if they decide to switch runways.

However, controllers use this technique to help the pilots. We will generally keep the departing aircraft on a heading close to the direction of departure. Once you tell a controller the runway you are using, advise the controller if you decide to change. Many controllers don't care which runway you will be departing, so they don't ask. But the ones that do ask want to know for a reason!

When controllers issue headings for departure, it does not take into account any traffic flying via Visual Flight Rules (VFR) in the area. As controllers, we do our best to notify the pilots before they depart if we observe any traffic which could be a conflict. However, the heading is assigned based upon the situation for IFR separation only.

The controller then issued my clearance, "N12345, cleared from the Mount Pleasant Airport to the Mount Pleasant Airport via direct Charleston Executive Airport - direct. Maintain 3,000, departure frequency 119.3, squawk 4207. Hold for release."

I responded, saying "N12345, confirm you want us to climb and maintain 3,000 feet as we only filed for 2,000 feet."

Somewhat combatively, he countered, "N12345, affirmative. I have traffic, so climb and maintain 3,000."

As a pilot, I am always in the mindset that higher is better, so I accepted the 3,000-foot assignment. But realistically and wearing my "controller hat," I think the supervisor made a mistake and didn't notice the 2,000-

foot request for a final. To cover for the error and protect his ego – and we can all agree that both controllers and pilots have some fairly large egos – he maintained his clearance instead of correcting it.

That happens, but at the end of the day, we were safe at 3,000 feet.

If something doesn't add up, or even more importantly, if you are not sure you can do something ATC is instructing you to do, it is perfectly acceptable to either say "unable"[11] or to ask them to confirm the clearance[12] as I did in this instance. But as long as you can safely accomplish what they ask, then you should accept the clearance.

CHAPTER 3

AIRBORNE IFR PICKUP

In March 2019, I was training on the West Radar position at Charleston, South Carolina (CHS) TRACON. A Pilatus PC-12 departed VFR from the Lowcountry Regional Airport (KRBW), some 30 miles away in Walterboro, and checked onto my frequency - requesting to pick up their IFR clearance. As instrument-rated pilots know, this is typically easier than calling the TRACON on the phone to get a clearance while on the ground.

On this particular day, the ceiling was around 1,200 feet mean sea level (msl). In that area, the minimum vectoring altitude (MVA) was 1,600 feet msl. I found their flight plan and asked if they were able to maintain terrain and obstacle clearance until reaching 1,600 feet.

To my surprise, the pilot answered "negative."

If a pilot departs VFR and cannot maintain their own terrain and obstacle clearance up to the MVA, then, as controllers, our hands are tied.

I advised the pilot to maintain VFR and that I cannot issue an IFR clearance until they are leaving 1,600. Therefore, "say intentions" – which is pilot-speak for "what do you want to do now?"

Unrelenting, the pilot retorted that he wants his IFR clearance! As that option was not on the table, I went back and told him that, unless he can provide his own terrain and obstacle clearance through 1,600 feet or declares an emergency, I cannot issue the IFR clearance.[13] I further stated that if he wanted to return and land back at KRBW, I could issue him a clearance on the ground…

Airports have specific parameters met for ATC to issue IFR clearances on the ground.[14] We cannot guarantee those same parameters will be met for an airborne aircraft located below the MVA or MIA – the Minimum IFR Altitude.

Back when I was working at Cleveland ARTCC, there was a small cargo company that flew out of Stoltzfus (OH22), a private airfield with no instrument approaches. Since there were no published approaches to this airport, this pilot group was notorious for requesting cruise clearances when flying in Instrument Meteorological Conditions (IMC) so they could descend to the minimum IFR altitude. This technique got them into the airport probably 90% of the time...

One night during a midnight shift at Cleveland ARTCC (ZOB), one of their aircraft departed Stoltzfus, heading north. He departed VFR and wanted to pick up his IFR clearance. Sadly, he was in the same situation as this PC-12; he wasn't able to maintain his own terrain and obstacle clearance up to the MIA.

I instructed the pilot who departed Stoltzfus to maintain VFR and say intentions. He asked me to standby, and he radioed his boss for advice. When the pilot returned on frequency, he wanted to land at Wayne County (KBJJ) airport – a destination just slightly out of his way. Once there, he would request a clearance on the ground.

I gave him the direct line phone number to the ARTCC's supervisor desk. Once he landed, he called and I issued an IFR clearance. Now armed with a fresh IFR clearance, his strategy ultimately worked out well for him.

However, the pilot of the PC-12 departing KRBW told me he wasn't going back to land!

In that case, "maintain VFR," I directed him. The pilot continued VFR towards his destination while staying below the clouds.

Approximately 20 miles later, the pilot called again and asked if all he needed to do was ensure obstacle and terrain clearance up to 1,600 feet.

---

* In the ARTCC environment, it is called Minimum IFR Altitude as radar coverage is not required. TRACONs use Minimum Vectoring Altitude (MVA) which requires radar coverage at those altitudes.

I told him yes. He replied that he thought he could do it.

Now, when you are flying, never say you think you can do something when asked by ATC. If the answer is vague, we have to interpret the answer to be "no." For controllers, it must be a clear "yes" or "no" answer.

Other than at airports with control towers, controllers do not know where the current cloud layers are. We have access to automated weather information systems like AWOS and ASOS, but those only get updated on our displays once an hour, similar to how an ATIS is reported to your electronic flight bag.

However, I could tell by the tone of this pilot's voice that the ceiling was not lifting. Further proof was his altitude was precisely the same as when he initially called - not climbing any higher. Therefore, I asked him if he really wanted this, well, let's call it what it was – a lie - on a recorded frequency!

He said he could maintain terrain and obstacle clearance to 1,600, so he is ready for his clearance.

At that point, legal liability shifted over to him. I did not technically know if he could or couldn't, nor is it my job to police the frequency. I issued him an IFR clearance.

As far as I am aware, nothing more came of the situation. I suppose he got lucky.

As a pilot myself, I understand why the PC-12 pilot took off VFR. The controller MIAs/MVAs are not published for pilots to use in the cockpit, and he was able to climb at least a hundred feet above traffic pattern altitude from his departure airport. I'm not sure he had Class Echo cloud clearances, but I could see him thinking that departing VFR would have been a safe bet.

To get more familiar with local air traffic procedures, I recommend pilots schedule a tour with your local air traffic facility.[15] Ask what their MIA/MVA is in the area of your home airport, as they can show you the altitude map on either a paper copy or the radar scope! Many different altitudes make up a facility's MIA/MVAs. Sometimes, it is one altitude for a whole section of airspace, and other times, there is an obstacle like a radio tower which dictates a higher MVA with a diameter of only a few miles.

Just know MIAs/MVAs change at times for different reasons!

Either way, when departing VFR to pick up an IFR clearance, I would recommend that the ceiling be high enough to climb to around 2,000 feet agl and possibly higher in mountainous terrain. Otherwise, it is probably in your best interest to receive your IFR clearance while on the ground before you depart.

CHAPTER 4

YOU ARE THE PILOT-IN-COMMAND!

On January 23rd, 2017, a Beechcraft King Air 300 crashed immediately after takeoff from Runway 11L at Arizona's Tucson International Airport (KTUS).[16] The automated weather reporting ATIS reported the surface winds from the south (180 degrees) at 15 knots. However, the wind check issued with the takeoff clearance was from 220 degrees – the southwest - at 17 knots, gusting to 23 knots. The crosswind component – the calculated effect of the wind in relation to the runway direction - was 19 knots. I checked the Aircraft Flight Manual for the King Air 300, and its demonstrated crosswind component was higher than 19 knots.

The part I found interesting was a Cessna 172 departed from Runway 11L five minutes before the King Air. The Cessna 172 has a published demonstrated crosswind component of 15 knots.[17] Granted, that is demonstrated – meaning has been shown to be possible to safely land by a test pilot at the Cessna factory - and not a limitation.

As I reviewed the initial report on the King Air's accident, it included mention of the Cessna's departure. This was because, when controllers see a less capable aircraft perform a maneuver, they tend to believe that it is okay for the more capable aircraft.

For example, on one summer afternoon when I was working the radar approach control at CHS, we had pockets of light, moderate, and heavy precipitation in the area – the typical seasonal, scattered storms. There was some light-moderate precipitation starting about three nautical miles from the final approach leg and extending past the airport.

In the sky, we had a Boeing 717 and an Embraer E-145 decide to wait in a holding pattern for the precipitation to clear, but we also had several Canadair Regional Jets (CRJs), a Socata TBM 850, and even a Beechcraft Bonanza fly through the rain and land safely. One of the controllers thought the two aircraft in the holding pattern were being ridiculous because the smaller aircraft made it through just fine.

I'm not sure if any of the investigators talked to the flight crew of the Cessna 172 that departed KTUS, but I started thinking about other situations where you can tell by the response from the pilot that ATC was inadvertently having them do something they weren't comfortable performing. I could see how a runway assignment by ATC would have many GA pilots not liking the situation but accepting the clearance because they feel it is their only choice.

Airports have been following Runway Use Programs for many years. The current FAA Order was drafted in 1981[18] – but only applies to turbojet aircraft (not turbofan) and is seriously outdated. The FAA has been working on an updated order, which was recently released and put out for public comment. However, I have not seen any updates since.

Airports – of all sizes - receive aircraft noise complaints all the time. It is a common campaign platform for congressional candidates to pledge to address them as a concern to their electorate as there tends to be a lot of public pressure to reduce the noise around airports - even though these airports are in the same place before people built and moved into houses near them.

A fellow controller once told me that Los Angeles International Airport (KLAX) in California has their Runway Use Program in place. In it, controllers will keep using the westbound runways until their third arrival aircraft performs a go-around due to the wind. This procedure keeps the aircraft noise over the ocean as much as possible.

However, if a pilot requests the opposite direction due to the winds, they will accommodate that aircraft and create a hole in the arrivals large enough for it to land or depart.

In general, controllers do not have time to ask pilots if they can do something. There would be too much back-and-forth over the radio frequency, wasting precious time for everybody. Controllers expect the pilot-in-command to either accept or deny the clearances they issue.[19] Usually, the first plan is what we try first to help expedite your aircraft along.[20] If a pilot informs us they are unable, we will go with a backup plan. That second plan may simply have you level for a few minutes or get vectored a slightly off course, but, at the end of the day, it is much better to take a delay for a few minutes than to perform a maneuver you are not comfortable with.

Professional pilots seem to be reasonably comfortable telling ATC "unable." Most companies have standard operating procedures (SOPs), which require their pilots to perform a certain way. Therefore, these SOPs force them to say "unable." Typically, GA pilots do not have SOPs, so more decision-making is in grey areas using their best judgment. Add the ATC intimidation factor that many pilots experience, and I can see how it can be difficult to say no.

However, I have seen professional pilots sounding like they weren't sure if they should accept the clearance.

One day, I was working the East Radar position at Charleston TRACON. The West Sector had several aircraft inbound to CHS, and a TBM-850 was established inbound on the RNAV Y Runway 21 - already switched to the Tower frequency.

At the same time, a Boeing 737-800 was being vectored to final for the same approach.

Since the TBM is a lot slower than the B738, the controller had to add a few miles of spacing so the faster B738 wouldn't catch the slow-poke in front. To accomplish this, the controller assigned the B738 a speed of 170 knots and had them on an eastbound vector to add space between the two aircraft. At that point, the controller was relieved for a break.

After receiving the Position Relief Briefing and assuming the position, the new controller turned the B738 inbound a little too soon. The controller instructed them to slow by 10 knots until the final approach fix. There was hesitation in the pilot's voice, but they accepted the clearance.

Controllers are allowed to slow turbojet aircraft to 170 knots if they are within 20 flying-miles of the airport.[21] Apparently, this new controller didn't realize the B738 was already slowed to 170 knots, and he actually slowed it lower than allowed without asking the pilot if they could do it.

Just because the order says something doesn't mean controllers won't try to go outside the parameters in certain situations. When doing so, controllers will generally say something similar to "Boeing 1234, maintain 160 knots. If unable, advise."

Ultimately, the B738 landed safely without being vectored out for another approach. I would presume the pilots were able to make the speed safely... Otherwise, they would have told the controller.

My condolences go to the loved ones of the pilot and passenger in the Beechcraft King Air.

At Cleveland ARTCC, a controller had two aircraft that would eventually conflict with each other at 11,000 feet msl.

The controller asked one of the aircraft, a Cirrus SR-22, if they could accept 13,000 feet msl, and the pilot replied they could do it for a little while. The controller issued the climb clearance and considered the matter resolved.

About 20 minutes later, the pilot asked how much longer they needed to remain at 13,000 feet. The controller responded that they had passed the original traffic he moved them for, but there is additional traffic, so he will show 13,000 feet as their final.

The pilot responded that they will eventually need to descend, and the controller replied he had their request - and went about other business.

About five minutes later, the pilot asked if they could descend yet. The controller got a little upset — as five minutes in an ARTCC sector is nothing! The controller reminded the pilot that he had his request for lower.

At that point, the controller started to complain to the rest of us in the area. Of course, he didn't mention how long the Cirrus had been at 13,000 feet, but I suspected I knew why the pilot was asking.

Concerned, I asked, "How long has it been since he took the climb to 13,000 feet msl?"

He gave me a blank stare, so I rephrased my question.

"Is it getting close to the 30-minute mark since you climbed him?"

"Yes, probably about a half-hour."

"I bet he doesn't have oxygen on board," I said with a cautious tone. "Regulations only allow pilots to be between 12,500-14,000 feet msl for 30 minutes or less."[22]

The controller looked completely stunned.

Promptly, he asked the pilot if he needed to descend due to negative oxygen on board, to which the pilot responded in the affirmative. The controller then vectored the other aircraft that was traffic for the Cirrus and descended them back to 11,000 feet msl.

Most controllers do not know about many regulatory, aircraft or pilot's personal limitations for any given situation. It might have helped the Cirrus pilot if he answered the original question by saying he could accept 13,000 feet for only 30 minutes or less. He could have said due to having no supplemental oxygen available, but the reason isn't necessary. If he had, the controller could have planned better and got the Cirrus descended sooner rather than later, probably with a smaller turn for the aircraft at 12,000 feet.

I would estimate only a small percentage of controllers are pilots - nor do they need to be. Therefore, as the pilot, you need to realize there are times when pilot jargon is not understood.

In those situations, try to communicate a basic but brief (emphasis on brief!) description of what you are trying to say. Even if, at the 25-minute mark, the Cirrus pilot would have said that he would legally have to descend due to negative oxygen in 5 minutes or less, it would have cleared things up for the controller.

Either way, you are the pilot-in-command. You are the final authority for the safety of your aircraft. If a controller is giving you a clearance that jeopardizes the safety of your aircraft, simply tell them you are unable and offer what you could do instead.

CHAPTER 5

SPATIAL DISORIENTATION

During one of my previous work assignments, I worked in Air Traffic Safety Oversight at FAA headquarters in Washington, D.C. One of my job assignments was to attend the daily meeting at the Office of Accident Investigation and Prevention, discussing all the aviation-related accidents and incidents from the day or weekend before.

During one meeting, the group was briefed on a FAR Part 135 Pilatus PC–12 medical flight that had crashed after departing Amarillo, Texas, around 11:48 p.m. on April 28, 2017.[23] They were on a repositioning flight to pick up a patient from Clovis Municipal Airport (KCVN) in New Mexico. Sadly, three people died, including the pilot and two medical flight crewmembers.

The wind at Rick Husband Amarillo International Airport (KAMA) was reported out of 360 degrees at 21 knots, gusting to 28 knots, so Runway 4 was in use. The controller instructed the pilot to turn right on course and cleared him for takeoff.

The airport was instrument flight rules (IFR)[24] with the cloud ceiling reported at 700 feet broken and 1,200 feet overcast. After the aircraft departed, the controller noticed the PC–12 was not squawking the correct code, so he told the pilot to reset the transponder and squawk 4261. The pilot tuned in the correct transponder code, and the controller instructed him to contact departure.

While still turning on course, the pilot checked in to departure's frequency, climbing to 6,000 feet msl (2,395 feet agl). The controller radar-identified the aircraft and, about one and a half minutes later, informed the pilot he was no longer receiving the aircraft's transponder.

The pilot did not respond, and radar contact was lost shortly after.

During our meeting, a senior accident investigator commented the FAA would investigate this accident to its typical high standard. However, this accident has all of the earmarks of the pilot experiencing spatial disorientation.

Spatial disorientation is when the body feels that you are oriented in one direction, but in reality, are oriented in a different direction—you don't know which way is up. It is the same feeling kids get when they close their eyes, spin in circles, and then try to stand up straight, usually resulting in them falling down. Of course, you can find several technical and in-depth definitions from different sources, but this is sufficient for a general understanding.

At that point, the flight surgeon spoke up and said this accident was an exact scenario the FAA uses for one of its spatial disorientation simulators called 'The Vertigon.' He explained that the Vertigon is a large moving box that has a cockpit simulator inside where the pilot/student sits as it simulates IMC. An instructor issues ATC instructions to the student through the intercom, and as the student is flying the simulator, the instructor initially directs the student to make a turn in either direction. Once the student is established in the turn, the instructor gives the student one of three tasks: change radio frequency, change transponder beacon code, or pick up a pen off the floor. Each one of those tasks requires students to move their heads. Once a person is in a bank and moves their head without having a visual reference to the ground or horizon, 100 percent of the time, that person will experience spatial disorientation!

As I listened, I realized I had received training on spatial disorientation as a pilot, but I did not remember any training on it as a controller. I decided to submit a FAA safety recommendation to change ATC procedures and add training for controllers.

In my opinion, the most significant risk of spatial disorientation is single-pilot aircraft operating in IMC, since it would be rare for both pilots of a dual-piloted aircraft to experience spatial disorientation simultaneously. My recommendation was to change ATC procedures for single-pilot aircraft, requiring the pilot to report "wings-level" from a turn before issuing a frequency change, beacon code change, or any amendments to their route of flight.

The safety recommendation was denied because the FAA determined it was the pilot's responsibility to take precautions to avoid spatial disorientation. Therefore, as the pilot, you can apply the same principles when flying in IMC. If a controller issues a clearance that would force you to move your head while in a bank, simply tell ATC to "stand by." I realize many pilots have never told ATC to stand by; it goes against what feels normal! Resist the feeling to comply automatically. Controllers tell pilots to stand by all the time. This phrase is perfectly acceptable for pilots to use as well.

If you have any hesitation because you think you'd be a burden to ATC, let's think about it a little further. Most single-pilot general aviation aircraft flying in IMC will be one of only a few aircraft in the area.

GA aircraft typically fly in and out of smaller airports, both towered and nontowered. Most of these aircraft only fly in visual conditions. Therefore, the controller workload is significantly reduced most of the time when the airport is IFR. You should never worry about telling ATC to stand by in normal circumstances, let alone in IMC. Even if you are flying out of a nontowered field, the TRACON or ARTCC controller is typically less busy as well.

There are special rules for military single-pilot aircraft to aid pilots in avoiding spatial disorientation.[25] ATC is required to limit instructions, including frequency changes, below 2,500 feet agl. According to the ground track from the NTSB final report, the Pilatus in the 2017 accident should have been nearing the end of its turn on course. Since the aircraft was at 2,395 feet agl, there is a good chance the military procedure may have helped.

When I give presentations to pilot groups, I always discuss communication during emergencies. When practicing emergency maneuvers, I advise pilots to practice saying the exact words they would use over the radio, simulated with your CFI. As a student pilot, I had CFIs expect me to give them an overview, telling them "I would advise ATC," but never simulating the exact transmissions. Just like practicing other emergency procedures, creating muscle memory for phraseology during maneuvers will help in real-life situations.

I believe instrument-rated pilots should regularly practice spatial disorientation training under the hood with an instrument flight instructor. VFR pilots also should practice this at least once to raise their awareness in case they ever inadvertently fly into IMC. If you fly an aircraft with a wing-leveling autopilot, use the wing leveler in some of your practice scenarios. I highly recommend you practice telling ATC to stand by during those simulations with your CFII.

The NTSB final report was published on the Pilatus PC–12 accident with the probable cause: "The pilot's loss of airplane control due to spatial disorientation during the initial climb after takeoff in night instrument meteorological conditions and moderate turbulence."

The accident pilot held an airline transport pilot certificate with ratings in single- and multiengine aircraft for both land and seaplanes. He was also a CFI, CFII, and multiengine instructor and logged 5,866 total hours. If such a highly experienced professional pilot succumbed to spatial disorientation, imagine the level of risk you are susceptible to when flying IMC or during a dark night.

According to the FAA brochure, "Spatial Disorientation: Why You Shouldn't Fly By the Seat of Your Pants,"[26] between 5 to 10 percent of all general aviation accidents can be attributed to spatial disorientation, and 90 percent of these accidents are fatal.

My sympathy goes to the family members and friends of the victims of this tragedy. I hope pilots can learn from this accident in order to avoid spatial disorientation.

CHAPTER 6

"CLEARED DIRECT" CONFUSION

One afternoon, I was working the West Radar position at Charleston TRACON. I had a Cessna 172 call through the Remote Communications Outlet (RCO) at Charleston Executive Airport (KJZI), South Carolina, requesting her IFR clearance. The flight plan route was from KJZI direct to Newberry County Airport (KEOE). I didn't recognize that airport, so I asked what her on-course heading to KEOE was, and she told me 303 degrees.

Charleston TRACON was split into two sectors: West and East. The boundary line between the two sectors is the extended centerline for Runway 33 at Charleston Int'l/AFB (KCHS), a joint civilian/military use airport. Located a few miles west of the boundary line in West Sector's airspace is Charleston Executive Airport. Therefore, KJZI departures will be worked by either the West or East controller, depending on their flight route.

Since she would be remaining in my sector, I released her for departure to enter controlled airspace heading 270, climbing to 3,000' msl. She checked on my frequency a few minutes later, and I radar-identified her.

Knowing her on-course heading to KEOE was 303 degrees, I kept her on the westbound heading for a couple of minutes to keep her separated from some IFR traffic I had on downwind for the main airport. Once clear of that traffic, I cleared her direct KEOE.

I continued working on some other traffic and issued a few clearances.

As my radar scan brought me back to her aircraft, the Cessna 172 wasn't on the 303° heading I expected - she was heading northeast bound. I tried to run a route line on the radar display, but the airport wasn't programmed into the Standard Terminal Automation Replacement System (STARS) – a radar system that only has a few airports which are programmed into the TRACON systems, usually the more popular airports.

Concerned, I asked her to confirm she was direct KEOE, and she replied, "affirmative."

I asked her to say heading, and she replied 040. I wasn't sure why she told me her on-course heading was 303, but at that point, she was headed towards the East Sector's airspace. I coordinated with the East controller and handed her off. I then changed her frequency to the East Sector.

Several minutes went by, and as she was only a few miles north-north-west of KJZI, she started making a left-hand turn. I mentioned it to the East Sector controller so he could say something to her to get her back on course. Luckily, I didn't have any traffic in the vicinity of her aircraft.

I came to find out she was flying the 040-degree heading to intercept the original GPS course from KJZI to KEOE - which is one heck of an intercept angle!

Since she was turning to the original 303° heading, the East Radar controller flashed the handoff back to me. I took the handoff again, and she was shipped back to my frequency.

When she checked on again, I told her that I had cleared her direct KEOE, and, for her information, that means present position direct.[27] I told her not to create her own intercept angle to rejoin the original course. She acknowledged my statement and flew the rest of the route properly while inside my airspace.

I have not seen this happen in all my years as a controller. It obviously surprised me, especially as it seemed like she was solo - but that seems a little crazy to make that type of mistake when having an instrument rating. Maybe the CFII wasn't paying attention.

CHAPTER 7

CALL SIGN MIX-UP

I was working the Toledo/Pandora (TOL/PAN) Sectors D-Side at Cleveland ARTCC. The R-Side was certified on both sectors but was still training on other sectors in the area. Because of the airspace layout, TOL and PAN were often combined into one position, which means the controllers must use two frequencies. Overall, pilots are used to this type of configuration: the controller can hear the pilots from both frequencies, but the pilots can only hear other pilots on their same frequency. It is commonplace at both TRACONs and ARTCCs as they are dynamic based upon anticipated traffic levels.

The TOL Sector had three Standard Instrument Departures (SIDs) from the Detroit area headed southbound, while the Pandora Sector was positioned south of the TOL Sector with a single line of arrivals northbound towards Detroit. Of course, there were overflights and arrivals/departures from the smaller airports near their airspace in addition to those routes.

On this particular day, it started to get busy. The R-Side took a handoff on a Cessna Citation, N12345. The Citation departed a satellite airport of Detroit and was heading southbound on the Fort Wayne Departure. When N12345 checked on, the R-Side climbed them to Flight Level 230.

Shortly after the Citation checked on, we had another Citation, N89345, check onto the PAN frequency at FL200. At this point, we had similar sounding call signs, and both aircraft were Cessna Citations. To make matters worse, they were talking to the same controller but on different frequencies - one on TOL frequency, the other on PAN frequency.

The PAN Sector was supposed to start a descent for aircraft landing Detroit. N89345 had traffic at FL190, so the R-Side instructed, "N345, turn 20 degrees left, radar vectors for traffic."

Well, as you can imagine, both N345s answered!

Since they were on different frequencies, neither pilot could hear the other aircraft's reply. I told the R-Side both aircraft answered, and he needed to advise each aircraft of the similar-sounding call sign.

Air traffic controllers are to notify each pilot concerned when communicating with aircraft having similar sounding identifications or call signs.[28] In my experience, it can be pretty difficult to identify similar sounding call signs before they check-in on a frequency, especially when they are in different locations of the sector. Usually, our first clue is when two aircraft answer an instruction simultaneously. This is especially true when we get busy.

When this happens, we usually say something similar to "Okay, two aircraft answered the last call - that call was for American 121 only. American 121, turn 20 degrees left for traffic." Once we get the proper readback, we typically go to the other aircraft to confirm they are not performing the wrong control instruction.

On a side note, I've had many pilots ask me why we use multiple frequencies when we combine up sectors instead of using a single frequency. There are a few reasons why we do this:

First and most important -each sector has a frequency assigned that has been tested for coverage. There are often locations within the adjacent sector's airspace where the signals may not be strong enough.

Secondly, we tend to combine and de-combine sectors frequently throughout the day. If we go to de-combine a sector, once we program the computer to change the position, we don't have to go through and tell each aircraft to switch to the correct frequency. This technique helps tremendously as we often de-combine sectors when it is starting to get busy for a single controller. Adding the task of switching every aircraft to the correct frequency would be a lot of wasted time.

After a pilot's initial check-in, controllers can abbreviate call signs when no similar sounding call signs are on frequency.[29] However, pilots often forget that they are supposed to wait for the controller to abbreviate first.[30]

At that point, the R-Side told both aircraft about the similar-sounding call signs. However, he reverted back to abbreviating the call signs during the next transmission, as that was the habit he developed through this point in his career. He said, "N345, turn 20 degrees left, radar vectors for traffic."

And once again, both aircraft answered and started the turn. The major problem was the first aircraft, N12345, climbing southbound, had traffic to their left.

I brought it to his attention again, which I did in the middle of that transmission. Without unkeying his frequency, he quickly corrected himself.

Then, he issued a third clearance to N345. By that time, the pilots had realized what was happening. They started asking, "Was that for N12345?"

Finally, N89345 was exiting our airspace, and he used the full call sign to switch their frequency.

I have heard so many pilots always abbreviate their call signs, no matter the situation. They use their abbreviated call sign during their initial check-in and even when I use their complete call sign due to similar sounding call signs.

Please, ONLY abbreviate your call sign if a controller does first.[31]

Get into the habit of using your full call sign during every initial check-in, which will also keep it fresh in your mind. As with so many aspects of aviation, there can be real consequences for a simple mistake! When things get busy or confusing, it is human nature to revert our behavior to how we always practice.

I remembered when I first saw duplicate call signs. I was a senior in college and was touring Dayton ATCT/TRACON (I'm from Ohio, so

Dayton is close to home). As the manager was escorting me, a controller said they had duplicate call signs with an aircraft on short final and another aircraft holding short of the runway, waiting to take off.

The manager took the two flight progress strips and called the airline dispatchers to let them know, as they are responsible for flight number assignments. Up to that point, I had never thought that could be an issue, and I asked the manager if that happens often.

He told me that, overall, the airlines do a good job. However, when a flight is delayed, sometimes one falls through the cracks.

Several years later, it happened to me at Cleveland ARTCC when I was training on my first two D-Sides. Detroit TRACON called my sector over the 'shout line' (the landlines with other facilities come across the loudspeaker, so several sectors can all use the 2-3 total landlines). I answered the line, and they performed a manual handoff.

A manual handoff is when the controller calls the next sector and verbally references the aircraft's location, current altitude, assigned altitude, and call sign. They are required when the computer system will not allow an automated handoff for some reason. As computer systems have improved over time, manual handoffs are becoming rarer. Even though the computer will not allow an automated handoff, it usually has the flight plan on file. If the flight plan is not on file, the controllers have to verbally give the flight plan information, which takes a lot more time.

The Detroit TRACON controller told me they had a manual handoff. He also said they could not input a "Departure Message" into the system, which activates the flight plan, so the computer knows the aircraft is airborne. I found the aircraft's flight plan in the system, told the Detroit TRACON controller, "Radar contact," then hung up the line.

I entered a Departure Message for the flight plan, and the system rejected it.

I tried it again, and, once again, the system refused it.

My trainer looked at the error message, and it said there was already an active flight for the call sign. My trainer suggested for me to change the call sign by adding a letter at the end.

The computer system allows multiple flight plans to be filed, but only one can be "departed" (active) at a time.

On another day at Cleveland ARTCC, I had Jet Link Flight 1234 – a regional airline for Continental Airlines, with an ICAO airline designator code of BTA. Our computer system allows a maximum of seven letters/numbers for a call sign, so I dropped the last number and added "M."

I told the pilot that due to the same call sign already in the system, I was changing their call sign to BTA123M. The pilot accepted it, allowing our computer system to work normally.

One afternoon at Chicago ARTCC (ZAU), the West Area was busy with weather deviations. As the Front-Line Manager (FLM), it was my job to coordinate different issues with the Traffic Management Unit (TMU). I had walked down to TMU to have them implement some restrictions for the Chicago area departures.

As I returned, one of the controllers told me they had to take a manual handoff from Chicago TRACON for Southwest Airlines Flight 1234 since the computer said there was already a flight plan for the same call sign and the automation wouldn't work.

I asked the controller if they had changed the aircraft's call sign. He said they dropped the "W" from SWA to SA, which made it different in the system so that they could do it.

I asked him how they differentiated the two aircraft with the same call signs in the same sector. He said he informed both pilots of the situation then referred to them by Southwest 1234 landing Midway or Southwest 1234 landing Las Vegas. It seemed to work well enough to get both aircraft to their next sectors respectively.

The aircraft headed to Las Vegas had already flown into Minneapolis ARTCC's airspace. Since they were headed in opposite directions, there wouldn't be any further issues once they left our area. Therefore, I informed TMU of the situation so they could call the airline's dispatch and considered the problem resolved.

TMU got back to me saying the airline's dispatchers said they sent the message to the aircraft to change the call sign just before they left the gate. The crew must not have received the message in time. It was nice to know the dispatchers knew about the situation before and tried to fix it.

I was working the Shenandoah Sector at Washington ARTCC, and I had a Cessna Citation jet, N710LC, heading north to Toronto – with a flight plan that had a route I hadn't seen before. More importantly, there was preferred routing in which I was required to issue.[32] The computer automatically assigns preferred routing and is reflected on the D-Side computer showing the new route highlighted in blue.

I was working several aircraft, but they were all spaced out, and I didn't feel busy. I waited for the Citation to enter my airspace, and I said, "N0LC, I have routing, advise ready to copy."

The pilot's reply was very weak and scratchy, but I could make out they were ready to copy.

I issued, "N0LC, cleared to your destination via direct RICCS, direct OXMAN for the LINNG3 arrival."

The pilot responded, but the transmission was even more scratchy and unreadable.

Puzzled, I said, "N0LC, I'm sorry, I couldn't understand that, please say again."

I intensely focused on what was being said, but he was still tough to understand. I thought I heard him say he was unable RNAV arrivals, but I wasn't sure.

I continued: "N0LC, your transmission is still weak but did you say you are 'unable RNAV arrivals?'"

It was still weak and scratchy when the pilot responded, but it was the clearest he'd been. He said, "yes, we can accept RNAV arrivals."

Relieved, I said "roger," and I reissued the route.

The pilot keyed up, and the transmission sounded just as bad, if not worse, than the first time. The only thing I could make out again was "unable RNAV."

Then suddenly, his transmission became loud and clear, with him questioning the route.

That's when I realized something was wrong, and I thought two pilots might have been responding. I started scanning my data blocks that's when I noticed I had similar sounding call signs. I had an N220LC also on my frequency.

Usually, it is easy to know when two aircraft respond to the same clearance. However, this time, the pilots must have keyed up and then finished both of their transmissions simultaneously, making it sound like a weak radio instead of two separate transmissions.

Using the full call signs, I said, "OK, I see the problem here, I have both N220LC and N710LC. N220LC, remain on your previous route and be advised I have N710LC also on frequency."

Then I said, "N710LC, did you copy the route?"

The pilot responded, "N710LC, unable RNAV arrivals."

As he said that, I thought, *Yes, I did hear him correctly before!*

Even though I'm sure he already heard, I realized I didn't advise him of the similar-sounding call signs. I said, "N710LC, remain on your previous route and, be advised, I have N220LC also on frequency."

I called the next sector to let them know the pilot was unable RNAV arrivals, and they approved the non-standard route. I quickly switched N710LC to the next sector's frequency.

I proceeded to advise N220LC the aircraft with the similar-sounding call sign had left heading north, and they shouldn't be on the same frequency again during this flight. Often, similar sounding call signs are used on aircraft following one another.

Noticing similar sounding call signs can be difficult to notice, especially when you have several aircraft under your jurisdiction. However, this was the first time I've seen pilots respond so in sync that it sounded like a weak radio instead of two responding simultaneously. I'm glad I figured it out before it became a real issue.

Back when I was newly certified on my first two radar sectors at Cleveland ARTCC, I was working one afternoon, and it was relatively slow at this point. The sector owning the airspace above me initiated a handoff for an aircraft going to Pittsburgh with the call sign CPZ. I had not seen this call sign before.

I looked at the flight plan to see if they put their call sign telephony in the remarks section, like "DAL- Delta." Many companies do this when they know they will be flying to an area where the controllers are not used to seeing their call sign. I recommend pilots and dispatchers to this as it really helps us. The remarks section in the ARTCC's shows up in the flight plan readout on the radar scope or the EDST (En Route Decision Support Tool – the electronic flight strip) – the D-Side's computer. At the ATCTs and TRACONs, it prints on the bottom of the strips. This is a lot easier to find than trying to search a database on a side computer.

I took the handoff, and the pilot checked on a short time later. I tried to listen to the call sign specifically, but I couldn't understand the pilot. I wanted to respond quickly, so the pilot didn't think they made a mistake and went back to their last frequency.

I went to grab the En Route Information Display System (ERIDS), a touch screen computer mounted on an extension arm above the sector that has several databases in it we can quarry. As I pulled the ERIDS down to search the system, I asked the other area controllers if they knew what the call sign CPZ was.

Dave, a fellow controller who had trained me a few times, immediately responded, saying it was "Chimpanzee."

I keyed up and responded to the pilot saying, "Chimpanzee 1234, Cleveland Center, descend and maintain Flight Level 230."

Before I even finished issuing the clearance, Dave started laughing hysterically. At first, I didn't even realize he was laughing at me.

Of course, since I didn't use the correct telephony, the pilot didn't respond. When I turned and asked Dave if he was messing with me, he started laughing all over again. He could barely say that he made it up, and he had no idea what CPZ was. I learned then to be very cautious at trusting other controllers...

For what it's worth, CPZ was the airline designator for Compass Airlines, a regional carrier for Delta Air Lines. It went bankrupt and ceased operations early in the wake of the COVID-19 pandemic.

There is a BIG difference between Compass and Chimpanzee.

Same goes for Chautauqua (a now-defunct regional airline) and Chihuahua.

CHAPTER 8

STEEP TURNS GONE CONFUSING

One day, I was working at Cleveland ARTCC on the D-Side of the Briggs/Hopkins Sector. There was a Dassault Falcon 20A that departed IFR from Pittsburgh International Airport (KPIT) in Pennsylvania, headed westbound on a demonstration flight as part of the aircraft's sale process. In their flight plan they requested 16,000 feet. They checked on our frequency. The radar controller climbed them to their requested altitude and, after several minutes, they called and requested 'steep turns' in each direction before returning to Pittsburgh.

The radar controller, who was not a pilot, did not understand what the pilot was requesting, so he asked again. The pilot responded, saying they wanted a steep turn to the right, then immediately into a left turn, then they would be ready to return to KPIT.

We didn't have any traffic in that area, so it should have been an easy approval. Instead, the radar controller remarked in line with "what on earth" and looked confused. I thought maybe he just didn't hear the pilot, so I told him they wanted steep turns.

He then asked me, "What are steep turns?" That's when I realized he didn't understand what it meant.

I told him they would do a steep, 45-degree or more bank angle, tight right turn for 360 degrees circle, then immediately turn into a tight left steep turn for another 360 degrees, and then roll wings level on their current heading.

I sat there in disbelief as he ignored what I told him and again asked the pilot what they wanted (remember the chimpanzee call sign and why controllers may distrust each other?).

By this time, the pilots were fed up with asking for steep turns and changed their request to return to KPIT without doing the maneuver. The radar controller gave them a clearance back to the airport, and that was the end of it.

Pilots need to remember that most controllers are not pilots. In this situation, the ARTCC controller doesn't work traffic down to the ground except for during midnight shifts. Therefore, he had not dealt with pilot training maneuvers.

If the pilot had explained it in plain language, such as I did, the radar controller would have likely approved it. Sadly, controllers have a severe lack of trust at times for other controllers, so my efforts were wasted and the pilot didn't get to perform the maneuver.

CHAPTER 9

MY DEAL

Separation standards at the ARTCCs are either 5 nautical miles later-ally[33] or 1,000 feet above/below vertically.[34] A new addition, Track Based Display Mode (TBDM), utilizes ADS-B equipped aircraft as the primary surveillance source, which now allows 3 nm separation at and below FL230.[35]

At the Terminal facilities, it is only 3 miles laterally. However, both facility types have rules which allow for closer standards in certain situations. When the separation standards are not maintained, it is officially called an "Operational Error," but controllers usually refer to it as having "a Deal."

Even though controllers strive every day to ensure these safety standards are maintained, the sad reality is that many controllers will have a deal at least once during their careers.

After only roughly a year and a half into my career as an air traffic controller, I had my "deal". I had finished training on all of my D-Sides at Cleveland ARTCC, and had checked out on my first two Radar positions.

I was working both the Briggs and Hopkins Sectors at the same time; the airspace between Cleveland and Pittsburgh from 9,000 feet to Flight Level 230. The sector located north of them is the Youngstown Sector, because the Youngstown-Warren Regional Airport (KYNG) is located approximately 7 miles north of the sector boundary line.

The Youngstown controller had a Learjet depart KYNG going direct to the Dryer VOR (DJB), westbound and climbing to Flight Level 230. They initiated the handoff to me and, when I saw it, I thought the Learjet would not be in my airspace for long.

Initially, I wondered why they didn't do a Point Out – where one controller gets permission to allow their aircraft to go through another sector without performing a handoff or switching frequencies.

Either way, I took the handoff and waited for the aircraft to check-in on my frequency.

Shortly after that, another aircraft - a Northwest Airlines (NWA) DC-9-30 (DC93), level at FL230 and flying from Detroit to Pittsburgh - started to be handed off to me from the same sector. I took that handoff as well.

On my screen, I ran out my leader lines, where the computer estimates the position of aircraft up to eight minutes out. The program projected out that the DC93 and the Learjet would be close. Since I was a newly certified radar controller, I didn't want to tell a senior controller how to do his job.

A rule in the air traffic job order says one sector cannot give a "deal" to another sector.[36] This means the first sector (Youngstown) must ensure all aircraft are separated before handing them off to the next sector (my sector). Even though that rule is in place, we still look out for each other because controlling is very much a team effort. The first controller may have a plan to provide separation, but maybe they just didn't foresee the conflict, especially since you never know what is going on in a different sector.

I called the Youngstown Sector via the landline: "I can take N12345 (the Learjet) at Flight Level 220."

That controller responded, "ah---pproved."

I said "XI" - my operating initials – which is how we end all landline calls - and hung up. I then changed the temporary altitude in the data block from FL230 to FL220, since I already had the handoff and controlled the data block.

After that, the NWA DC93 checked in on my frequency. I acknowledged them and advised them of the Learjet climbing to 1,000 feet below their altitude, to which the DC93's flight crew replied that they were looking.

I watched the Learjet's altitude go to FL220. Then, I saw their altitude went to Flight Level 223. That's when I decided to broadcast in the blind to check on it…

"N12345, confirm you are level at Flight Level 220." I did this thinking maybe the Learjet finally switched to my frequency but didn't have a chance to check on it yet. More importantly, if a pilot gives an altitude report, that altitude reported is considered accurate and would supersede the Mode-C readout.[37]

The Learjet replied, "N12345, negative. Climbing to Flight Level 230."

Astonished, I immediately keyed up: "N12345, negative! Descend and maintain Flight Level 220. Traffic, five o'clock, two miles, southeast bound at Flight Level 230 is a DC-9!"

The good news is that I knew both aircraft were already passed each other and would not collide. However, I still needed to re-establish legal separation as quickly as possible, which is why I descended the Learjet back down to FL220.

Whenever there is a loss of separation, the controllers are removed from their positions while management investigates the situation. Knowing I tried to help the Youngstown controller, I was confident in my actions.

After about an hour, the Operations Manager paged me into this office. He informed me I had the "deal." They reasoned that I did not use standard phraseology on the landline when I called the Youngstown Sector to offer FL220 as a way out for the other controller. The Youngstown controller had changed the Learjet to my frequency about 90 seconds before I made the landline call to him.

If I would have said, "Stop the Learjet at Flight Level 220," the Youngstown controller would have told me he had already changed the Learjet to my frequency and was my control - allowing me to make changes to it while still in his airspace. Then, if I tried the Learjet on my frequency and it didn't respond, we would have turned the DC93 away from the Learjet to ensure separation.

Either way, my lousy phraseology was the problem and, therefore, the "deal" was assigned to me.

Since Quality Assurance was involved due to the Operation Error, they had no choice but to turn the Learjet pilots into their Flight Standards District Office (FSDO) as a "Pilot Deviation" for not checking onto my frequency as they were instructed several minutes before I asked them to confirm they were level at FL220. Whenever a controller tells a pilot to contact an air traffic facility on another frequency, it is a control instruction and must be executed upon receipt.[38]

Fast-forward to a couple of years later, I was working the midnight shift and I had this same Learjet come through my sector inbound to Youngstown. I asked if they had time for a question, and they said they did.

I asked if they had been with the company for a while and told them I had an operational error with their aircraft. I further remarked that I recalled hearing it got turned in as a pilot deviation, but I hadn't heard anything since – as controllers generally don't.

The pilot replied that he was, in fact, the captain on that flight and that, yes, he did have to make a trip to the FSDO. He recounted that the FAA inspectors sat him down, listened to the tapes, and instructed him not to forget to check-in on a frequency again. And then, luckily, that was the end of the meeting.

I was elated that there was no action taken against the pilots. Most controllers do not like turning in pilots, and we usually hold the attitude of No Harm/No Foul. However, whenever there is a loss of separation due to a pilot deviation, it will always be sent to the FSDO.

CHAPTER 10

PILOT DEVIATIONS

As I mentioned before, most controllers are not eager to file pilot deviations. Even though we don't typically hold back our displeasure over the frequency, we do tend to avoid taking any further action.

I think part of this mindset has a lot to do with an old policy from several years ago. Back then, whenever a controller would report a possible deviation to management, management would listen to the voice recordings starting from 30 minutes before the reported event to 30 minutes after the event. Now, how often do you think a controller uses perfect phraseology for an hour straight?

Enough controllers got into trouble for their phraseology, and most do not want the possibility of management critiquing their work when it is not required.

The other part of this is the out-of-sight/out-of-mind theory. Once the aircraft has left the sector, it imposes no further risk for that controller. When the controller gets relieved for a break, do you think they would want to spend that time doing paperwork or decompressing outside the control room?

However, there are times when reporting pilot deviations are beyond our control. For example, any time there is a loss of separation because of pilot error, a pilot deviation will always be filed.

Another type of deviation that must be reported is what we call NORDO, meaning "No Radio." If we were talking to you, and for some reason, we no longer get a response, then this is considered a security issue.[39]

Depending on your flight's specific situation (heading, altitude, location) will affect how the security office decides to handle it.

If you remain NORDO for a certain length of time, you will probably be intercepted by a military aircraft.

If you ever are intercepted, and the frequency you are on doesn't work since you are out of range, change to the guard frequency (VHF 121.5 or UHF 243.0) so you can receive instructions. I would recommend you review the intercept procedures regularly![40]

Those are the two most common situations that are mandatory for the possible pilot deviation to be turned into the FSDO.

To date, I have only turned in one pilot. It was a few years into my career at Cleveland ARTCC. When I came back from a break, I was told to open the Mansfield Sector D-Side position since it was about to get busy.

The Mansfield Sector had two lines of arrivals northbound to Cleveland Hopkins International Airport (KCLE) and a string of southbound departures. This was back when Cleveland-Hopkins was a hub airport for Continental Airlines, so it got pretty busy during the pushes. When we have a line of aircraft that are all the same type of aircraft and all climbing on the same departure route, we assign them similar airspeeds to keep them evenly spaced out until they can get a turn to split them up.

On this particular day, we had a line of Embraer E-145s (E145) all flying CLE...HERAK...APE. The radar controller assigned the first E145 an airspeed of 290 knots or greater, and then 290 knots to the rest of the aircraft in line.

One of the things we have to be very diligent about is watching the ground speeds on aircraft that are following each other. We cannot see an aircraft's indicated airspeed, so we rely upon the radar computer to generate a ground speed based upon the difference in location of the radar target. We have to watch the speeds closely as, two-thirds of the time, the "Conflict Alert" will not indicate an overtake situation until standard separation has already been lost.

As I scanned for speeds, I noticed the first aircraft was about 35 knots slower than the E145s that followed. I told my radar controller to ask the first aircraft what their airspeed was

The copilot keyed up and said, "250 knots increasing to 290." The problem was we had assigned the 290+ knots 4 ½ minutes before we asked. According to the Aeronautical Information Manual (AIM), "…When ATC issues a clearance or instruction, pilots are expected to execute its provisions upon receipt."

For the record, 4 ½ minutes later is not executing upon receipt!

The radar controller told them he assigned them 290+ knots and he expects them to do it, so they need to increase now to 290 knots as there is traffic behind them and separation is being degraded due to compression!

When the Captian keyed up, I heard perhaps the most arrogant response I have ever heard a pilot say on frequency: "We are only doing 250 knots, if you don't like it, you can turn us out, but we are only going to do 250 today."

The tone of voice the Captain used was unbelievable to me, as if he was putting us in our place.

So, we ended up turning them out and letting the aircraft behind fly past.

If the Captain had said they could only do 250 knots, when we assigned the 290+ knots, we would have changed to Plan B and made it work. However, blatantly ignoring a control instruction jeopardizes the safety of the National Airspace System (NAS), and to me: that is unacceptable!

After the traffic died down, I went out on a break. The more I thought about this situation, the more it bothered me. I decided to call one of my airline pilot friends who worked for the same airline. I asked him if he had online access to see who the flight crew was for a specific flight number.

He looked it up and told me, "Oh, that guy. The Captian on that flight hates management so much. He does whatever he can to make every flight he is assigned to fly as late as possible. All of the First Officers hate being assigned to fly with him."

That told me this Captain wasn't just having a bad day - this was an attitude problem that needed to be addressed!

I went back into the control room to talk to my supervisor and told him I wanted to turn this pilot in for a pilot deviation. He turned it into the operations manager, who turned it over to Quality Assurance (QA).

A few months later, I saw the QA specialist and asked him about it. He said he spoke to the company's chief pilot – who he said was extremely upset by the information and promised to take care of the situation with the offending pilot. The QA specialist decided the chief pilot could handle it and did not turn it over to the FAA Flight Standards District Office (FSDO) to investigate. I never heard what happened after that, but I hope the Captian learned that he could not accept a clearance then ignore it!

I was working at Charleston TRACON and had N12345 – Mooney (M20P), which departed KCHS VFR headed westbound to KRBW. Upon departure, the tower controller issued a heading, turning them NNW. Shortly after takeoff, the local controller switched them to me in the TRACON.

The pilot checked onto my radio frequency and sounded really upset. He said they just had the engine changed, and they wanted a circling climb over the airport in case something goes wrong, and said they had told the last controller.

I called the local (tower) controller on the landline to get control of this aircraft so I could turn him from his assigned heading, as they owned a halfcircle of airspace on the departure side of the runway.

Honestly, I was a little forceful with the controller and told him that the pilot wanted a circling climb over the airport until he reached his cruise altitude. The local controller gave me control and started to explain. I cut him off telling him we'd take care of it later as I wanted to get the M20P his turn.

I turned the M20P left, heading 180, as I had a Southwest Airlines' Boeing 737-800 (B738) on final to Runway 03. I planned to keep him close to the airport, and, by the time he would be about a mile south of the airport, the B-737 would have landed. He was climbing the whole time, so he should have remained within gliding distance. Once past the B738, I could allow him to remain directly over the airport. I needed to keep the separation in case the Southwest plane had to perform a "go around," an aborted approach to landing - because that would become a big problem.

I was busy working several other aircraft when this happened, I then issued a couple of instructions to them. After that, I noticed the M20P appeared to be flying southeast-bound. I told the pilot to confirm he was on a 180 heading, and he replied that he needed to circle until reaching his cruise altitude and that's what he is doing. At this point, he was over the top of the B738. Even if the B738 started to climb, they would be out in front, so I just let it go. Once the M20P reached 3,500' msl, he proceeded westbound towards KRBW.

Early in my ATC career, I was told by a senior controller that you can be absolutely positive you said something on the frequency or landline, but wait until you hear the audio recordings because there is an excellent chance you remember it wrong.

I was relieved off my position shortly after this happened, and I went into the office to listen to the frequency recordings to see what actually happened, starting with clearance delivery.

The pilot did, in fact, tell the controller he wanted to circle. He said it numerous times to clearance delivery, ground, and tower, but he only phrased it as he "wants to circle" - he never said anything about a circling climb over the airport or just having had a new engine installed!

The controllers told him they had his request for circling but would take care of it after he departed. It was only after he switched to departure and started speaking to me that he became agitated and told me about the circling climb request and the new engine.

After determining it wasn't an issue with controller performance, I really wanted to have a conversation with the pilot to explain what happened. Since he already landed, the only way to do that would be to involve the FSDO.

Over the last few years, the FAA has been leaning towards educating pilots instead of simply violating them. This concept works better for everybody involved. I wanted the FSDO to contact the pilot to have a conversation about the miscommunication on his part and his blatant disregard for control instructions within Class Charlie airspace. I did not want to violate him. However, I found out that the FSDO typically won't even reach out to pilots if the pilot didn't receive the Brasher notification (*"N12345, Possible Pilot Deviation. Advise you contact Charleston Approach at 843-414-2800"*). Therefore, I was advised not to pursue contacting the pilot.

I learned a big lesson that day. Even if I want to have a simple conversation, I need to issue the Brasher notification. The FAA JO 7210.632 states "This notification, known as the "Brasher Notification," is intended to provide the involved flight crew with an opportunity to make note of the occurrence and collect their thoughts for future coordination with Flight Standards regarding enforcement actions or operator training."

The name "Brasher" comes from the pilot who, in 1987, argued that the FAA had failed to warn him of their belief he was flying unsafe – and that the lack of warning waived the FAA's right to impose any sanctions against him. The National Transportation Safety Board's Administrative Law Judge agreed.[41]

Hence, a Brasher notification allows the pilot to file an Aviation Safety Reporting System (ASRS) report with NASA, allowing for immunity.

Sadly, we were not able to communicate with the M20P pilot to let him know to be clearer over the radio with his requests. I'm sure he has no idea that he never said anything other than "circle" until he was talking to departure. Either way, that does not give him the right to go against control instructions as he was obviously not in an emergency situation – declared or otherwise.

CHAPTER XI

EMERGENCIES

One day, I walked into the area at Chicago ARTCC, and one of our trainees just had an aircraft check-in on his frequency and said, "Chicago Center, Cessna 123."

The trainee's response was, "Last aircraft calling Chicago, you got this frequency in error; go back to your last." Now, this is a technique controllers use in Class Alpha airspace – the high airspace which requires pilots to talk to ATC - when we are really busy. When we are not so busy, we will do our best to find out which frequency the aircraft should be on, and issue it.

As pilots know, this is how many pilots make an initial call for VFR flight following. As mentioned before, I would guess most controllers are not pilots. Therefore, it is generally difficult for controllers to put themselves in the shoes of the pilots, even though they do try!

Of course, before the trainee unkeyed his microphone from that transmission, his On-the-Job Training Instructor (OJTI) told him that he doesn't know what that aircraft wanted or where they are located. He needed to find out.

The trainee went back and said, "Last aircraft calling Chicago Center, say again."

"Chicago Center, Cessna 123, we lost our engine, we are going down."

At that point, the sector team starts working the emergency procedures such as radar identifying the aircraft, getting the number of souls on board, and as much actionable information as possible.[42]

Luckily, it was a good outcome. They were VFR, flying above the TRACON's airspace and were monitoring the ARTCC frequency, so it was easy to make their call. The pilot was able to land their Cessna 172 in a field, and he and his wife, the only passenger, were able to walk away from the aircraft without injury.

The trainee learned a big lesson that day: that he cannot simply tell an aircraft to return to its last frequency without knowing precisely what is going on.

Now, I want you to think about this from the pilot's perspective: If you lost your engine, what exactly would you say? Can you think of a better way to phrase your radio transmission to avoid the 20-30 second delay this pilot experienced?

Obviously, this controller did not handle the situation properly at the beginning. However, I can't say the time delay is uncommon in regards to how the pilot started his communication. If a controller believes you are a VFR popup, you are automatically their last priority, which is true for all radar facilities. How many times have you had to wait for ATC to get back to you when you've made these calls? Has it taken several minutes for the controller to assign you a beacon code to be radar identified?

What if the pilot would have said, "Mayday, Mayday, Mayday, Cessna 123 is over Dubuque at 9,000', we've lost our engine and we are headed towards the Dubuque Airport." Or maybe "Chicago Center, Cessna 123, declaring an emergency, we've lost our engine and we are going to land on the highway northbound." Either of these statements would have gotten the attention of ATC immediately and resulted in you becoming the priority over everybody else![43]

Now, think how busy the cockpit gets when training for emergencies. Imagine adding the stress of a real-life emergency to the mix. Would that extra 20-30 seconds be beneficial to you as the pilot to work the emergency?

Of course it would!

There are only two words (phrases) in the Pilot/Controller Glossary that communicate distress: 'Mayday' and 'Pan-Pan.'

In my experience, I have only heard a few recordings of pilots using

'Mayday,' but I have never heard the term 'Pan-Pan' used. Both words are legal words to use according to both the FAA and the International Civil Aviation Organization (ICAO), so use them as the situation dictates. If you do use either term, be sure to say them three times. Once, I heard a 'Mayday' call where another pilot stepped on their first two 'Maydays' and only the third 'Mayday' was heard.

Of all the emergencies I have worked, the pilots, mostly airline pilots, used plain language: "Center, [call sign], we are declaring the emergency due to…"[44]

Airlines have Standard Operating Procedures (SOPs) that require them to declare an emergency for specific items. I have personally worked a few emergencies. Mostly, they were medical emergencies where a passenger needed to get to a hospital.

I once had a Hawker jet declare an emergency due to a high oil temperature light on their right engine.

Another time, I had a regional jet, climbing through 16,000 feet msl, lose their secondary hydraulic system and return to the field.

And then there's the time a Boeing 737 had a passenger's Personal Electronic Device (PED) start smoking- which I will discuss later. All of these crews requested the airport rescue and fire-fighting equipment to be standing by at the runway.

Airline pilots never seem to hesitate when declaring an emergency. Maybe it is because they are required by their SOPs, so there is no gray area during the decision-making process. Or, perhaps they have enough passengers who need medical assistance that they have gotten used to it. It may simply be they have practiced it so much throughout their careers, it has become second nature. Either way, I think it is good how airline pilots handle emergencies.

However, my experience with general aviation pilots is the exact opposite. Most of them try to avoid declaring the emergency to the maximum extent possible. I assume this is because they are afraid of the FAA. I can tell you, if the thought of declaring an emergency even crosses your mind, then you probably should go ahead and declare it. I have heard GA pilots hemming-and-hawing on frequency, trying to communicate their problem without declaring. It is almost as if you can hear the pilot thinking "emergency" over the frequency, but they refuse to say it.

In those situations, I've declared the emergency on behalf of the pilot.[45] I don't think most pilots realize controllers have that authority, but we do. Most of the time, when controllers make that decision, I don't think those pilots ever find out the emergency has been declared.

When an emergency is declared, air traffic gets extra help to assist you in whatever means they can. The supervisor or TMU starts making phone calls to the airport of intended arrival to coordinate emergency equipment or whatever else the pilot requests. At the ARTCC, we generally add a D-Side if that sector currently does not have one. We limit changing other aircraft to the affected sector if needed. Regardless, several things happen behind the scenes to help a flight crew!

If you ever have to declare an emergency, you may be directed to submit a written report to the Administrator (or their designee) of the situation.[46] Well, if the emergency ends up in an accident or incident, you will for sure have to deal with the FAA and/or NTSB.

One friend of mine, who has been flying for more than 20 years, told me he has declared more than a dozen emergencies. Only one of those situations required him to submit a NASA Aviation Safety Reporting System (ASRS) report. He said after a different emergency, the FSDO called to make sure everybody was okay after having smoke in the cockpit.

If there is any kind of mechanical failure, that information needs to be communicated with the FAA as they keep a database. If there are too many problems with the same aircraft type or part, they may require operators to make changes for the whole fleet. I believe most emergencies do not require any follow-up paperwork if the flight ends with a good outcome.

In a different situation, I was working the Mansfield Sector D-Side at Cleveland ARTCC. I got a call from the sector that controlled the airspace above us, telling me she had an emergency airline aircraft that had an issue and was diverting to Cleveland-Hopkins Airport.

She told me they had already gotten all of the required information - number of souls on board, fuel remaining in hours and minutes, and more - and asked me what I wanted her to do with the aircraft.

I gave her a lower altitude for them to descend into our sector, got control from her, so we can turn the aircraft while still in her altitude stratum, and told her to put the aircraft on our frequency.

After I hung up with the other controller, I told my radar controller what was going on, what to expect, and that the last sector already got the information we must collect for emergencies. Then, I notified my supervisor that we had an emergency coming our way!

The aircraft checked onto our frequency, and my radar controller acknowledged their transmission and started asking them all of the emergency item questions. As he unkeyed from that transmission, I told him the last sector had already gathered the information and turned it into their supervisor. He responded, saying he wanted to get the information again because what if the previous sector screwed it up.

The pilot came back and started giving the information, and I could tell by the tone of the pilot's voice he wasn't happy about answering it all again. Being an airline, he had to find the manifest with the crew and passenger count again - while trying to get the aircraft configured for the diversion.

If you are ever in an emergency, please give this information if you can. It is designed to help search and rescue efforts if the worst happens. However, if you already gave the information and know the controller received it, you do not need to provide it again. Only spend additional time if the controllers did not receive it the first time, like due to a blocked transmission, or is trying to clarify the information.

If you know they have it and you are busy, you have two options: The first option you always have as pilot in command (PIC) during an emergency is simply ignoring the controllers. Pilot training teaches to "Aviate," "Navigate," and then "Communicate." You can always choose to ignore ATC while you fly the airplane. Realistically, the controller will assume you didn't hear them and keep asking. If you choose to respond, an easy way to handle the situation is to say, "I gave that information to the last controller - I'm too busy - pull the tapes." That will get most controllers to back down and give you more time to work.

Now, I'd like you to imagine that you are the controller in an emergency. Controllers want to help pilots as much as possible, but the only thing we can do is "Communicate." Whenever there is downtime on the frequency, minutes feel like hours. Even with the best intentions, sometimes we end up doing more than we need to. Other times, the pilots have said hearing ATC really helps. I personally try to give professional pilots as much room to work as possible because they are trained to work emergency situations as a crew. It is situationally dependent with general aviation pilots if I feel the need to talk more.

When flying in the ARTCC environment or a large TRACON with multiple sectors, you will probably be issued frequency changes. The frequencies are tested for only the confines of the sector boundaries. Especially if you are flying a faster aircraft such as a turboprop or jet, you will cross several sectors before reaching the airport of intended landing.

If you are in a situation where you don't want to change frequencies, you can request to stay on your current frequency. The controllers are well aware of frequency weak and dead spots. They will tell you if it is going to be a problem. If you don't want to make any further changes, simply change to the emergency "Guard" frequencies of 121.5 VHF or 243.0 for UHF. Unless there is a maintenance issue, all air traffic facilities monitor these frequencies.

Every ARTCC has emergency frequencies which provide coverage for all their airspace. However, these facilities are broken down into Areas, usually between 4-8 Areas per ARTCC. Some areas may not have the emergency frequency, but the Supervisor can coordinate with the sector in their building who does.

★ ★ ★

I realize most general aviation aircraft do not monitor Guard on their secondary radio, but I highly encourage you to make that a routine practice - as discussed later in Chapter 28. The airlines monitor it and are usually the ones that first report ELT signals. Monitoring these frequencies can help you be ready to make an emergency call yourself, or it can help with NORDO (no radio) situations.

One of the first things we try when an aircraft goes NORDO, is try to raise them over Guard frequencies. With the airlines, we have additional options. We can call their dispatchers and have a message sent through their Aircraft Communication Addressing and Reporting System (ACARS) or by sending a CPDLC message – discussed later. Many business jets include their satellite phone number into their filed flight plan's remarks section, which we can call. For most of GA, the only option we have is to use the Guard frequencies, which is ironic since they are the ones who monitor those frequencies the least. Often enough, fighter jets have been dispatched to intercept GA flights when we cannot contact them.

If you are talking to an Approach or Tower controller, there should be no radio reception issues unless you are flying in mountainous areas. If you request to remain on your current frequency, they should have no problem accommodating your request. It is probably more manageable for the controller if you switch, but if you are busy, tell them you don't want to.

Never hesitate to declare an emergency, it will only help you. Once you do, keep ATC advised as much as practicable but be sure you fly your airplane all the way through landing - that is your highest priority! Just never forget, the pilot in command is the final authority during emergencies.

I was working the Mansfield and Marion Sectors combined at Cleveland ARTCC. The controller behind me - there are sectors on the left and right side as you enter the area - was working the Toledo, Pandora, and Sandusky Sectors combined, so he owned 11,000 feet msl to Flight Level 300. He announced he had an emergency aircraft.

My sector was slow, so I "Quick Look" -ed - a key stroke which will let me see all of the data blocks from his radar scope on mine – his sector. We'll do this to help as an additional set of eyes to make sure the other controller doesn't get fixated on a single aircraft or situation and miss something else due to having tunnel vision. We do the same thing when another controller is busy, but our sector is not. It is a way to protect the team.

Luckily, the controller only had a few aircraft, so that he could dedicate almost all of his attention to the emergency aircraft.

The aircraft was a Piper PA-46 Malibu, a single-engine turboprop aircraft. The pilot declared the emergency due to the loss of his only engine, and he was some 40 miles southeast of Toledo, Ohio, at FL260 headed northwest-bound.

He asked where the closest airport was located and its reported weather. The first airport the controller issued was IFR, so the pilot asked about two other airports, which were also both IFR.

At this point, the Malibu started squawking "7700" – the transponder code reserved for emergencies. When this happens, the plane's data block starts to blink on all of our radar scopes. The controller asked everybody in the area why he was squawking emergency when he had already verbally declared, and I replied it is just part of his emergency checklist he is running. I added that it had been my experience pilots are trained to do that whether or not they are talking to ATC.

The benefit of squawking any of the three emergency codes – 7700 for emergencies, 7600 for lost communications, and 7500 for a hijacking - is it will show on everybody's radar scope which is viewing that location, including TRACONs and ARTCCs -instead of only the sector working the aircraft.

The pilot was still on his original northwesterly heading. It appeared he had established a shallow glide as the altitude was only changing by a standard rate. It seemed like this pilot was taking a long time to decide where to divert. However, altitude was still on his side, and I thought that had to be one of the worst situations to be in: to lose your only engine, and all the airports are IFR.

The pilot asked about the weather for a fourth airport, and the controller read the weather for that airport, plus informed him of the Toledo Airport ahead - though it was probably too far. Still, it did have better emergency services available if they could make it.

Then, as if by a miracle, the pilot reported the engine had restarted, and he wanted to climb back up to his original cruise altitude and continue to his planned destination. He said it as if nothing had even happened.

We were all surprised that the pilot didn't want to divert to have his aircraft checked out. The controller even asked the pilot, and he said negative. As the controllers were discussing this, I said the only way I would feel comfortable, as a pilot, was if I knew exactly why the engine had failed, and it was something I had control over, like if I forgot to change fuel tanks.

But this pilot apparently felt different, and never told us what the problem specifically was nor how he remedied it. He just continued on his flight.

I searched the NTSB's and the FAA's database, and I didn't find any incident on file. I'm sure Cleveland ARTCC management entered the landing time into the facility log, but that was probably the end of the event. Even though I was not involved with the process after, I'd be surprised if there was any further communication about the incident.

Hopefully, it was just a simple error and easily remedied. I'm glad he declared the emergency and asked air traffic about the weather and airport information. Either way, I'm sure he learned something from that day!

CHAPTER 12

TERRORISTS & INTERCEPTS

In September of 2017, I had been working at FAA Headquarters with Air Traffic Safety Oversight (AOV) for about a year and a half. I often took breaks with a fellow controller named Steve Collison. I first met him when I started working at AOV, as he was assigned to train me into my new position. I liked Steve, and we often walked to different places during our breaks to get out of the office and stretch our legs.

One particular morning, Steve said he needed to swing by the convenience store a couple of blocks away during his lunch break, and I agreed to join him.

When lunchtime finally rolled around, I walked over to his cubicle by the window. He was focused on his computer and had obviously lost track of time from working so hard. I asked if he was ready to go.

He looked up and said, "is it that time already?" He saved his work then grabbed his coffee tumbler so he could get a refill from the coffee shop on the way.

As he was standing up from his chair, I told him that today was September 11th and I couldn't believe it had already been 16 years since the terrorist attacks. Quietly, he agreed.

As we started walking through the rows of cubicles towards the hallway, I said that 9/11 is a day that most Americans who were old enough will vividly remember for the rest of their lives. I remarked that, in 2001, I was a sophomore in college when it happened. Knowing Steve had worked at a handful of ATC facilities, I asked where he was on that fateful day.

He told me he was the controller working the radar at Washington National Airport in the Terminal Radar Approach Control (DCA TRACON) when American Airlines Flight 77 crashed into the Pentagon. Today, the area radar facilities in that region are consolidated into Potomac TRACON.

Now, at this point, I had been working with Steve for a year and a half. I had no idea he was involved with the 9/11 terror attacks to this level. I froze as I felt a wave of emotions pummel my body. I could hear my heartbeat. I was nervous that he may be avoiding discussion of the topic, and I just brought it up to the controller working traffic and who could look out the window and possibly see the crash site!

I heard some controllers didn't come back to work after that experience. I knew Steve worked traffic right up to the age of 56, the mandatory forced retirement for controllers, but then he was able to get an office job at Headquarters, which allowed him to remain employed. I thought that even though he continued to work traffic after 9/11, was this a topic he avoided talking about? Would this completely ruin his day, his week, or longer?!

Whenever September 11th was discussed at Cleveland ARTCC, the controllers in my area, Area 8, did not work any of the hijacked aircraft. The one controller in the ARTCC who was last to talk to United 93 was in Area 4, but I never spoke to him about it. The controllers in Area 8 said it was eerily slow during the days to follow when the National Airspace System was shut down, except for the military aircraft flying.

With all of this racing through my mind, and knowing he hadn't told me about it before, I asked him if he was okay to discuss it. In a very casual manner, he said he was okay talking about it. His answer sure was a big sigh of relief for me! At that point, I told him I would love to hear his story, and he obliged.

On the morning of September 11th, 2001, Steve was working the West Departure radar position, with everything seeming normal. At some point, he got a call to keep an eye out on his radar for abnormal targets.

At 9:29 a.m. EDT[47], there was an untracked target approximately 35 miles west of DCA, coming from the Armel VOR/DME (AML) area, located at the Washington Dulles Airport.

Steve recalled that he wasn't too focused on the primary target as it was located within the Arrival Sector's airspace, not his. In general, arrivals turn north towards Frederick, Maryland, circling north of the airport and make a big right turn east.

About a minute later, the tower at Andrews Air Force Base (KADW – now named Joint Base Andrews) in Maryland called for an IFR departure release for GOFER06, a Lockheed C-130H Hercules operated by the Minnesota Air National Guard, routed over Martinsburg, West Virginia (KMRB), headed to Minneapolis, Minnesota.[48] With ease, Steve issued the release to ADW tower.

Now, in the interests of complete accuracy, I have reviewed the radar video replay to get exact times and locations.[49] At this point, in the background of the audio recordings, you can hear two other controllers coordinating on the landlines, "You got a primary target heading for P-56 (Prohibited Area airspace around the White House) to the west, ten west, fast-moving."

The other controller responds to the primary target call with "He's radar contact." Just after that, the primary target makes a right turn heading south.

Air traffic control uses two different types of radar. Primary radar is the original technology from World War II-era which sees a piece of metal, and other things in the air. Secondary radar is the system that sends out a signal that prompts an aircraft's transponder to broadcast its identification and altitude information. Via this secondary radar, the information is received, and the beacon code and altitude readout are displayed on the radar screen. But when a transponder is turned off, such as with American 77, we still see a primary target, albeit without its tagging.

Less than a minute later, GOFER06 departed ADW and checked onto Steve's frequency.

According to Steve, the arrivals routed over AML are always in conflict with westbound departures from KADW. That area is a major corridor, and, to his surprise, there was a fast-moving target – clearly nothing like a wayward Cessna. Coming from that direction screamed, "keep an eye on me!"

The unidentified primary target continued its right turn, eventually doing a 360° turn. At that point, Steve climbed GOFER06 to four thousand.

Meanwhile, there was another controller who tagged the fast-moving radar target.

Anytime a controller wants to watch a primary only target, it is easier to tag them up – meaning click on the target and create a data block by typing in a call sign. If we don't have one, we make something up that wouldn't be used by anybody, such as "WATCH" or, in this case, the controller used "LOOK." The computer system will create a data block (tag) and display the call sign, ground speed, and anything else the controller types in - such as a destination or type aircraft. Trying to watch a primary target without a data block continuously is very difficult, if not impossible, when performing the normal radar scan. This is the same procedure controllers use when a VFR popup checks onto their frequency.

At 9:36 a.m., Steve said, "GOFER06, traffic is eleven o'clock in five miles, northbound, fast-moving, type and altitude unknown."

The pilot responded, saying, "GOFER06, we have the traffic in sight twelve o'clock," referring to the position difference showing just how fast the aircraft was moving.

Steve said, "Do you know what kind it is? Can you see?"

"Looks like a 757, sir… it looks like he is low altitude." Moments later, the pilot continued, saying, "that traffic… is still in a descent now… Looks like he's rolled out, northeast bound."

Steve starts to clear GOFER06 to climb, but management directed to have the military aircraft follow the target - telling GOFER06 to "turn right and follow the traffic please."

At 9:38 a.m., GOFER06 keys up: "… that aircraft is down. He's at our twelve o'clock position… Looks like it's just to the northwest of the airfield."

Replying, Steve said, "… thank you, descend and maintain two thousand."

Acknowledging the altitude change, the pilot continued: "… it looks like that aircraft crashed into the Pentagon, sir."

"… GOFER06, thank you…"

"The pilot of the C-130 says that it just flew into the Pentagon," Steve remembered as we continued our walk. "Of course, you get kind of a chill that comes over you because now you're in some kind of surreal situation. This can't be reality."

GOFER06 asked to circle around the Pentagon, and Steve approved the request. Informing his supervisor, Steve asked, "this aircraft is circling over the Pentagon. What do you want me to do with him?"

The supervisor advised Steve to go ahead and send him on his way, as there wasn't anything else that could be done. Steve cleared the Hercules on course.

"After that, we worked things sort of normal for a little while, if you could call it normal after something like that," Steve recalled. "Eventually, we stopped departures. It wasn't long before they stopped arrivals into National Airport. They didn't want anything aimed at our area anymore. We have other things in the area that are important: the Capitol, the White House, Congress, all of those things that are nice targets in DC."

"It was a strange situation and very sad, but you didn't feel it at the time," he said with a sigh. "I've been a controller for a long time, and I've worked a lot of emergency situations. You're trained to work through."

"And so, you work through it," he continued. "We've all worked a lot of emergencies; then after a while, things go back to normal. You start working traffic again, things start picking up - where on this day, that didn't happen. We worked what traffic we had, cleared the airspace - and then that was it."

Having been interviewed several times for books, Steve recollected, "Nobody ever said not to talk about it. I talked to that lady who did the book, and that never seemed to be a problem."

That surprised me: "There's a lot of conspiracy theories around this particular crash, and nobody said to hide any part of the story?"

"No," Steve remarked. "I was in a management class in Oklahoma City. You get people from all over the country there. There were people there who worked for the FAA who could pretty much find out whatever they wanted to find out. They believed in this conspiracy theory that a rocket or a missile hit the Pentagon."

Steve continued "I was like, 'well, don't worry about that because there were people who saw it happen,'" he continued. "I didn't see it happen: I just saw the radar target, and I was talking to the captain of an aircraft that witnessed it happen."

The controllers in the tower would not be able to see it crash into the Pentagon because of the way the tower is situated. "I'm sure they could see it as it was descending," he claimed. "The 757 is a pretty big airplane. Controllers are trained pretty well to see airplanes."

"It would have gone down below the skyline, and they wouldn't have been able to see it," Steve recalled. "You can't see to the ground over there; you can't even see the Pentagon from the tower. There are just too many buildings in the way."

I mentioned it sounds like there was great teamwork on behalf of the controllers and management, to which Steve observed: "Everybody pulls together when something like that's going on. We had some really good controllers back then. Those guys were really sharp. Some of the older controllers had been around long enough to have worked untracked targets. And some of the military controllers were used to it, a lot better than I was, that's for sure."

Before the ATC computer systems could display data blocks, they would only show the targets on the radar screen. There was no computer system coupled up with the radar data to display data blocks - information such as the call sign, altitude, destination, etc. Those old radar screens laid flat, and the controllers would write the call sign on small plastic pieces referred to as "shrimp boats." They would manually move the shrimp boats as the radar target moved across the radar scope. To me, that sounds horrible, and I'm thankful for modern technology!

Steve said, "At National Airport, we had routine air taxis coming and going. It made up about half of our traffic. We didn't have any real GA traffic. All of our traffic was professional pilots, all working air carriers or air taxis. So, it's a different environment there."

"Things changed a lot after that," he recounted. "You become a lot more sensitive once you have a situation where there might be terrorists. Maybe they'll come back in a week, or maybe they'll come back in a month, so you don't want to let your guard down. You put in procedures to help."

"And so, they didn't have any more air taxis into the airport and no more GAs," he concluded.

"[The FAA] set up a system for if someone wanted to come in, they had to land outside the area, had to be checked, then they could fly in," Steve said. "Even though they had that system in place, there wasn't very many that followed it because they didn't want to bother."

"They instituted that you can't get out of your seat within 30 minutes of landing at National. They had that in place for a long time," he continued. "They put beacon code assignments into effect for certain aircraft that were going to be allowed to be in the area. If an aircraft wanted to come in, then they would be given a beacon code that the tower would have so we would know that they were okay to come in. And you didn't want to come in without that beacon code!"

I worked up the nerve and asked Steve when he heard about the World Trade Center: "There was a rumor that came through the TRACON that someone said 'we don't have this verified, but we think an aircraft has crashed into the World Trade Center.' Of course, as a controller, you're like, 'Oh my gosh, who did that? Who vectored an aircraft into the World Trade Center? How do you live with yourself after something like that?'"

"That's because, in my mind, that's not going to happen by accident," he observed. "An airplane isn't going to be there by accident. No air carrier pilot is going to fly there by accident. So, you're milling over all these different ideas in your mind about how that could have possibly happened. Of course, no one thought about terrorists at the time. That's why it worked, I guess. Because no one would think about terrorists. Who would think about a terrorist doing something like that? Nobody."

"There's no other reason for the 757 to have done that, to make those maneuvers and come back," Steve concluded. "Obviously, their target was the Pentagon. That was a sad day."

As one would expect, after 9/11, there has been heightened awareness for possible terrorism involving aviation. New policies were developed and implemented. Security is on the forefront of most of these policies.

Over my years as a controller, I have worked a few F-16 interception flights. The fighters launch with a pre-coordinated plan, then tell ATC what they need. In those situations, they get priority and we help them in any way we can.[50]

The real-life scrambles I've seen have been mostly due to the Track of Interest (TOI) pilots becoming hypoxic. Those pilots may have been unconscious but probably passed away before the fighter aircraft intercepted them.

In June 2021, I had the pleasure of flying in an aircraft being intercepted by F-16s. I was asked to fly as Mission Observer (MO) for a vital homeland security mission with Civil Air Patrol (CAP). Named "Fertile Keynote," the mission is for military interceptor aircraft to practice their procedures on another aircraft.

Even though I am a qualified CAP Search-and-Rescue Mission Pilot (MP), the U.S. Air Force and CAP generally want pilots to fly as a MO before flying as the MP.

The day before our mission, we had a conference call with the aircrews for both the USAF and CAP. We reviewed the exercise layout and expectations, and the pilots asked us to upload any videos to them after the flight so they could get some visual feedback on their performance.

The plan involved two Air National Guard F-16s and three CAP aircraft consisting of two Cessna 182s as Tracks of Interest (TOI) and one Cessna 172 at 8,000 feet msl in a visual holding pattern as High Bird. The High Bird aircraft's purpose is to relay radio communications between the mission aircraft and CAP's Virginia Wing headquarters in Richmond and be a backup TOI if needed.

There were four scenarios for the F-16s to fly, alternating between the two CAP C-182s. The plan was to intercept my aircraft on the second and fourth scenarios.

That night, I reviewed the standard Intercept and Escort[51] procedures. Honestly, I had not reviewed these procedures since preparing for a check ride many years ago.

The following day, I arrived at the Leesburg Executive Airport (KJYO) early at 6:15 a.m. We planned to be wheels-up at 8:00 a.m. I got my headsets, ADS-B Receiver, and iPad set up. A fellow CAP pilot let us use her GoPro cameras for the mission. She met us at the airport at 6:30 and set them up while the MP completed the preflight inspection.

Shortly thereafter, we were on our way!

The weather was nice for a late spring morning, with a mild temperature of 60° F, calm winds, and a broken cloud layer at 12,000 feet.

After engine start, I called for our IFR clearance. Since I was in the right seat, I ran the checklists and radios. Once released, we departed KJYO via Runway 35 and, after a few minutes, we were cleared on course, cutting through the Class Bravo airspace just west of Dulles International Airport (KIAD).

We were on our way to the Restricted Area R-4006. Once we were close, we called "Baywatch," a military controlling facility, to get clearance into R-4006. Once in, the F-16s announced "Fights On!" over the predetermined simulated guard frequency for our first scenario.

A scattered cloud layer had formed around 1,500 to 3,000 feet msl. We climbed to 5,000 feet msl to allow plenty of room for the fighters to operate in visual meteorological conditions (VMC).

For this first scenario, we were to simulate an aircraft with a broken electrical system. Therefore, we turned off all of our exterior lights, set the autopilot to maintain straight and level flight, and ignored their radio calls once they started trying to reach us.

Once I knew we were on course and the aircraft was configured properly, I started looking for the ADS-B In traffic on my iPad.

During our phone briefing the day before, the pilots said their aircraft were not equipped with "ADS-B Out." Automatic Dependent Surveillance-Broadcast (ADS–B) is a surveillance technology in which an aircraft determines its position via satellite navigation or other sensors and periodically broadcasts it, enabling it to be tracked. Using "ADS-B Out," each aircraft regularly broadcasts information about itself, such as identification, current position, altitude, and velocity, through an onboard transmitter. ADS-B Out provides air traffic controllers with real-time position information that is, in most cases, more accurate than the information available with current radar-based systems.

"ADS-B In" is the reception by aircraft of other traffic data systems and ADS-B data such as direct communication from nearby aircraft. The ground station broadcast data is typically only made available in the presence of an ADS-B Out broadcasting aircraft, limiting the usefulness of purely ADS-B In devices.

Nevertheless, the fighter pilots said their transponders would remain on during the exercise, and the ATC system will rebroadcast their information through the ADS-B In system. I noted a few times when they were not displayed on my iPad, but overall, it was a pretty good feed.

The F-16s initially approached us from behind, offset to the right. As they passed us, I was amazed at how far away they were from us. I have never flown in formation, having only observed formation flights at air shows, but obviously, this was not a Thunderbird demonstration. But I'm not sure I would have seen them during their first pass if I genuinely had electrical issues with focused attention trying to troubleshoot the issue at hand.

The next approach was a lot closer, but again, still a lot further than I would have expected. The F-16 was obviously in slow flight with the pitch-up attitude as they flew past with only a slow overtaking speed. This time, the pilot announced over the simulated guard frequency, saying our N-number, that we had been intercepted and were instructed to land immediately.

Per our scenario instructions, we ignored this radio call as well. We watched as the single F-16 flew past us. Then, the second F-16 flew past us in the same manner and location off our right wing as the first. Since we were simulating the electrical failure, we were ready to respond to them by rocking our wings.[52] However, they declared the scenario was terminated and started the next scenario before using the prescribed non-verbal communication methods.

After they intercepted the other CAP C182, they declared "Fights On" with us for Scenario 4, which had us simulating a slow drone. I admit, I had not thought of them being scrambled for drones, but it makes sense for them to practice.

We dirtied the aircraft up and flew slowly, just like a Cessna can do. Again, we kept our heading and attitude straight and level. I watched them on my iPad but did not see them – although I later realized I had the "Hide Distant Traffic" setting selected.

Finally, I saw the ADS-B targets getting close.

The first F-16 flew higher than us, which due to our Cessna being a high wing aircraft, we could not initially see. Once that F-16 was in front of us, he turned left, crossing in front of us, which we did see.

We were looking for the second F-16. I looked at my iPad, and it appeared to me it was going to be off our left wing, so that is where we were looking. The video footage later showed the second F-16 flew past us on the right at a higher altitude, then turned right, flying away from us.

As we completed the intercept mission and were flying back to Leesburg, I thought about how the Aeronautical Information Manual (AIM) states they will only conduct the intercept if they deem it to be safe.[53] The F-16 pilots did an excellent job at this, as I never felt unsafe.

Post-flight, I knew I still had some homework. I fly in the Special Flight Rules Area (SFRA) which encircles Washington, D.C. for security purposes. I believe some intercept missions are flown by helicopters instead of F-16s, so I need to brush up on my intercept procedures and communication signals for helicopter interceptors. Either way, it is nice to know we have aircraft standing at the ready to defend the skies over our great country!

CHAPTER 13

HYPOXIA

AUTHOR'S NOTE: During my ATC for Pilots seminars, I show the video which includes both the radar data and frequency recordings of Kalitta 66 (audio-only versions are available online). In preparation for this book, I interviewed Jay McCombs, now retired Cleveland ARTCC controller who was working the Franklin Sector. According to him, the audio recording I use was enhanced significantly. "What we were actually hearing in our headsets was very garbled, very scratchy, very difficult to understand," Jay remarked.

I have transcribed the enhanced audio recording to write this chapter. Therefore, as you read this, when the exchanges between the controller and the pilots don't make sense, keep in mind the controllers could not hear or understand what the pilots were saying.

On July 26, 2008, a couple of years after I started working at Cleveland ARTCC, there was a situation in Area 5. In that era, whenever there was anything abnormal, management briefed the situation to the whole controller workforce during the daily meetings. Most of the time, these types of briefings were reviewing Operational Errors. This day was different. We were reviewing a "controller save" involving a Learjet 25 flown by Kalitta Air (KFS) Flight 66 from Manassas, Virginia (KHEF), to Willow Run Airport (KYIP), in the township of Ypsilanti just west of the Detroit Metro Wayne County Airport in Michigan.[54]

After KFS66 departed, they were issued a climb instruction to Flight

Level 270 by Washington ARTCC. They were handed off to the Imperial Sector in Area 6 at Cleveland ARTCC.

Approximately 50 miles southeast of the Johnstown VOR (JST), Kalitta 66 checked onto Cleveland ARTCC: "Center, Kalitta 66 with you at Flight Level 260 for 270."

The Imperial Sector controller replied, "Kalitta 66, Cleveland Center. Thanks, climb and maintain Flight Level 3… make that Flight Level 320," although the pilots originally requested FL340. The pilots read the clearance back normally.

About a minute later, as the aircraft was climbing through FL288, the controller told the pilots, "Kalitta 66, a little routing change when you're ready."

The pilot responded by saying, "Ah, negative, standby." However, that transmission's sound level was extremely low, and it appears the controller did not hear what the pilot said.

About another minute later, the controller asked if they were ready for the new routing.

And again, the pilot responded, "Negative."

The controller issued the new route, and the pilot didn't respond to the clearance. By now, the aircraft had leveled off at FL320.

Another minute passed, and the controller asked, "Kalitta 66, did you copy that routing?"

"Negative," the pilot continued to assert.

At this point, the controller countered: "Kalitta 66, I can't understand you. You're coming in extremely weak, and I'm not picking up any of your transmission."

Finally responding to the clearance, the pilot replied: "Could you read the clearance again? Kalitta 66."

The controller answered, "Kalitta 66, it is unreadable. Try a new microphone or a new radio."

About 20 seconds later, the pilot made a transmission. Even with the enhanced audio recording, I can only hear the pilot say his callsign. At this point, for the first time, there was now an alarm in the background during the pilot's readback transmission.

The controller replied, "Okay, if that was Kalitta 66, I just got a noise in the background - no voice."

"Okay, we'd like a readback of the clearance again," the pilot reacted.

The controller then issued the flight's clearance: "Kalitta 66, after HAGUD intersection, cleared direct Dryer (DJB), LEEOO Two arrival to Ypsilanti. Let me know if you get that."

The pilot started the readback: "HAGLR, DRYER, next fix."

The controller repeated, "Kalitta 66, after HAGUD, its Dryer VOR, LEEOO2 arrival to Ypsilanti."

This time, the pilot's voice is even slower and more sluggish: "HAGLR, Dryer, HAGUD arrival, Kalitta 66."

The controller obviously could not hear what the pilot was saying enough to realize the pilot said the wrong initial intersection - HAGLR instead of HAGUD. He also said the wrong arrival - HAGUD arrival instead of LEEOO2. Again, even with the enhanced audio, it took me several times to determine what he said.

The controller replied, "Okay, Kalitta 66, you definitely need to get your radios worked on. They're very, very weak!"

"Roger, we will have that done," the pilot quipped without a second thought.

There are many times aircraft radios sound weak or scratchy. We'll inform the pilots when that is the case, but - most of the time - the pilots switch to their other radio, which solves the problem. Other times, they talk into their headset microphone instead of the handheld microphone.

Either way, if a controller tells you it is an issue, please take the information seriously. I understand a lot of aircraft owners don't want to pay for radio work prematurely, but there have been some awful-sounding radios we've been forced to deal with. It can be a serious distraction, but we do our best.

When Kalitta 66 was a few miles from the JST VOR, the Imperial Sector controller handed the aircraft off to the Franklin Sector. After Franklin accepted the handoff, the Imperial controller called the Franklin Sector and said, "Hey Franklin, Imperial. Kalitta 66, the radio is really bad, and he does not listen very well, so just keep your eyes on him."

This is an excellent example of how controllers talk to each other. When anything is out of the ordinary, we make sure to let the next sector know about it so they can pay special attention.

During the phone call, the Franklin controllers were in the middle of a position relief briefing. Jay McCombs was in the process of taking over the sector to relieve the controller who had been working the position up to that point.

After the Imperial controller hung up from the landline call, he directed, "Kalitta 66, contact Cleveland Center 119.72."

"Nineteen seventy-two, Kalitta," the pilot acknowledged.

Jay had assumed complete control of the sector when Kalitta 66 changed onto the Franklin Sector's frequency.

When KFS66 checked on to Jay's frequency, the alarm was still sounding in the background of the aircraft, and their radio was still very weak. Jay was relatively busy as he had numerous aircraft in his sector.

Approximately a minute and a half later, Kalitta made a transmission that was so weak and garbled, nobody could understand it! During that transmission, another pilot keyed up and said, "stuck mic."

The Kalitta transmission continued for a few seconds past the other pilot's stuck mic call. After the Kalitta pilot unkeyed, Jay - who could not hear anything except background noise, said, "Kalitta 66, I believe occasionally having a stuck mic there. Be careful."

The Kalitta pilot responded: "Kalitta 66, aircraft control problems, declaring emergency," which was still extremely weak with background alarm noise.

Jay keyed up: "Kalitta 66, Cleveland. How do you hear?"

The pilot responded in a forceful tone, "five by five."

"Kalitta 66, roger. You're keying your mic, and it is staying on their frequently - so please be careful."

The pilot then said, "Kalitta 66, declaring an emergency."

A pilot of another aircraft joined the exchange, as he apparently could hear the Kalitta flight's transmissions clearer: "Sir, he is declaring an emergency with his flight controls."

Strongly, the Kalitta pilot agreed: "Affirmative."

"Yes sir, he said affirmative on that," the other aircraft's pilot relayed.

"Alright, Kalitta 66, roger. What are your intentions?" Jay calmly asked.

The ATC frequency equipment only utilizes one transmitter/receiver antenna at a time, although there are additional backup sites. I'm not sure where the transmitter being used for the Franklin Sector frequency was located, but it sounds to me that the other pilots must have been physically closer to Kalitta 66 than the location of the controller's antenna. They were all at a high enough altitude, and the terrain would not have been an issue.

Whenever a pilot declares an emergency, the whole dynamic changes, and the pilot is in charge[55]. Controllers typically use the phrase "say intentions" so we can understand what you need in order for us to move other traffic out of your way and prepare the airport you intend to land.

The Kalitta pilot said: "request vectors Ypsilanti."

The other helpful pilot keyed up, relaying: "Sir, he's looking for vectors."

They are still tough to hear and understand, so Jay replied: "Alright, Kalitta 66, understand an emergency, you want a vector to Cincinnati, is that correct?"

The pilot replied, "negative, vectors Ypsilanti," to which the helpful pilot again relays.

Several seconds pass as Jay types YIP into his computer system to populate a heading and then issues a heading of 310 for Ypsilanti. The pilot reads back very slowly and slurs the words "three one zero, Kalitta 66."

Jay was still relatively busy with all the aircraft in his sector. About twenty seconds later, the data block on the radar scope showed Kalitta's altitude dropped to FL317 from the assigned altitude of FL320. "Kalitta 66, are you able to maintain altitude? What assistance can I give other than that vector?"

The audio from Kalitta was still extremely difficult to understand – as its pilot keyed up and very slowly said, "Unable to control altitude, unable to control airspeed, unable to control heading, Kalitta 66. Other than that, everything A-OK!"

Looking back in hindsight, Jay recollected to me, "It sounds a little humorous but at the time, [it's like] what in the world is going on here?!"

"Okay, Kalitta 66," Jay told the pilot. "Understand you're not able to control this aircraft, is that correct?"

The pilot - with long pauses between each word, claimed, "That... Is... Correct..."

"Kalitta 66, there's other airports closer than Ypsilanti that might be more of a benefit to you," Jay informed the pilot. "Pittsburgh Airport about 30 miles southwest of your position and Cleveland Airport about 70 miles northwest of your position." At this point, Kalitta 66 is at FL310 even though they are still assigned FL320.

Less than a minute later, the pilots didn't respond to his offer of a closer airport - so he repeated the statement.

The Kalitta pilot responded with a very long, slow-paced announcement which, even with the enhanced audio, some of it is unintelligible...

"Prefer to land aircraft at destination airport as the aircraft is empty—no possible damage to any part of the aircraft or crew. So, we are slowly, ever so slowly, regaining control of the aircraft and the aircraft, if we are given the time to slowly reengage all members, all actions of the autopilot, which is what we are attempting to do now. We have been getting over-speed warnings as well as other warnings continuously, making it more than a little – probably [difficult] to control the airplane. However, we will be able to continue the flight..."

The alarm in the background stopped sounding towards the end of this transmission. Also, during Kalitta's long transmission, Jay put the radio receiver on the overhead speaker instead of through his headset so other controllers in the area could hear it and hopefully help figure out what the pilot was saying.

Luckily, Jay's tactic worked. Another controller in the area heard this pilot over the loudspeaker and she said, "it sounds like he has hypoxia."

"As soon as she made that comment everybody's eyes got wide open because we all knew about the Payne Stewart incident,[56]" Jay recalled. "We all knew what that could possibly mean and what the consequences of that might be. It changed the demeanor of everybody in the area from thinking 'something isn't sounding right' to, 'oh my gosh, is this guy going to make it?!'"

"When she said hypoxia, everybody knew exactly what had to be done," he continued. "It was just the matter of, 'okay, how do we accomplish this given the traffic' and also the fact the guy has just said nothing on his airplane works, he can't control anything!'"

"It was a little bit concerning [that I'm going] to give him a descent clearance with an airplane that might not be controllable. You have all of those other thoughts in your mind that 'okay, this guy can't control his airplane now I'm going to give him a control instruction hoping that he'll get control at some point.'"

Over the radio, Jay said, "Kalitta 66, are you able to descend?"

"Say again?"

"Kalitta 66, if able, descend and maintain Flight Level 260." Struggling, the pilot read it back: "descending now to Flight Level 260, Kalitta 66."

There was a concern among the controllers that once the pilot started his descent, he may not stop and crash because of it!

Jay thought a bit and said, "When he was at thirty-two thousand, I didn't give him a clearance down to ten; I stepped him down. One of the reasons I decided to do that was to keep him engaged with me as he was starting down."

Looking at the situation and as I was listening to Jay tell me this, I have to admit - I would have never thought about doing that. It was a brilliant strategy!

"There were some other airplanes we were trying to get out of the way," Jay continued. Jay got approval from those lower sectors to descend the Kalitta into their airspace. The controllers working the airspace under Jay's altitude stratum, automatically started moving their aircraft away from the vicinity of the Kalitta aircraft – another outstanding example of how controllers work together to help a pilot in distress.

Approximately a minute later, as Kalitta was descending through FL292,

Jay said, "Kalitta 66, descend and maintain Flight Level 180."

The pilot started to sound slightly better and said, "Okay, we are now descending to Flight Level 180, Kalitta 66."

In another amazing example of ATC teamwork, as Kalitta 66 descended through FL249, Jay advised: "Kalitta 66, descend and maintain one-two thousand, Pittsburgh altimeter 29.93." As he was issuing the descent below the flight levels, another controller working a low altitude sector yelled out the altimeter setting, so Jay didn't have to take the time to look it up – only low altitude sectors are required to display altimeter settings.

Another voice on the audio recording, presumably the Kalitta co-pilot, chimed in: "Flight Level 120, Kalitta 66."

As Kalitta was descending through Flight Level 195, Jay asked: "Kalitta 66, are you still requesting a vector for Ypsilanti?"

As the pilot keyed up, the alarm in the background was sounding again for the first few seconds of the transmission, then stopped. The captain replied, "Affirmative, we sure are. We've got the aircraft back under control, but it would help us immensely for a heading to reprogram the GPS."

Jay then issued: "Kalitta 66, if able - fly a heading of 330."

The ARTCC computer systems are pretty good. Controllers can type a couple of commands, then click with their trackball mouse - and the system will provide a range and bearing. The further from the airport or fix the aircraft is, the more of a guess it will be for the controller, as the system does not consider the winds. Therefore, controllers will periodically update the issued headings. Since most aircraft have GPS, this technique is used less often, a lot of the times being during emergencies such as this one.

About a minute later, Jay advised Kalitta 66 of precipitation ahead. The pilot, sounding a lot better, responds by asking for a deviation right of course.

The aircraft descends through the assigned altitude of 12,000 and shows 11,300 when Jay says, "Kalitta 66... are you able to maintain one-one thousand, eleven thousand?"

"Affirmative, Kalitta 66, eleven thousand."

The aircraft continued to 10,800 feet, and Jay asked again, "Kalitta 66, are you able to maintain altitude at one-one thousand?"

In reply, the pilot remarked: "Affirmative, Kalitta 66, one-one thousand, is this transmitter working alright?"

"Roger, eleven thousand, Kalitta 66," the co-pilot added.

"As he got lower," Jay recounted to me, "he started sounding better. When he got down, everything sounded normal again - a huge sigh of relief for everybody in the area and all the supervisors who had been monitoring the situation."

Once the aircraft was level, Jay asked: "Kalitta 66, roger. Say intentions."

The co-pilot answered, "Kalitta 66, destination Ypsilanti."

A short time after that, the captain added, "Aircraft stable now, thank you."

The pilots flew the rest of the flight to Ypsilanti at low altitude without incident. According to Jay, the whole time this was happening, he had moderate traffic levels and was constantly issuing control instructions to other aircraft. After Kalitta 66 left his airspace, the traffic level started to come down, and Jay was relieved from the position within 5-10 minutes.

"Of course, after it happened, I did get relieved," Jay noted. "Then all the pats-on-the-back and everything started coming. After it was over, it was pretty exciting. During it, it was pretty hair-raising to say the least."

Jay expressed just how thankful he was that the one controller had hypoxia training as a pilot and suggested it as the potential problem. He reiterated how impressed he still is at the teamwork from all the controllers in the area, who all pitched in to help in their own way.

"Now, again at the time, she says hypoxia which turns out to be what the case was, but there is also that one chance in 100 maybe that he really did have an airplane that he couldn't control," he concluded. The alarm in the background was an alarm on the airplane due to low pressurization.

I can understand his hesitation because controllers are trained to help the pilots during emergency situations, never providing control instructions unless asked. That is why Jay said "if able" during the initial clearance.

According to FAA information, "the captain was a 67-year-old retired airline pilot. He had little recollection of the event, and the co-pilot was believed to have been unconscious. The captain had been trying to engage the autopilot but was unsuccessful. If it would have engaged it, it is entirely possible he would have also passed out, which would have led to a different outcome for the worse."[57]

In retrospect, Jay finds it interesting that at least 15-20 other pilots were on frequency while this was happening. Whether they thought of it or not, none of them said anything about hypoxia, or any other ideas for that matter.

The controllers involved, including Jay, received the prestigious National Air Traffic Controller's Association's Archie League Award for Safety for the Great Lakes Region.

I reached out to Bill Salazar, M.D., a now retired FAA Regional Flight Surgeon, who has accident investigation experience. I asked his thoughts about KFS66 and hypoxia in general. In an email to me, he remarked:

"As with anything medical answers are never black or white because symptoms depend on the makeup of the human. In general terms, 'hypoxic hypoxia' will lead to symptoms ranging from mild to severe. Mild to moderate symptoms might include: temporary memory loss, reduced ability to move your body parts (sluggish or incoordination), restlessness, confusion, shortness of breath, difficulty paying attention, or difficulty making sound decisions. Severe symptoms range from seizures to coma and death.

With respect to being hypoxic and staying on task depends on the individual. I have witnessed multiple altitude chamber flights at CAMI, where some people crapped in minutes and other people who stayed focused for 15 minutes or more, albeit not at 100%. The constitutional makeup of the person is critical. Bottom line is when I gave recommendations on hypoxia for private pilot groups, I tried to think of how to keep that "weakest link" person out of trouble. Some basic recommendations:

- First and foremost, don't get yourself into situations that could make you hypoxic, i.e., follow FAA rules on altitude and oxygen use - for pressurized aircraft check oxygen and pressurization systems on every flight.

- Consider carrying supplemental aviation oxygen for flights above 10,000 feet (even if not required) – for pilots with chronic respiratory illnesses they might consider this for lower altitude flights. Remember that hypoxia impairs night vision early on.
- If you have any kind of respiratory condition such as asthma, emphysema, etc. or if you are a smoker, recognize that you are susceptible to hypoxia at lower altitudes.
- Never forget your passengers – they can become a liability if they become hypoxic.
- Understand and recognize the stages and symptoms of hypoxia (a good website is Mountain Flying LLC at https://www.mountainflying.com/Pages/mountain-flying/hypoxia.html) – as soon as a pilot recognizes something is not right, they should go on oxygen and/or descend.
- Consider using a finger pulse oximeter in flight (they are very inexpensive) to monitor your oxygen levels. Hypoxia for most people hypoxic symptoms start at around 92% oxygen saturation with more severe symptoms at 89% or lower."

CHAPTER 14

SMOKING BATTERY

On March 8, 2020, I was working the Shenandoah Sector at Washington ARTCC. The traffic had died down, but I was still working thirteen aircraft. I took the handoff on United Airlines Flight 355, a Boeing 737-800 flying from Newark Liberty International Airport (KEWR) to George Bush Intercontinental/Houston Airport (KIAH) level at Flight Level 360. The pilot checked on saying, "Washington, United 355 level 360."[58]

A little over four minutes later, the pilot said, "Um, Center, United 355."

I responded, "United 355, go ahead."

"Sir, we're going to need to declare an emergency and divert to Dulles," the pilot replied. "We've got um, a personal, or a passenger's personal device, electronic device is smoking."

"Uh, United 355, roger. Cleared to the Dulles Airport via direct, descend and maintain Flight Level 340. And what's the reason again?" I did not specify which direction for them to turn as, at the time, Dulles was pretty much directly behind them. As I initially didn't have any traffic for them, I left it up to the crew to pick which way they'd like to turn.

The pilot acknowledged, "Uh, direct to Dulles, maintain Flight Level 340. We've got a passenger's, ah, personal electronic device is smoking."

"United 355, roger. I assume you want the uh, um, [fire] equipment standing by?"

"Yes, please. And we're initiating a left turn back to Dulles," he concluded.

As I was coordinating this emergency, all I could think of was a time back in college when we were studying Air Canada Flight 797; a Douglas DC-9 that exploded some 90 seconds after an emergency landing at the Cincinnati/Covington Airport (KCVG) as passengers were evacuating.[59] The professor told us that if there is smoke or fire, it is not if, but when, will the aircraft explode. Alarmed, I informed the supervisor on duty of the situation.

At high altitudes, the turn radiuses of aircraft can be very wide. Wahoo Sector owns the airspace to the east, at the same altitudes, and Shenandoah and Wahoo Sectors sit side-by-side, so I put a data block on her scope, pointed at it, and told her "Point out," and they are turning left to Dulles - meaning, they will fly into her airspace.

The Wahoo controller had an aircraft at FL340, bound to the south-west. I thought the two aircraft might get a little close, so I told the Wahoo controller that she may want to turn that aircraft.

She agreed and turned her aircraft left 20 degrees, and had another aircraft several miles behind that, also at FL340. I told her I would miss that traffic with UAL355.

The next order of business was to get United 355 to a lower altitude. The Tech and Gordonsville Sectors were combined, and they own the airspace below mine. I hollered over to the controller (not through the headsets) that UAL355 was in a left turn direct Dulles and asked how low can I descend them.

He said FL280 - which is the floor of that section of airspace.

I descended United 355 to FL280, then switched their frequency to Tech/Gordonsville.

As the aircraft was on the Tech/Gordonsville frequency, the controller received an update from the flight crew that it was a passenger's personal device that was smoking, and they did have it inside a fireproof bag.

At the time of this writing, the FAA has not approved any fire suppression bags. There has been a lot of concern about the lithium-ion batteries catching on fire. In 2018, the TSA was days away from implementing rules mandating passengers to put any lithium-ion batteries in checked luggage, but the FAA stopped it with the mindset that if any device does catch on fire, it needs to be in the main cabin so the crew can do something about it.

When you change frequencies, I recommend checking in, saying something similar to "Washington Center, United 355, emergency aircraft, Flight Level 330 descending to Flight Level 280." The controller is already going to know you are an emergency case. However, the other aircraft on the new frequency have no idea. As you would imagine, when other pilots hear an emergency aircraft, most of them will limit their radio transmissions to keep the frequency clear for the emergency aircraft.

For example, after I switched United 355 to the Tech/Gordonsville Sector, a pilot was asking for a new cruising altitude. The timing of that request happened about the same time United 355 switched frequencies, and instead of checking in, I think they were busy getting set up for the diversion.

After establishing communications, the Tech/Gordonsville controller coordinated with the sector below him and descended UA355 to Flight Level 230.

The supervisor was standing behind the Tech/Gordonsville Sector, talking on the handheld phone with the Traffic Management Unit (TMU), who were coordinating with Potomac TRACON and Dulles ATCT. The controller asked, "United 354," misspeaking the plane's callsign, "do you know how many souls on board and if anybody is on oxygen?"

"One hundred, forty-nine souls on board and nobody on oxygen that we're aware of," the pilot replied.

The controller started to switch UAL355 to the next sector's frequency but stopped. As he keyed up, the next sector approved UAL355 to descend to 16,000 feet and didn't need to talk to them, saving the pilots the extra step.

Under the guidance of a supervisor, the controller asked about the fire: "United 355, is the fire contained in the cockpit currently?"

"It's in the cabin, it's in the thermal containment bag, but it is contained in the bag. We just need to divert."

"Roger," the controller replied before switching UAL355 to Potomac

TRACON.

Upon checking onto Potomac TRACON's frequency, the controller asked UAL355's pilot which runway they preferred at Dulles, to which the pilots selected Runway 19C.

As the aircraft was abeam the airport on a downwind leg, the controller said, "UAL355, and ah the tower said they have all the emergency vehicles on 19L, um, do you need 19C or are you okay with 19L?"

"19L is fine, ah UAL355."

The controller asked the pilot about switching runways. As an emergency aircraft, the pilot-in-command is in control and dictates whatever they need.[60] This flight has a professional crew who accepted the runway change. If you are ever in this situation and even hesitate a little, it is okay to tell ATC no.

I don't know how long the emergency vehicles would take to drive to the Center Runway, but UAL355 still had several minutes of flying time left before they would land. I would bet the equipment could have made it to the Center Runway with time to spare.

As UAL355 crossed the runway threshold, emergency vehicles followed them down the runway. As UAL355 turned off the runway and stopped past the hold-short line, it switched frequencies to monitor fire/rescue and the ATCT. The emergency vehicles surrounded the aircraft to check its exterior.

After some time, the pilot called, "and uh Rescue, uh, this is UAL355."

"Go ahead for airport ops," the ground operations crew replied.

"Yeah, um, we'd like to get to the gate as quickly as we can. There's not a fire," the pilot exclaimed. "There's a device that was giving off some smoke and some fumes. It's under control, it's in the bag, but it's still giving off some fumes. But we need to get to the gate because uh because of the fumes.

"Ops copies."

The pilot continued, "and it was okay, and it was located by the aircraft aft right door, and if we could speed this up, I sure would appreciate it."

This is an excellent example of a pilot being assertive to tell others what they need. If you ever need it, don't hesitate, you should make this type of statement to ATC!

It did take a bit longer for the emergency vehicles to clear the aircraft, but UAL355 was able to make it to the gate.

After this incident, I started thinking like a general aviation pilot.

I spoke to Robert Ochs, Ph.D., Manager of the Fire Safety Branch at the FAA Technical Center in Atlantic City, NJ. He has conducted studies with lithium-ion batteries.

First, Robert said "I give lectures and I usually start off by saying there's seven lithium-ion batteries on my person when I go on an airplane, and that's common. My watch, my phone, my tablet, my computer, my earbuds, the case the earbuds go in, it's all got lithium-ion batteries."

I realized that when I fly, I have several lithium-ion batteries with me personally, plus whatever any passengers I have with me. I always have my phone, tablet, ADS-B receiver, handheld VHF transceiver, and a backup tablet battery. And that doesn't include any video cameras I mounted for the flight!

Robert continued "Lithium itself is a highly reactive metal. It's very reactive and that's why they are good batteries. They'll discharge fairly quickly when they're in use, they'll recharge pretty quickly as well, they have a lot of potential energy within them."

He continued "Inside the battery, depending on the construction, it's a cathode and anode separated by a thin film layer. Everything is fine when they're used and put into equipment, but there could be small microscopic latent defects that don't really manifest themselves in that separation layer. Over time it could break down [or from] over use – charging and discharging."

"Once you have the cathode and the anode short circuited within the battery, now it's an internal short and it will just get hotter and hotter until it reaches thermal runaway - what that is called."

"[The battery] could be dropped and that could force it to happen quicker."

"We assume any Lithium battery has potential to go into thermal runaway which would cause smoke and flames."

Robert said that smoke and fire are the same chemical reaction, but fire doesn't produce as much smoke. It just burns it up! When it burns, it burns around 2,000 degrees Fahrenheit.

The second thing which stood out to me is he said is we should always treat lithium-ion batteries as if they will explode.

Therefore, the official FAA recommendation uses a Halon extinguisher to extinguish the flames. Halon has been found to degrade the ozone layer and is no longer produced, but it is still sold from recycling old extinguishers. There are a couple of replacements called Halatron and Halatron BRX.

When I was going through my private pilot training, my instructor told me only to use the fire extinguisher if absolutely needed as it puts so many chemicals into the air that I wouldn't be able to breathe. I asked Robert about that, and he said that is an old theory and tests have proven otherwise.

Halon is very good at extinguishing the flames. However, the problem with lithium-ion batteries is they reach thermal runaway if they are not cooled. Halon does not cool them. Therefore, dump water on the battery to cool once the flames are extinguished. If you don't have water, use whatever non-alcoholic liquid you have.

After you have cooled it with liquid, if you can, submerge it in water to further cool. However, never submerge in ice. Ice will trap the heat and risk reigniting the battery- basically the Igloo effect – from acting as insulation and keeping the temperature from dropping further.

I asked if the FAA has done any studies for lithium-ion fires with general aviation. He said, not to his knowledge. I told him that I have my iPad mounted via suction cup to the window when I fly, and it hangs over my left leg.

There are no studies that have tested ambient temperature, so they do not know if the hot summer days on the tarmac without air conditioning will have an effect or not. In addition, they have only done testing on fully charged batteries and do not know if a partially-charged battery changes fire susceptibility.

I asked him about the fire suppression bags. He said "we really don't have any advice for the burn bags. The problem is, I guess, they could lead people to believe they can handle a device that is in a thermal runaway event and put it in a bag because that's safer."

Robert stated the FAA officially does not certify fire bags. The official FAA recommendation is to use Halon to extinguish the fire, cool the battery with water, or any non-alcoholic liquid, then submerge the battery in liquid. Be mindful to avoid using ice. At that point, according to Robert, if you want to place it into a fire suppression bag, you can.

He recounted some testing at the Tech Center with fire suppression bags. The FAA had professional firefighters in full turnout gear, their flame-resistant uniform, on hand and following the directions from the fire suppression bags. Once the batteries ignited, the firefighters attempted to put the device in the bag. However, the tests didn't go as planned. When they tried to put the device into the suppression bag, the battery on fire fell out of the device onto the floor, and the firefighters didn't even notice!

One tricky part of these bags, Robert noted, is a lot of them come with gloves to handle the device. Unfortunately, the battery can explode, and the rest of your body is unprotected, making for a very uncomfortable situation. He continued "Even if the kits did come with that much equipment, by the time you put all of that on the event will probably be over anyway."

Therefore, the best way to handle it is to follow the FAA's Safety Alert for Operators (SAFO)[61], extinguish the fire with Halon, and cool it with water.

Imagine your tablet caught on fire as you had it mounted in the airplane. The fire burns at approximately 2,000 degrees F right in front of you. Imagine how much longer it would take to get the fire suppression bag from storage, put the gloves on, try to remove the device from the mount – which holds the device very firmly and can be challenging to remove in everyday situations - and place it into the bag.

To me, it makes perfect sense to have the fire suppression bags on larger aircraft where people can move easier. It was successful in containing the smoking device on the UAL355 emergency.

But in small GA aircraft, there isn't much room to move. So, at a minimum, in addition to the installed fire extinguisher, consider having a bottle of water with you when flying with your devices.

The FAA keeps a database of "Events with Smoke, First, Extreme Heat or Explosion Involving Lithium Batteries."[62] In 2021, when airline traffic was low due to COVID-19, there were 54 events reported to the FAA. Categories include personal electronic devices, e-Cigarettes, Cell Phones, Battery Packs and Laptops.

I have to admit, this is more of a problem than I ever expected.

CHAPTER 15

"IMMEDIATELY"

Imagine you decided to take a flight for that $100 hamburger, or more realistically, it's now several hundred dollars. Recently, you heard about a great restaurant located approximately 200 miles from your home airport. You think it would be fun to make a day of it to fly the long cross-country, perhaps next Saturday. You invite your two closest family members or friends to join you, and the weather is forecast to be "extreme" VFR.

The morning of your planned flight, the forecast was spot on: absolutely perfect! Even though it is VMC, meaning the weather is good enough for VFR flight, you file an IFR flight plan. You make it to your airplane, complete the preflight and takeoff. You climb up to your cruise altitude, and the conditions are perfect - not even a single bump in the sky. You configure the plane just right.

About halfway to your destination, you are chatting with your passengers and are thoroughly enjoying the flight. At this point, you think to yourself: *this flight is simply perfect.*

Then, the air traffic controller observes traffic that just popped up on the radar scope! Maybe the other pilot's transponder was malfunctioning, or perhaps that pilot just realized they forgot to turn it on and finally pushed the button switching from STBY to ALT. The traffic is at your 12 o'clock, same altitude, opposite direction, type is unknown. At this exact moment, all that matters is the controller tells you about the traffic, so you have time to get out of their way.

The problem is your traffic is so close, the controller only has one chance to tell you about it, so you have time to maneuver out of the way. If you ask the controller to "say again," it will be too late.

What would you need that controller to say during their transmission so you understand that a collision is imminent and you need to perform to avoid the other aircraft?

The Pilot/Controller Glossary defines only two words to be used to describe urgency:

"IMMEDIATELY. Used by ATC or pilots when such action compliance is required to avoid an imminent situation."

"EXPEDITE. Used by ATC when prompt compliance is required to avoid the development of an imminent situation. Expedite climb/descent normally indicates to a pilot that the approximate best rate of climb/descent should be used without requiring an exceptional change in aircraft handling characteristics."

According to the definitions, "Immediately" is used to *avoid* an imminent situation, and "Expedite" is used to *avoid the development* of an imminent situation.

The "Expedite" definition goes further to describe what it means when it is issued for a climb or descent because controllers use it often.

The reason "Expedite" is used often is because it will be more efficient for the aircraft involved. For example, let's say I have a jet that wants to climb to Flight Level 230, but I have distant crossing traffic at 14,000 feet. I know if the jet climbs at a decent rate, they can continue to Flight Level 230 without having to level off.

I would issue "N12345, expedite through one five thousand for traffic. Climb and maintain Flight Level 230." I have seen some controllers that instruct every aircraft to expedite, which waters down the meaning. That is why I always tell the pilots why I need them to expedite.

Recently, there was a change in the ATC Job Order, allowing controllers to instruct pilots to leave an altitude within a given number of minutes. I use this more often now than "expedite" since "expedite" is subjective and doesn't provide positive seperation like a crossing restriction.

The AIM states: "When ATC issues a clearance or instruction, pilots are expected to execute its provisions upon receipt. ATC, in certain situations, will include the word "IMMEDIATELY" in a clearance or instruction to impress urgency of an imminent situation and expeditious compliance by the pilot is expected and necessary for safety."[63]

The AIM is very specific, stating all situations, including normal ones, you should execute a clearance upon receipt. Therefore, if *immediately* is used, you would need to complete the maneuver quicker than you usually would since you can't initiate the clearance any sooner than "upon receipt."

Before I get into the next part, I would like to ask you a favor. Will you keep an open mind and read this chapter until the end before you make any judgment or allow any previous experience to bias your thoughts?

Yes?

Great, here we go!

On July 7, 2015, there was a midair collision between a United States Air Force F-16C Falcon, callsign "Death 41," and a Cessna 150M, registered as N3601V, near Moncks Corner, South Carolina, approximately 17 miles north of Charleston Int'l/AFB.[64]

The F-16 was on an IFR flight plan being vectored for a practice approach at KCHS. The Cessna 150M departed the Berkeley County Airport (KMKS), an uncontrolled airport, on a VFR cross-country eastbound.

The controller vectored the Falcon southwest-bound and descended him to 1,600 feet, the minimum vectoring altitude (MVA). The F-16 was headed close to KMKS on his way to KCHS.

The controller observed VFR traffic at KMKS but assumed they were going to remain in the airport traffic pattern. Once she noticed the VFR traffic climbing above traffic pattern altitude, she started to advise the F-16 of the traffic.

She said, "Death 41, traffic twelve o'clock, two miles opposite direction 1,200 indicated, type unknown."

The pilot responded, "Death 41, looking."

"Death 41, turn left heading one eight zero if you don't have that traffic in sight," the controller continued.

Death 41 then responded, "confirm, two miles."

"Death 41, if you don't have that traffic in sight, turn left heading one eight zero immediately!" The response from the F-16 was garbled, but he did start turning left.

At the last second, the F-16 pilot saw the Cessna 150, which he speculated was within 500 feet of his aircraft. He applied full back pressure on the control stick, but it was too late: the F-16 collided with the Cessna 150. The F-16 pilot tried to keep his aircraft under control but ultimately had to eject to survive.

The Cessna pilot, a 30-year-old man, and his father as his passenger, both perished in the accident.

The National Transportation Safety Board, in its final report on the accident, concluded the probable cause(s) of this accident to be: "The approach controller's failure to provide an appropriate resolution to the conflict between the F-16 and the Cessna. Contributing to the accident were the inherent limitations of the see-and-avoid concept, resulting in both pilots' inability to take evasive action in time to avert the collision."

For full disclosure, part of my duties at FAA Headquarters were to attend the NTSB hearings and presentations, which is how I learned the details of this accident. I did not start working at CHS TRACON until 2018, three years after this accident.

The NTSB had several issues with how the controller instructed the F-16. I want to be clear by saying I think the controller made mistakes, and I don't believe anybody would argue that fact.

Nevertheless, there are a couple of expectations the controller had, which I can understand.

The NTSB had significant problems with her use of If/Then Clearances. I could see an argument made for the amount of time wasted since the controller said, "If you don't have the traffic in sight, turn left..." Honestly, I have used those types of clearances regularly throughout my career but have never used them in this same situation. I used this technique far before the two aircraft ever got that close to each other. I turned the aircraft I was controlling well before it could become an issue.

That said, after discussions about this accident, I no longer use this technique.

According to the report "the controller stated that when she issued the command to the F-16 pilot to turn left "immediately," she expected that the F-16 pilot would perform a high performance maneuver and that she believed that fighter airplanes could "turn on a dime."

Further, the NTSB recognized the controller's belief was in line with FAA Orders, but held different meanings between her and the pilot.

To communicate her objective, the NTSB said the controller should have said, "Death 41, turn left immediately heading 180, expedite your turn." However, this would be an illegal clearance.

"Immediately" and "Expedite" are two defined words in the Pilot/Controller Glossary which have different meanings. I believe the NTSB did well identifying the difference of expectations between the controller and the F-16 pilot. In spite of this, I don't think they realize how common of an expectation among controllers this happens to be.

I have spoken to several of my colleagues, asking them what they would expect a pilot to do if they used "Immediately" in a clearance. I was cautious about asking in a manner that would allow for an accurate answer without leading them in a specific direction. All of them I spoke to said they would expect a fighter jet to perform a high-performance maneuver. They phrased it differently, but the intent was the same.

While at Cleveland ARTCC, I remember my trainer discussing "Immediately" with me, and he told me that if I need to use "Immediately," then definitely use it! But I need to understand the consequences...

If I instructed one of the airliners we were currently working out of Detroit to climb or descend immediately, he said, the pilots would make an evasive maneuver so that anybody who wasn't wearing a seatbelt, such as flight attendants, would probably have broken bones. He said the maneuver would be so evasive, it would possibly put those people on either the floor or ceiling. Pilots will maneuver as far as their aircraft will allow, according to him, without jeopardizing the integrity of that aircraft!

He further said if one of the Air National Guard F-16s out of Toledo were told to climb immediately, the pilot would point the aircraft straight up. If they were told to turn immediately, the pilot would do a knife-edge turn since fighters have that capability.

Controllers are taught words mean things. In the F-16 and Cessna scenario, by saying "Immediately" as part of the control instruction, I believe most controllers would have expected the F-16 to perform a higher-than-normal maneuver.

In hindsight, I should not have been shocked by this issue. As my ATC trainer explained his expectations, my first thought as a pilot was I would not have taken evasive action . However, what they were saying was logical and made sense. Therefore, I tried to learn from it as both a controller and a pilot.

During the NTSB presentation, there was a discussion that the controller's tone of voice was a factor. I can understand how most pilots would think this, but again, I strongly disagree. Controllers actively train themselves to keep a calm, clear voice when busy and stressed. When they don't do this, most of the time, the pilots come back with "say again," forcing the controller to repeat the clearance and putting them further behind. It may sound robotic, but it saves time. Expecting a controller to change how they train for something during a stressful situation is naive. In fact, controllers are known for remaining calm during emergency situations, which can be comforting for pilots.

With that being said, I've seen probably 50% of the controllers maintain that calm, cool nature in actual high stress situations. Knowing that controllers strive for it, do you want to rely upon getting one of the 50% which does change their voice inflection even though they've trained not to?

I think the NTSB stopped their investigation short of discovering the real problem: Pilots and controllers use the same Pilot/Controller Glossary but interpret these definitions differently. Even if they want the pilot to respond less evasively to "Immediately," what does that leave the controller to rely upon?

After the NTSB's final report was published, the FAA developed training instructing controllers not to allow two aircraft, including both IFR and VFR, to get too close together. It essentially treats VFR aircraft similar to IFR aircraft. I agree that is good training to provide as in the past there were always a few controllers who only separated between two IFR aircraft. However, I don't believe that corrects the underlying problem. There has not been any training about expectations for the use of "Immediately."

Being an air traffic controller means that you are constantly fixing different situations. What happens when the controller accidentally lets two aircraft get too close to each other? "Immediately" obviously cannot be relied upon and there are no other defined words in the Pilot/Controller Glossary to aid in the situation.

As of right now, interpretations of words are by definition only, and that has unknowingly been taken away from the controller. I would really like to see a scientific study to see how this matter can be better handled, which could drive the needed change within the FAA Orders.

When I was a controller at Cleveland ARTCC, we were reviewing an operational error (OE) within the facility. One OE that I was briefed upon was a controller who keyed up to transmit to an aircraft. As he started talking on the frequency, he saw two other aircraft conflicting with each other. He stopped his first clearance mid-sentence, remained keyed up and said, "Oh f**k, Learjet 12345, CLIMB!"

The Learjet responded, "Center, Learjet 12345 is climbing at 8,000 feet per minute. Tell us when to stop!"

I can honestly say, if I am ever in a situation where I need a quick response from a pilot, I will probably use "f**k" in my clearance, as that is the only thing that I can guarantee will work. I will not rely upon a pilot to interpret my voice inflection properly.

The NTSB held a briefing to bring attention to midair collisions, and I agree with them on this concept. They have videos on their YouTube channel that shows computer simulations from inside the cockpit of both the F-16 and the Cessna 150.[65] They believe the see-and-avoid concept is physically impossible. Their simulations show, for the F-16 pilot to have seen the Cessna in time to maneuver out of the way, he would have had to look down and to the right through the bottom of his aircraft. And in order for the Cessna pilot to have seen the low profile F-16, he would have to see through the wing strut on his side of the aircraft.

Obviously, there is no way for either pilot to have accomplished this while in routine flight.

The NTSB believes traffic technology could have aided both aircraft to see their respective traffic in time to maneuver out of the way, as neither aircraft had Automatic Dependent Surveillance-Broadcast (ADS-B) In. The F-16 had a military version of radar, which he had configured to 20- and 40-mile range, manually alternating between the two ranges. There was no traffic advisory equipment in the Cessna.

With some exceptions, ADS-B Out is now required for aircraft operating in the designated airspaces within the United States. However, there is no requirement for the pilot to have ADS-B In. At least some ADS-B transponders have Bluetooth capability to transmit ADS-B to your electronic flight bag. Even if your aircraft doesn't have the equipment installed, you can get a portable ADS-B In system for only a few hundred dollars.

Personally, I bought the Stratus 3 to place on the dash of the aircraft, and it displays traffic on my iPad. Whichever method you choose, I highly recommend that pilots have ADS-B In viewable while flying their aircraft.

I want to be very clear: I do not blame this F-16 pilot. I believe this is a systemic issue where most pilots interpret the definition of immediately one way and the controllers interpret it the opposite way. My big question is: what can be used to communicate the urgency of a situation, especially when the controller only has enough time to say the clearance once, ensuring everybody is on the same page? Whether the word is "Immediately" or not, we need a legal form (not f**k) without relying upon a controllers' voice inflection to make the communication standard. Right now, we have no legal words we can use to guarantee the pilot will understand the severity of the situation.

I submitted a Safety Recommendation to expand the definition of "immediately," similar to how "expedite" describes climbing and descending.

The FAA decided to deny my safety recommendation as some are afraid if we expand on the definition of "Immediately," then some pilots will overstress their aircraft trying to comply.

The other reason they didn't want a change is they looked at how "Immediately" was being used at the time.

After I had submitted the safety recommendation, I heard a few controllers at Washington National Airport (KDCA) use it. They told several aircraft to "line up and wait and be ready for the immediate takeoff." Then they cleared them for the immediate takeoff.

The only other time I heard it issued was when an instructor took over from a trainee, which issued a bad vector to an aircraft. Those are the only times I've witnessed "Immediately" used in real life.

Now, if I was the pilot flying and I received a clearance to turn immediately, how I would respond would depend on the flight conditions at the time.

If I were in VMC, I would put the aircraft into a steep turn.

If I were in IMC, I would probably only go slightly steeper than a standard rate turn because I do not want to induce Spatial Disorientation. Whatever you do, DO NOT create a new problem trying to avoid the first problem!

So my question to you: if you were flying for that $100 hamburger, per the example at the beginning of this story, and the aircraft just turned on their transponder, does it really matter how that airplane got there, or do you only care about getting an ATC instruction which would allow you to get out of the way in a hurry?

Of course, every pilot out there would want to be told about the traffic so they could get out of the way.

Shouldn't there be a standard way that clearance is issued and not based upon the controller's tone of voice as the sole means of communication?

My sympathy goes to the family and friends of the father and son in the Cessna, to the F-16 pilot, and to everyone invloved.

CHAPTER 16

THUNDERSTORMS

There is no event better known for pilots than the Experimental Aircraft Association's annual gathering in Wisconsin, the EAA AirVenture Oshkosh! It's the pilot's version of New Year's, Christmas, and the Fourth of July – all rolled into one week. Hundreds of thousands of pilots and aviation enthusiasts gather for the more than ten-thousand aircraft that arrive at Whitman Regional Airport (KOSH) for the world's largest air show.

My first trip to AirVenture was in July 2012. One of my college friends was a controller the FAA brought in to work the heavy air traffic for the event. He had to work one of the days I was there, so I attended the show solo.

I was walking around, enjoying the static display exhibits, when I came across the Piper Aircraft setup, which had several different models in their area.

One of the sales associates saw me looking into the Piper PA-46 Malibu Meridian window and headed my way. As I noticed him approaching, I said hello and noted that I'm not currently a buyer as much as I would like to be, and I didn't want to waste his time.

That was okay by him; he had plenty of time and asked if I had any questions.

I told him I was a controller at Cleveland ARTCC, and I worked with Malibu pilots regularly. It was nice to be able to see one in person.

We discussed a few things then we eventually came upon the topic of weather radar. He told me that out of all the planes he had sold over the previous few years, only two were sold equipped with onboard radar. According to him, the people purchasing the aircraft ordered them with XM Weather which showed next-generation weather radar (NEXRAD) precipitation on their displays, and that was as good.

I was shocked by that. I mentioned that was interesting because, as a controller, I had always heard the onboard radar was way more accurate than NEXRAD, which is also displayed on our radar scopes as it could be up to 15 minutes delayed.

A few years later, I was working at FAA Headquarters, and I showed up early for a meeting that included some people from other offices. Two guys I'd never seen before were sitting there, so I struck up a conversation and found out they were engineers that worked with the weather radars.

Remembering my conversation from Oshkosh, I explained that I had always been told the precipitation displayed on our radar scopes could be delayed as much as 15 minutes. I never had an opportunity to ask somebody who worked on those systems, so I wondered if that was correct information.

They said, yes, it could be delayed 15 minutes, but in reality, it is not when we need it. They explained how the system worked as inside the radar dome, the dish starts at the lowest angle and rotates 360 degrees. Then, it adjusts up to the next angle and rotates 360 degrees. It repeats this process until it has captured all the angles – a process that takes 4 minutes to capture the data. Then, it sends the information to the computer systems, including our radar scopes.

Furthermore, there are two different settings for how often the system updates:

- In Precipitation Mode, it will update every 4 minutes.
- In Clear Air Mode, it will update every 11 minutes, which helps prevent wear and tear and cut down on electrical expenses.

Therefore, since it takes the system 4 minutes to run through all the different angles to capture the information, the displayed data is somewhere between 4-8 minutes old; it should update by the 8th minute and the lower altitude angle is the oldest data included in the update.

However, it takes an additional 4 minutes to beam the information up to the satellites and back down to the aircraft using XM Weather. Therefore, some of the XM Weather displayed in the aircraft is a minimum of 8 minutes old!

Now, imagine you are stuck outside somewhere when a thunderstorm approaches. How long does it take for the storm to move across the street to where you are?

Once it starts, how long does it take before the intensity levels change?

If you think about it, they can move really quick! Especially in the 4-8-minute window, the storm's leading edge can be several city-blocks away. Not to mention, the storm can change a lot in how it builds and dissipates in different sections.

Ideally, I believe it is best to have both systems. Onboard radar will give you a picture of what is happening right now. You can use XM Weather or the free ADS-B In Weather for the big picture.

During the summer of 2020, COVID-19 affected everybody's lives. Airline traffic was down significantly. Even though there were not as many "pushes" throughout the day, the ones we had could get busy. The FAA created special work schedules for controllers, splitting us into three different crews. We worked five days on, then ten days off. This allowed any COVID outbreak among staff to be secluded to only 1/3 of the workforce at any given time.

Due to this scheduling format, the number of controllers on duty was drastically lower in comparison to regular times. Since traffic counts were down, it mostly worked well.

During the evening shift on Aug 6, 2020, we took a couple of sick leave hits to our small crew. We had thunderstorms in the area, making our workload higher due to complexity. At the beginning of the shift, we knew it would be an "interesting" afternoon and evening.

As a result of low staffing, we worked 3 hours 15 min on position before getting offered a short break. Typically, we are offered a break no later than 2 hours on position. I know this sounds excessive, and when traffic is light and the weather is good, it can be. However, it is not nearly enough when working heavy traffic and/or bad weather.

On bad weather days, I've walked out on a break and have been so wound up it was hard to relax. I've also had my neck muscles so tight due to those sessions that I could barely move my head left or right. When it is that bad, it can be very difficult going back in to control again after a short break that wasn't long enough to even partly calm down.

After my short break, I returned to my area and plugged into the Wahoo Sector, relieving the controller currently working it. There were enough airplanes where it needed to be split by itself, especially since those aircraft were deviating due to weather inside the sector boundaries. At that point, it wasn't overly busy.

However, that didn't last.

After a while, the traffic levels started going up, and with the complexity due to deviations, it got busier but still manageable on my own without a D-Side.

As the Washington Metro departures (KDCA, KIAD & KBWI) checked onto my frequency, I climbed them into my altitude stratum and informed them of the weather. All of them requested deviations, which I accommodated.

It didn't take long and it was busy! I had several aircraft headed southwest-bound, mostly at flight levels 340, 360, and 380. It crossed my mind to ask for a D-Side, but I thought it was still manageable on my own. A bit later, I had a couple of aircraft ask for a shortcut to avoid the weather. I explained I could offer deviations, but I had to get them to the Greensboro VOR (GSO) before they turned south because there were several lines of traffic in the sector next to me.

By now, some aircraft were starting to step on each other on the frequency. I responded: "Multiple aircraft calling at once, N926AL, did you check on?" I use this technique to maintain control of the frequency so all the aircraft that stepped on each other the first time wouldn't do it again. I usually have a good guess at who is checking on based upon the handoffs I took. However, when it is an aircraft already on my frequency, that is a little longer to scan through all the data blocks to find them.

The first aircraft I asked did respond, saying they were climbing to Flight Level 330. I climbed them and advised them of the weather, issuing the deviation.

Then, I broadcasted, "Other aircraft calling Center, say again." It was an aircraft I was already talking to that wanted to deviate further than the 20 degrees they requested. I approved their new request.

Next, I got a call on the landline.

Landline calls from inside the ARTCC are a hotline directly into the other controller's headset. Outside facilities come across a "shout line" over the loudspeaker, which we have to hit the button to answer. This call automatically connected into my headset, and I hit the override button on the VSCS comm system to change the frequency audio from my headset to the loudspeaker above the radar scope so I could separate the conversations and be able to understand the people talking on the landline.

On the line was a controller calling, from the adjacent sector, pointing out one of their deviating aircraft who was going to cut into my airspace, so I approved the 'point out.' But while I was offline, I heard somebody check-in over the loudspeaker, but I missed the call sign.

After the landline call was complete, I hit the VSCS button again - moving the frequency audio back into my headset. I keyed up and said, "I was offline, last aircraft calling Center, say again."

With an annoyed tone, the pilot said, "For the third time, Airbus 1000, our dispatch wants us on a new route."

I started looking through all of the data blocks to find the call sign. I finally found them in the middle of my sector. As I was looking, she continued her transmission listing all of the fixes they wanted as their new route to Florida, but I wasn't ready for that.

At the ARTCCs, we type everything into the system - making pen and paper nearly extinct. Generally, the only time we use them anymore is for a route request including fixes we don't use every day. Most of the time, we have to get it from the supervisor's desk.

Since I missed the first few fixes while I was trying to find their aircraft data block, and I didn't have a pen and paper anyway, I had to sit and listen to her long broadcast wasting precious time until she was done.

I responded, "Airbus 1000, roger. Sorry for the delay - I am a little busy here. Unable your route request as I am too busy, but you can make your request with Atlanta Center, who you'll be talking with in a few minutes. If you need to deviate before then, let me know."

She said, "Okay," with a tone of voice that was extremely upset.

In addition to the time it takes to type in the new route and clear the aircraft, we also have to check with TMU, especially when bad weather is involved. That can take 5-10 minutes or more to get approval. When it is busy, we have to focus on keeping aircraft separated, and everything else is considered an additional service. Requests for new routes take the longest amount of time compared to all other requests, so it is the first one dropped when we are busy.

Then, I had another airliner say they have a request. I asked for their request, and they said they were looking for three different fixes to tie into arrival due to the weather.

"Unable," I replied, as I again had no pen and paper, nor the time to call TMU.

I cleared them direct to SLOJO as that's the best I could do, and told them if they need deviations off that heading to let me know.

Just as that finished, Atlanta ARTCC's High Rock Sector called over the loudspeaker on the shout line, saying unable to take Regional 2000 CRJ 700 (CRJ7) at FL360 – and N12345 – a Gulfstream at FL430 – the first two airplanes I had in handoff status.

I clicked on the line and asked if he can't take only the two aircraft he named or if I'm in the hold for everybody.

He didn't answer, so he must have been so busy he only had time to make the statement and then hung up.

Obviously, the answer was I was shut off completely. I yelled over to the supervisor that High Rock shut me off and I needed a D-Side!

The supervisor paged the only controller who was on a break back, and he had been out for less than 10 minutes after his marathon session on the lower sector!

I learned, early in my career from a controller I respected, that there is no shame in asking for help, called a "D-Side." He taught me to ask for help before you genuinely need it because it gets harder to ask when you are hyper-focused on the traffic. To be honest, I waited longer on this day than I usually do because of the short staffing. That was my mistake, but I did ask the minute I truly needed it.

The Gulfstream was the closest aircraft to the boundary line: "N12345, Atlanta Center just shut me off due to saturation so you can expect holding. For now, turn right heading 010, radar vectors for the hold."

"Center, N12345," the pilot replied. "You want us on a 010 heading? We are going south." I think I sighed in disbelief because even though I had been busy before, it was about to get a lot more complex, especially with pilots questioning their clearances after I had already explained the reason why.

However, we always tell pilots to ask for confirmation if they didn't get a clearance:[66] "N12345, Atlanta Center cannot take you due to saturation so you can expect holding, turn right heading 010, radar vectors for the hold!"

After the second telling, he accepted the clearance.

But at this point, another aircraft asked for a new route.

"Attention all aircraft," I announced! "I have to start spinning airplanes as Atlanta Center just shut me off due to saturation. Please do not call me unless you need a deviation!"

Of course, just after that, a pilot asked about the rides – meaning the amount of turbulence being reported... In disbelief, I honestly don't remember if I answered or not.

Next, I turned the CRJ7 to the same heading. I had to turn both of these aircraft because they were getting too close to the Atlanta ARTCC boundary line, and due to how these sector boundary lines are designed, putting them in present position holds would have infringed into the next sector. Therefore, I had to turn them around to get them away from the boundary lines to issue holding instructions.

The next three aircraft closest to the Atlanta boundary were all in line at FL380. One of them was able to accept FL400, so I climbed them. I descended another one to FL340 and issued present position holds to these three aircraft. After I vectored the Gulfstream and CRJ7 to the same general location, I issued them holding patterns as well. At this point, I had five aircraft in holding patterns at all the westbound altitudes from FL340 to FL430.

The D-Side, who was paged back arrived in the control room, sat next to me, and asked what I needed. As I pointed at the gaggle of aircraft near the Atlanta ARTCC boundary, I told him to make sure everybody was separated there. Since I was issuing headings, I wanted to ensure the winds were not pushing them back into the original line of aircraft I turned away from.

It was nice to have a second set of eyes. Luckily, the true craziness had already passed, but I was still busy and welcomed the help. It only took a few minutes for the D-Side to return to the control room, and all of this transpired during those few minutes.

I instructed all the other aircraft in the sector headed southwest-bound to maintain minimum practical airspeed as they can expect holding, once they get closer to Atlanta ARTCC.

After about 15 minutes, Atlanta ARTCC called and said they could take airplanes again. I started with the Gulfstream and went in order after that, issuing clearances out of their holding patterns.[67] I then issued normal speed to all the other aircraft.

As all of this was happening, the line of precipitation had moved into the middle of my airspace, forcing my traffic to deviate into the sector east of me. This is an issue because that sector works all of the arrivals into the DC Metro area, Philadelphia, and overflights to New England. Deviations are especially problematic when dealing with climbing and descending aircraft because they are not level at an altitude correct for direction of flight. Finally, TMU had stopped departures routed through my sector.

Almost instantly, things finally slowed down and the traffic levels were lower than when I sat down for this session - I thanked the D-Side for his help, and he went back out to finish his break.

Even though we were short-staffed that night due to the two sick leave hits and the COVID schedules, short-staffed shifts during normal operations happen often enough. Thunderstorms and other weather issues create complexity, and when traffic volumes climb, we may have all of the staffing on position and need more. High traffic levels can be predicted, but the complexity, in addition, makes it super busy quickly. By the time the D-Side got back to the control room on this day, it was mostly over. Other times, it lasts a lot longer.

As a pilot, try to be aware of what the controller is telling pilots. If they use the term "I'm too busy" or you hear them say "unable" to shortcut requests, try to limit your communications to necessary transmissions only. Don't ask for a shortcut because you are late (everybody is late when there is bad weather). Please keep your communications brief and avoid listing a laundry list of fixes without the controller asking for them. A lengthy pilot transmission can put the controller behind the 8-ball quicker than you think. The controller may not be issuing a constant flow of clearances, but may still be busy with several aircraft as they constantly scan and coordinate on the landlines.

The next day, I arrived to work for my afternoon shift, with thunderstorms forecast again. That summer, it just seemed like we had more bad weather than I could remember as we were getting our teeth kicked in every single day!

Later that shift, I worked the Shenandoah Sector, where a line of thunderstorms ran from the southwest to the northeast about 300 miles long

- going right through my airspace! The computer showed the tops in the low 40,000s, and I didn't have any aircraft get high enough to give me a cloud tops report.

But there was a single break in the line of precipitation where aircraft were going through to get on the west side of the weather.

It started getting busy. It became a race to get the aircraft level at an altitude as soon as possible so they could all go through the same hole. On average, there was an aircraft in line with the others at the same altitude about every 10 miles or so, and this was at all the westbound altitudes of FL340 through FL400. All of the pilots were doing a good job and, even though it was busy, it was working well.

At this point, Indianapolis ARTCC called on the shout line. I picked up, and they were APREQing – an Approval Request - a U.S. Navy F-18 fighter jet, negative RVSM (Reduced Vertical Separation Minimum), at Flight Level 370 to stay on top of most of the weather. He was going to Norfolk, which is supposed to be at Flight Level 330 or below because we have to get them to Flight Level 230 in roughly 50 miles.

There is a short list of non-RVSM aircraft which are allowed into RVSM airspace such as military, medevac, and foreign state aircraft.[68]

Anytime a pilot requests something because of the weather, I do my best to approve it. As the Indy controller was saying his APREQ, I was scanning incoming traffic and trying to figure out where I would put this F-18, especially since he was non-RVSM.

Being Non-RVSM requires 2,000 feet separation instead of 1,000 feet.[69] Therefore, since the F-18 was at Flight Level 370, I couldn't have any westbound traffic at Flight Levels 360 or 380. That takes away half of my available altitudes for however long it takes the F-18 to go opposite direction through the hole in the precipitation.

The Indy controller called early for the APREQ since he knew we were dealing with weather issues. I had to zoom out on my radar scope a few times to see where the aircraft was located. Being that far away, I wasn't sure where my traffic would be located when the F-18 entered my airspace.

I told the Indy controller that I didn't know if I could and told them the

APREQ is approved, but my control - meaning I can issue control instructions to the F-18 while the aircraft is still in Indy ARTCC's airspace. The Indy controller gave me control, and I hung up the line.

Once the F-18 got close enough to appear on my radar scope, I took the handoff. The pilot checked onto my frequency. I told him that I had several aircraft southwest bound at all the even altitudes. I asked him how high he would have to go to top the weather because otherwise, I may have to put him into a holding pattern to wait for a break in traffic. After all, I have a lot of aircraft going through the only hole in the weather.

Knowing he was a fighter jet, I didn't have any issue climbing him as I know he could descend extremely quickly once past the precipitation, allowing him to avoid conflicting with the other lines of traffic and meeting the altitude restriction for his destination.

The pilot replied that he sees all the opposite direction traffic on his radar, but he doesn't think he can get high enough to fly overtop. I instructed him to fly an easterly heading and expect holding instructions in a few minutes.

I turned my attention to some other aircraft checking on, requesting deviations.

Just as I was going to issue the holding instructions to the F-18, he requested a 30° left turn for the weather as he thinks he can get around the worst of it going that direction. I approved the deviation, which would take him into the Marlington Sector.

I then called the Marlington controller to tell her what was going on and initiated the handoff. Before she heard my call in her ear, she said, "Ah, negative RVSM." Non-RVSM aircraft have a coral box around the altitude marker.

I told her the F-18 said they couldn't climb above the weather and wanted to deviate to the left. I gave her control and hung up, then switched the F-18 to her frequency.

The F-18 ended up turning further to the left than 30°, and then climbed up to Flight Level 430 and went across the weather. I suspect the cloud buildups must have been lower further to the north, and, once he crossed the line, he dropped like a rock as he descended down!

In the end, it worked out for everybody.

When working during thunderstorms, each day is always different because every storm is different. The cloud tops, the width of the precipitation and turbulence associated with them are always diverse and dynamic. Sometimes, pilots report cloud "buildups" which, at times, sound pretty nasty.

In the ARTCC, even though we depict NEXRAD precipitation, we only have a couple sets of altitudes we can select so we rely upon pilot reports to get a good idea what is actually out there. NEXRAD only depicts precipitation and not clouds.

On one particular afternoon shift we had moderate traffic levels flying through the area and the side-by-side sectors Shenandoah and Wahoo were spilt.

The pilots who were headed southwest bound started checking on frequency and asking for left deviations around cloud buildups several miles ahead. Initially they were just inside the sector boundary line when they needed to turn, which was easy to approve.

The buildups must have been growing quickly because soon they needed to turn before they even left the Pinion Sector's airspace. I called the Pinion Sector to get control to turn the airplanes while they were still in their sector, which they quickly approved.

Finally, the clouds built up enough so the aircraft were starting to deviate well before they got to my sector. These clouds must have looked massive because all the aircraft were deviating 40-50 miles off their route to avoid them.

The Pinion controller was issuing their deviation instructions and then handing off the aircraft to me, at the Wahoo Sector. The ERAM computer system allows controllers to type in a message in the fourth line of the data block, up to 8 characters long. This allows us to avoid calling each other on the landlines for every aircraft which is not doing exactly as the flight plan dictates. On this day, the data blocks said "DL/GSO" or "DL/FLASK"[70] meaning "deviating left, when able direct Greensboro VOR (GSO)" or "deviating left, when able direct to the FLASK intersection."

Even though Shenandoah and Wahoo were split, I was getting all the aircraft for both sectors from the northeast as their deviations took them through my airspace. In addition, I had aircraft in other parts of my sector deviating as well.

I didn't have a lot of aircraft at the time, but I was moderately busy due to the complexity.

I had an aircraft make their way around the buildups and then advised me they were direct FLASK.

About a minute later, a pilot keyed up and started making an announcement to the passengers, or so he thought. He forgot to switch his comm panel to speak over the Public Address system, or "PA" to talk to the passengers, but instead was talking on my frequency.

After thanking everybody for flying with them, he started talking about the forecast weather in Dallas. As I looked at all of my data blocks, only one aircraft went to Dallas-Fort Worth International Airport (KDFW), a Boeing 737-800. For what it's worth, DFW is a central hub for American Airlines, but this was not an American Airlines flight.

He unkeyed for a bit, so I immediately tried to tell him he was broadcasting on my frequency. It didn't work. He paused his speech again, so I tried one more time with no luck.

Finally, after about two minutes, which is an <u>eternity</u> in ATC time, he ended his long-winded passenger announcement. Thank goodness!

Well, that is when all the other pilots started keying up and making fun of his mistake.

In the dozen times or so this has happened to me before, I've been lucky that it occurred when I wasn't too busy, and I got to laugh along as the other pilots made fun of the offending party.

After the third pilot added his jab on frequency, I keyed up - intending to ask everybody to please stop as I'm busy with deviations.

Well, the actual verbiage I said was, "Okay, everybody shut up, I'm too busy for this crap!"

As soon as I unkeyed, I thought, *did I really just say that? Whoops, I didn't mean to come off harsh like that.*

Then I thought, *oh well, I have no time to worry about it now,* and kept working.

Once things calmed down, I felt terrible how that played out, but I realized that even though I didn't like what I said, it was effective as nobody else keyed up in jest again.

Remember, controllers are people, too. We like to laugh and tell everybody the difference is that pilots fly the planes – and controllers tell them where to go!

CHAPTER 17

IN-FLIGHT BREAKUP

When I worked at FAA Headquarters, a controller from the Atlanta office was in town on official business. Before starting his job in Atlanta, Georgia, he was a controller at Memphis ARTCC (ZME). While there, he was on position when an aircraft crashed. After everything was finalized with both the accident and the legal issues, he developed a briefing to teach other controllers about the accident.

Since he was in Washington, D.C., he scheduled his briefing as a "brown bag" session - given during lunch so interested employees could attend - to present to people at Headquarters. He emailed a briefing invitation to the group, and I thought it sounded interesting - so I attended.

On October 26, 2010, the controller was working as the radar controller on Sector 14 at Memphis ARTCC. That morning, there were two lines of thunderstorms near Memphis, Tennessee, with both lines running from the southwest to northeast. One line was west of Memphis,[71] And the other line was approximately 70 miles east of Memphis[72].

Around 9:25 a.m., N8045Y, a Beechcraft B36TC Bonanza, departed Olive Branch Airport (KOLV), a satellite airport southeast of Memphis. There were two people on board; the pilot, who owned the aircraft, and his wife as a passenger. The pilot filed an IFR flight plan to Dekalb-Peachtree Airport (KPDK), a satellite airport near Atlanta.

At 9:37 a.m. Central daylight time, N8045Y checked onto Memphis ARTCC's Sector 14, climbing through 6,200 msl to 7,000 msl on a heading of 090.

The ZME controller said, "N8045Y, Memphis Center, good morning. Tops ahead of you are estimated at one-seven thousand. You are cleared direct Muscle Shoals (MSL), flight plan route, if you need something different, let me know."

The pilot then asked for Flight Level 210, and the controller acknowledged his request.

Then, the controller said, "8045Y, listen up next transmission. I have a Cirrus on the other side of the weather that just went through it, also inbound to Peachtree. Let's see what he says."

The pilot responded, "Okay, 45Y."

The controller asked the other plane: "N815SR, can you give us a pirep (pilot weather report) for traffic behind you, departing Memphis headed to Peachtree?"

The pilot of the Cirrus replied, "Ah, yeah, we just had light turbulence and ah, period of, ah, pretty heavy rain but only for about a minute. We went through ah, a little gap in it. It was yellow to green on our onboard radar versus red on either side of it. It was fairly good."

"815SR, okay," the controller followed up. "Thank you, sir, and of course you were at niner-thousand when you went through the weather, correct?"

"That's affirmative, sir," the Cirrus' pilot concluded.

The controller then switched back to the Bonanza: "8045Y, so you might be okay lower. I can approve whatever you want to do."

"Okay, we heard that pirep," the Bonanza's pilot replied. "We'll go ahead and, ah, stick at 17,000. When we get above this next layer, we'll see what, what we see and ah, we can get above it, so we don't really need to go through it, so we'll tell you."

As the Bonanza was climbing through 10,300 msl, the controller added, "Bonanza 45Y, for additional traffic, amend altitude, maintain one three thousand." The pilot promptly accepted the change.

A couple of minutes later, as the Bonanza was climbing through 12,600' msl, the pilot keyed up and said, "Center, 8045Y, can we, ah, go deviate about 15 degrees right?"

Now, this is a very common exchange between pilots and controllers. Pilots often request to deviate 15 degrees right, 10 degrees left, or whatever the number is. When a controller replies with "cleared to deviate right/ left, direct ____ when able and advise," that allows the pilot to deviate as far-right or left as they want. Just because they asked for a certain number of degrees doesn't mean they are only cleared for that number unless the controller specifies it in the clearance issued.

For example, if I had traffic right of this Bonanza at the same altitude, I might say, "Bonanza 45Y, cleared to deviate up to 15 degrees right of course…" Then, the pilot is only allowed to deviate to that number. However, if the controller doesn't specify, which we usually don't, you can turn further than that if you need.

Keep in mind, it is good practice to let us know if you are going further than you originally specified, especially if it is a lot further.

On another side note, when making a deviation turn request, please say it in the form of the number of degrees right or left. Please do not say a specific heading, especially in the ARTCC environment. We do not know what heading you are currently flying - except in the rare case we assigned you a specific heading.

Typically, when we vector for anything other than approaches where we own down to the ground, we usually say turn 30 degrees right or 10 degrees left. The winds can be so strong that if we issue a heading, there is a possibility you will turn in the opposite direction than what we need. Therefore, we generally stay away from assigning a specific heading.

The controller replied to the Bonanza, "8045Y, yes sir. Left and right deviations are approved, when able, cleared on course, ah, resume own navigation, when able direct Rome (RMG) now and advise Center."

The Bonanza pilot reached 13,000 msl as he replied to the clearance, "Okay, we're at ah deviate 15 right back on course, we'll get Rome, and we'll advise Center, 45Y."

The controller did not specify to the pilot that he could deviate further right or even left. I usually don't correct the pilots either in this situation as, the way I see it, the pilot came up with his plan and only needed the 15 degrees right. Even though I tried to give them the liberty to go further, I don't need to waste precious time explaining it.

As I reviewed the radar video replay, a little less than three minutes after the Bonanza leveled, it appears the aircraft was located a couple of miles west of where the moderate precipitation began. At that time, the controller issued a climb to Flight Level 210, and the Bonanza started climbing again.

As the aircraft climbed through 13,700 msl, it appears to have entered the area with extreme precipitation. The aircraft continued climbing to 14,800 msl, which was as high as it got. Then, it started a rapid descent for a couple of radar updates and, after that, radar contact was lost.

The controller tried calling the pilot several times and even had a nearby FedEx aircraft attempt to relay a call. The controller also tried on the emergency frequencies, all with no reply from the Bonanza's pilot or passenger.

The wreckage of the Bonanza was found scattered across 15 miles, and several parts of the aircraft were never located. The National Transportation Safety Board (NTSB) analyzed the radar data and calculated the Bonanza had at least a 4,800 foot-per-minute rate of descent.

The NTSB's final report stated: "A survey of the wreckage indicate that all fracture features were consistent with overload failure induced by airload or impact, and examination revealed no evidence of a pre-accident mechanical malfunction."

In other words, the aircraft broke up due to high loads on the airframe.

The NTSB findings held the pilot responsible for the cause of the accident, but also blamed the controller, saying: "While the [pirep] was provided from the same general area, it was provided 20 minutes earlier, 5,000 feet lower and several miles north of the point of the accident... No other information was provided to the pilot about the precipitation depicted on the controller's display."

The controller solicited the pirep from a Cirrus, the last aircraft to go through the precipitation. Therefore, it was the most current and best report that could've been relayed.

The JO 7110.65 states, "Controllers must issue pertinent information on observed/reported weather and chaff areas to potentially affected aircraft…"[73] and provides guidance on how to issue the information to the pilots.

The examples in the 7110.65 don't cover the exact phraseology for precipitation in a line such as this. Therefore, if I were to issue a report on the precipitation depicted from this storm, I might say, "N8045Y, there is a line of moderate to extreme precipitation east of your position by approximately 50 miles. It is a line running from the southwest to the northeast approximately 15 miles in diameter."

Now, thinking from a pilot's point of view: if I received that information, does it tell me exactly where to navigate to avoid the precipitation?

Does it tell the exact location? No, it is approximate. I think the reason why controllers issue the depicted weather is purely a "heads up" to the pilots that there is precipitation, and they need to formulate a plan on if and how they intend to deal with it. I can't tell you how often I tell pilots about precipitation, and they tell me they will take a look and let me know, sounding like they didn't realize it was close!

Based upon the Bonanza pilot's actions, do you think he was aware there was precipitation along his flight route? I think it is evident that yes, as the pilot requested a right deviation for the weather.

The NTSB talked to the owner/operator of the maintenance facility the pilot used. He said the pilot had totaled a different Beechcraft A36 and, in addition, had N8045Y (the accident aircraft) repaired for flying both into "heavy" weather. The accident report quoted the facility owner's recollection that "The second airplane was brought to the facility within 30 days of the first."

The maintenance owner said, "I ended up with both overstressed aircraft parked next to each other in front of my shop." He added, "In my 33 years of aviation, I learned when these things happen (the accident), we knew it would happen in advance. I worried about [the pilot] for two years. He was doing better and I started to quit worrying."[74]

★ ★ ★

The executor of the accident victims' estate and surviving family members brought a lawsuit against the United States of America, alleging the FAA "breached its duty of care in providing control services."[75]

They alleged the controller was required to advise the pilot of the depicted weather. Since that is the reason the NTSB cited, I can understand why they argued that point in their lawsuit, and they further argued several other points.

I am not an attorney, but in my opinion, their other points were not very strong arguments.

For example, they tried to say it was the controller's duty to vector the aircraft. In its ruling: "The court declines to apply the vectoring provision because, based on the information he had available, controller ... did not perceive any immediate safety issue. Even if the vectoring provision applied in this instance, it does so in the same capacity as other weather services generally – as an *additional service* subject to higher priority duties."

Of course, what happens in court versus the outside world are two different things. The training I have received has us issue "suggested headings" if an aircraft asks for vectors around precipitation.

The reason is the **pilot-in-command (PIC) is always the final authority.**[76] Therefore, it is the PIC's decision on if and how to deviate, not the controllers. Our job is to make it work so you don't collide with other aircraft. That's it! I have come across many general aviation pilots who think controllers will vector them where they should go, but that is not the case.

The estate also argued the controller should have issued a "Safety Alert." The JO 7110.65 states: "Issue a safety alert to an aircraft if you are aware the aircraft is in a position/altitude that, in your judgment, places it in unsafe proximity to terrain, obstructions, or other aircraft."[77] The attorneys "argued that weather constitutes an 'obstruction,' the court is not persuaded (and finds no law to support)."

Before the fateful flight, the pilot called the Flight Service Station (FSS) to file an IFR flight plan. The FSS specialist asked if he had the weather, and the pilot said he did. The SIGMET (significant meteorological information) describing the thunderstorm he flew through was published before that phone call.

The Bonanza was equipped with dual Garmin GNS-430s, with active XM Weather subscriptions. This, in addition to other factors, led the court to believe the pilot already had the information about the thunderstorm. In the court's opinion, if the controller had issued the depicted precipitation, it would not have made a difference in the pilot's actions.

The court order stated, in regards to the JO 7110.65, "¶2-4-6. Important here is the provision's use of a solidus or "slash" punctuation – a common substitute for the word "or" ... Hence, the provision reads that a controller must, unless requested otherwise by the pilot, issue information on either "observed or reported" weather. In this case, the court finds that controller .... Issued "reported" weather consistent with the proper provision..."

Ultimately, the whole case was decided on the fact that the "/" is considered to be a replacement for the word "or," and the controller issued reported weather which satisfied his obligation.

In 2016, Senior United States District Judge William C. O'Kelley ordered judgment in favor of the defendant, the United States.

The pilot and passenger's estates and the surviving family then filed an appeal with the United States Court of Appeals for the Eleventh Circuit, which upheld the original judgment.[78]

While the NTSB blamed the controller for not advising the pilot of depicted weather - two different courts decided the controller "acted reasonably under the circumstances."

It is always a tragedy to lose loved ones and my condolences go to the family and friends of the pilot and his wife.

CHAPTER 18

TURBULENCE & CHOP

In 2007, I was training on the Toledo/Pandora radar positions combined at Cleveland ARTCC. I had only worked with this instructor a couple of times before, so she asked random questions to check my knowledge levels.

She asked me the difference between "chop" and "turbulence," and I replied that the only thing I knew about were the different definitions of turbulence.

She told me that "chop" is when the aircraft rolls left and right, and "turbulence" is when the pitch changes up and down.

Her explanation sounded absurd to me, so once I went on break, I went outside and called Chris, an airline Captain on the Embraer ERJ-145.

I asked him about "chop" and told him I thought she was wrong. He said that her explanation was wrong, but chop does exist. He explained chop was the bounces which were rhythmic, and turbulence was more like hitting a hole. He added that he would much rather be in chop over turbulence.

I was working an evening shift at Washington ARTCC. There were several areas of thunderstorms over the Carolinas and the Atlantic Ocean along the coast. Therefore, the Atlantic Routes (ARs) were closed and all of the traffic headed to Florida was rerouted through our area. This is a typical Severe Weather Avoidance Plan (SWAP) strategy from the TMU.

In addition, we had continuous light chop everywhere with occasional-continuous moderate chop within approximately a 40 nautical mile radius of Montebello VOR/DME (MOL). This is typical due to the mountains in that area. Also, Indianapolis ARTCC (ZID) had thunderstorm deviations where they were routing aircraft into my sector which typically weren't there. It got busy quickly, and I asked for a D-Side to help.

A Boeing 737 asked where the moderate chop was, and I told them 20 miles behind them. Another aircraft gave a ride report as they were reading back their frequency change. I had three pilots who were extremely needy asking about the rides. As you can see, if the controller is not careful, this is how a controller loses control of the frequency very quickly!

I had a Hawker on a bad routing who I was issuing the preferred route. A split second after I unkeyed from reading the VERY long reroute, a Cessna Citation checked on climbing to Flight Level 330, saying "looking for higher," even though they still had about 5,000 feet before they would level.

Issuing new routing to an aircraft while busy is one of the most time-consuming tasks a controller must perform. To have another pilot screw it up by not pausing for a couple of seconds after tuning into the new frequency is aggravating, to say the least.[80]

In one of the rudest comments I've ever made over the frequency, I said to the Citation's pilot, "Did you really not just hear me talking to another airplane?!"

Thankfully, the Citation's pilot apologized, and then I asked the Hawker if they got the route.

Naturally, the Hawker's pilot said they got the first fix but needed it read again for the remaining six items. Sigh… I read it all for the second time and, once the Hawker pilot confirmed the new route, I climbed the Citation.

It was so busy, when a pilot would call who had already been on my frequency - asking about the ride or requesting a new altitude - it was challenging to find them on the radar scope, as they are not in the typical locations where aircraft check-in!

Further, I had an A320 request a climb to FL360, and I told them unable as I was too busy. About five minutes later, once things calmed down a bit, the A320 pilot again requested the climb, and I happily obliged!

This is just a singular glimpse of how ATC can go from having a few airplanes and everything completely under control to being crazy-busy due to a few needy pilots. ATC has to remain in control of the frequency in those situations, so if you ever hear a controller say they are too busy for something - especially if you hear it multiple times - do not ask for anything unless you absolutely need it, such as an emergency or an encounter with severe turbulence![79]

I remember a solo flight back in college. The flight went well and I was about 5 miles from the airport, already talking to the tower. It was a smooth day and, as I was maneuvering over our visual checkpoint, I had a single hard bounce of moderate turbulence.

The airplane bounced so hard, I hit my head on the ceiling of the aircraft, which really hurt since I was wearing my old metal headsets!

I always remember back to how much I didn't particularly appreciate flying through moderate turbulence. As a controller, I do my best to advise pilots where the known chop and turbulence is, and offer possible alternatives.

However, when it gets busy, the controller's primary responsibility is to keep aircraft separated, not find the smoothest ride for their comfort.

As I was working the Wahoo Sector one afternoon, the sector below me initiated a handoff to me for a Boeing 737-800 (B738) who was headed southwest-bound and climbing to FL330. I took the handoff, and once they checked onto my frequency, I climbed them to FL360.

As they got close to the Atlanta ARTCC (ZTL) boundary, I handed them off to the Hirock Sector, which took it. Then, the B738 reported moderate chop at FL360 and wanted to descend to FL340.

I told them I had their request and I started to coordinate with Atlanta.[81] But as I was waiting for the Atlanta controller to answer the shout line, I noticed the data block altitude changed to FL356.

Concerned, I hung up the shout line and keyed up my frequency, asking the B738 to confirm they were level at FL360. I assumed they started down without a clearance, but a pilot report always supersedes the computer readout, which is why I asked.[82]

I continued, saying, "if you only have moderate, it's not severe, is it? Because if not, I need you to maintain FL360!"

They replied that they were in moderate-to-severe chop and couldn't maintain altitude. I was taken back by their response and half-wondered if I gave them the excuse they needed to justify their change in altitude. But that didn't matter, as I had to act quickly because they would be inside Atlanta's airspace before they leveled at FL340, and I didn't know if Atlanta had any traffic which would conflict with this airplane!

I called the Hirock Sector again, as they own FL350 and above. This time, they answered quickly, and I told them the B738 was going down to FL340 due to moderate to severe chop.

The Hirock controller acknowledged and quickly hung up to turn an aircraft level at FL350, heading in the opposite direction and right at the B738.

At the same time, I called the Charlotte Sector, which owns FL240-340. That's when the data blocks start flashing on my screen – the collision alert was going off for an aircraft who was level at FL340, heading west!

The Charlotte Sector controller answered the line, and I told him what was happening. He instructed me to turn the B738 to a 170 heading. I promptly did, and I issued a traffic advisory.

When I was on a flight deck training trip, flying in an airliner's flight deck jump seat to observe and learn, I talked to some pilots about determining their highest altitude based upon aircraft weight. From them, I learned that when the computer tells the pilots they can make a certain altitude with only a few hundred feet above, they usually only want to go to that altitude if there are smooth rides because the bouncing causes their airspeed to fluctuate. If the bouncing causes their airspeed to drop below the required speed, they could stall!

I'm not sure if this was their concern or not, but I can tell you they should have declared an emergency if they were going to handle it like that!

After we ensured separation between all of the aircraft, I asked the pilots our standard questions when severe turbulence is encountered – including if there was any damage to the aircraft or if anybody was injured. The crew replied no to both.

Due to their proximity to the ZTL boundary and because I had already handed them off, it takes some time to coordinate an altitude change between the three sectors.

This B738 narrowly avoided a midair collision with not just one but two aircraft because they started a descent without a clearance.

I know moderate chop is not fun, especially for scared passengers. However, it is much better than having a midair. It may take some time for us to coordinate, but when aircraft are in moderate, most controllers do their best to accommodate pilot requests.

CHAPTER 19

TMU

In August of 2020, I arrived to work for my afternoon shift at Washington ARTCC. As I clocked in and reviewed the daily memos, the controller working the Wahoo Sector hollered over to the supervisor on duty.

The supervisor looked up and over to the controller, who said a pilot wanted his manager's phone number, so he gave him the area phone number. The supervisor said, "Okay," then turned to me and remarked, "this guy is unbelievable."

I asked what happened – and he said there is a Citation that wanted a shortcut to Florida. The Citation was given a 4-hour ground delay at Teterboro, and, understandably, the pilot was not happy.

Within each ARTCC, there is a team of air traffic controllers that focuses on traffic flow management processes - as opposed to separating traffic. This team, called the Traffic Management Unit or "TMU," coordinates directly with the Command Center that oversees the entire National Airspace System.

A while later, TMU opened up a "playbook" route. The playbook is a set of routes used when the preferred routes will not work. There are several options based on the situation, and the controllers got in touch with the Citation pilot, telling him if he could accept the new route, which was pretty far out of the way, they could let him launch. The pilot accepted the new route and was soon airborne.

After he switched to Washington ARTCC, he asked for a shortcut.

The controller told him "unable" since he was on TMU routing, but they would check.

When TMU routing is issued, the letter "T" appears beside the data block on the radar scope and also beside the route on the D-Side computer.

Whenever TMU issues a special route, controllers must leave them on it unless TMU instructs otherwise. It would defeat the purpose of having TMU issue special routing, and then the controllers give a shortcut, which puts that aircraft into the traffic situation they were trying to avoid.

These routes are usually used to avoid overwhelming controllers with too much traffic or high complexity. Some reasons which trigger TMU intervention include bad weather, special events such as major air shows or college football games, low controller staffing, or when an air traffic facility goes ATC Zero.

The supervisor talked to TMU and was instructed to leave the Citation on their current route due to weather and traffic saturation – and the jet made its way through the first sector. As that controller initiated the hand-off to the Wahoo Sector, he called to let the Wahoo controller know this pilot was upset they did not approve the shortcut, and they checked with TMU and was instructed to leave them on the route. The supervisor from Area 1 came and told the supervisor in our area the same story. The Wahoo controller took the handoff.

The Citation checked onto the Wahoo frequency and immediately asked again for a shortcut. The controller acknowledged the check-in and again told the pilot he was unable as TMU instructed him to keep the plane on their assigned route.

Then, the Citation pilot came back and said they needed the shortcut because they didn't have enough fuel on their current route.

The Wahoo controller relayed the information to the supervisor. The supervisor called TMU again, and the response remained adamantly the same.

Frankly, whether this was true or just an excuse, it upset a lot of controllers. The pilot knowingly accepted the TMU route in order to avoid a ground delay. He should have never accepted it if he didn't have the fuel to fly it. The controller told the pilot that he had to stay on the current route and, if he needed to divert for a fuel stop, to let him know.

Nobody likes having ground stops and restrictions which delay aircraft. However, it is a necessary component to keep the airspace safe. I can tell you TMU tends to be fairly reluctant to issue restrictions. For example, when a line of thunderstorms is moving across departure routes, they tend to wait until the deviations are getting close to the arrival lines. Many times, controllers tend to want more restrictions in place sooner than what TMU is willing to provide, but they really do try to accommodate as many aircraft as possible.

After the controller told the pilot to let him know if they needed to divert, the pilot got mad and asked for the phone number for the controller's manager. That's when the controller told the supervisor he gave the area phone number while I was standing there.

I finished my clock-in procedures and grabbed my headset. I ran the "break board" to see who was next for a break. I relieved the Shenandoah controller so he could go home for the day.

After I finished receiving the position relief briefing and signed into the position, the supervisor walked around his desk over to the sectors.

"You're not going to believe this. The pilot used the airplane's satellite phone and called to complain," the supervisor announced.

I asked, "What did he say?"

"The pilot was just making the same argument he was on the frequency," the supervisor concluded. "I told him that, if he didn't have enough fuel, he shouldn't have departed on this route. So, he got upset and hung up!"

By this point, the Citation was getting close to Atlanta ARTCC. Both the controller and supervisor called their counterparts for the next sector to inform them what happened, and the controller handed off the aircraft and switched their frequency to Atlanta. As a precaution, the supervisor then walked down to the Watch Desk to inform the Operations Manager (OM) of what happened.

As soon as the aircraft exited the Wahoo Sector airspace into Atlanta's sector, the airplane made a hard left turn. We were in disbelief they turned him after all that had happened!

The supervisor returned to the area after talking with the OM and TMU. The controller told him about the turn, and the supervisor said they knew about it, and TMU was having them put the aircraft back onto the original routing. I can't imagine that went well!

Furthermore, the supervisor noted that, between the OM and the TMU supervisor, supposedly they decided to turn the issue over to the FSDO to investigate.

I have not heard of a pilot calling to complain while airborne before or since that day. I don't know what happened with any FSDO investigation, but I can tell you as a pilot, that is not a conversation I would want to have!

One evening, the OM walked down and told us that the Indianapolis ARTCC would be going "ATC Zero," which is when a facility is unable to provide air traffic services or "zero services." My night was about to change from being routine to becoming quite interesting very quickly!

Supposedly there was a problem with the commercial electricity provider, and then their generators wouldn't take the electrical load. Therefore, they were operating on battery power – thanks to multiple layers of redundancy. But to avoid a spontaneous shutdown, they decided to clear their airspace until maintenance personnel got the generators working properly.

I was working the Shenandoah Sector, which airspace borders Indy ARTCC in the northwest corner. South of Indy ARTCC's airspace line is Atlanta ARTCC, where most of my traffic goes between the two.

It was late evening, and I didn't have too many aircraft, I would consider my traffic level a slow-steady flow.

A few minutes later, I got a call from the Atlanta ARTCC's Baden Sector: They had several aircraft on 090 headings to avoid Indy and asked if I needed anything different. I told him no, but "my control" upon radio contact for all aircraft for the next hour. He approved my request and hung up.

I took the handoffs on the first three aircraft. Their final destinations were Columbus, Ohio (CMH), Cleveland, Ohio (CLE), and Detroit, Michigan (DTW). These were my old stomping grounds at Cleveland ARTCC!

I looked in the route dropdown menu on the D-Side computer to see if there were any preferred routes I could use to their destinations. I was shocked that we didn't have any of the routes, but it made sense as each ARTCC only programs in the routes most often used in their own building.

A few years prior, in 2018, the Cleveland/Detroit Metroplex was implemented, creating new routes to and from the major and satellite airports. I was getting busy enough that I didn't have time to look up the appropriate arrivals to issue with the new routes.

I used to work the airspace at Cleveland ARTCC where these airplanes were going to fly through. Even though the arrival routes changed, I tried to remember some fixes I could use to route these aircraft around Indy's airspace.

The first aircraft I got from Atlanta was heading to Detroit. I programmed in direct the Briggs VOR-DME (BSV) then direct Detroit. The route line appeared on my radar scope, cutting through Indy's airspace. I needed to send them somewhere further east before BSV.

I could picture a VOR-DME southwest of Pittsburgh in my head, but I could not remember its name (Wheeling – HLG), and I didn't have time to look at the charts to find it.

The first aircraft was about 10 miles into my airspace, and I needed to get them turned. I told the pilot, "You can expect further routing to include an arrival from a controller down the line - but for now, you are cleared direct Elwood City (EWC), direct Detroit Metro Airport."

The pilot read back the clearance and made the turn north.

The following aircraft was a Southwest Airlines Boeing (SWA) 737-700 heading to Columbus. Indy controls the airspace partway between Columbus and Cleveland. Therefore, I needed to issue a route that would take them into Cleveland ARTCC's airspace, then south into Columbus Approach, which owns up to 10,000 feet.

I issued them direct EWC, direct Mansfield (MFD), direct Appleton (APE), and then direct KCMH. The pilot read the route back correctly, and I proceeded to issue similar routes to three other aircraft.

After that, the SWA B737 going to KCMH told me they didn't have the fuel for the route I issued to them. I replied that they shouldn't have to go all the way to EWC before making the turn to the west, but a Cleveland controller would have to issue the turn early, so they still avoid Indy ART-CC's airspace.

They asked if they could go direct if they descended down into approach control's airspace, which I thought was a brilliant question to ask. Unfortunately, I had to tell the flight crew no and explained that Indy ARTCC owned down to the ground between Columbus and Pittsburgh, south of Akron. Therefore, there were no approach controls to fly through, so we had to keep them north.

In a last-ditch effort, the pilots replied that they didn't have the fuel for it and asked if there was any chance of flying through Indy's airspace. I had to tell them no again as Indy was ATC-Zero and nothing could go in or out. If they needed to divert, I told them to please let me know, and we would make it happen.

They continued on for a little bit in hopes Indy opened back up before they needed to divert, and I handed them off to the sector north of me and switched their frequency.

Once they were notified of the ATC-Zero, TMU issued a ground stop for all aircraft arriving and departing airports within Indy ARTCC's boundary. I had to issue made-up routings to approximately a dozen aircraft before TMU caught up and issued new routes around Indy's airspace.

CHAPTER 20

CPDLC & TRAFFIC LEVELS

Controller Pilot Datalink Communications (CPDLC), or as some people refer to it as "DataComm," is a new system in the United States where air traffic controllers essentially text message clearances to the pilots.

The system added a bunch of fancy icons and buttons around the aircraft data blocks on our radar scopes, as well as on the flight plan on the D-Side computer to control the system.

For any new system, all the controllers have to be trained. A change as big as this involves both classroom and simulator training.

Around 2008, I started hearing the FAA was developing a system that would allow controllers to type commands to the aircraft. I would think about it from time-to-time, but never heard much more about it until I got to Washington ARTCC.

I was eventually scheduled for the three-day class. On the first day of the course, we were in the classroom and the controllers who were giving the class started briefing us on the system's capabilities. A few minutes into the lesson, I got excited for several reasons!

First, I thought, and still do, the function I would use the most would be changing frequencies. Frequencies are the most readback errors I catch. To send the frequency directly to the airplane, so there won't be any readback errors, is fantastic!

Second, I thought the function that would save me the most time would be issuing new routes. We use preferred routes every day, and luckily, most pilots file the correct routes as they should. However, when the weather becomes an issue, we often have to issue new routes to aircraft that are already airborne.

The third function I liked was using the system to instruct the pilots to contact us when they were NORDO (no radio). Without CPDLC, our only options are to try them on the Guard frequency, through their company if they are an air carrier, or to call their satellite phone if they put their number in their flight plan remarks.

A training course of this magnitude takes months to get all the ARTCC controllers through before turning the system on for live traffic. After it goes live, any controller who has not had the class cannot work an operational position until fully trained.

My class was scheduled a few weeks before they turned it on for use with live traffic in 2020.

In order to test the system, they turned it on for short periods of time. They started during the midnight shifts when traffic levels were low. They had CPDLC training cadre members who were active controllers from each area trained to provide the CPDLC classes to all other controllers. They were staffed separately to answer any questions we had and keep logs of any errors in the system.

It didn't take long to turn the system on full-time. A week or so later, I was busy with chop reports: all the aircraft were changing altitudes and asking for updated information. I handed off an aircraft to Atlanta ARTCC and, after Atlanta accepted it, I asked the B738 how their ride was. They replied they still had light chop, but it had gotten better.

I verbally replied, "Roger," then immediately clicked the arrow to the right of their call sign which sent the message to change frequencies.

As soon as I did it, I asked myself if it was rude to talk to them and immediately send a CPDLC message? That's when I realized that it saved me precious time so I could continue with my duties and not worry about them getting the frequency wrong.

Since then, I have used CPDLC for frequency changes as much as possible, as it is faster and reduces frequency change errors.

Then, on a stormy afternoon in July, the precipitation moved into my airspace resulting in most of the aircraft in my sector deviating. That's when I got the dreaded notification from TMU to issue new routes to a few aircraft due to weather problems down the line.

TMU sent the route to the aircraft's flight plan in my D-Side computer. Typically, we have to read the clearance over the frequency and right-click the route with our trackball so the system knows it was issued.

When you are logged into CPDLC, and I have control of your data block, it shows a solid white box to the left of your call sign. (See the data block on this book's front cover.) I've started to see several flight plans that have "CPDLC Equipped" in the Remarks section. This isn't necessary as the data block shows the active status, and it is easier for us seeing the data block instead of looking at the Flight Plan Remarks.

I looked at the first aircraft's route change that I needed to issue. That aircraft had the solid white box to the left of the call sign, which meant I could finally uplink the route using CPDLC!

As I clicked on the new route, the aircraft's pilot called to say there was weather ahead and asked for a shortcut. I told him I had just received a TMU reroute due to the weather, and I would uplink them the new route shortly.

With three clicks on the trackball on the D-Side computer, I uplinked the new route.

The data block on the radar scope showed the uplink line, meaning it was waiting for a pilot's acknowledgment. It can take several seconds to make it up to the aircraft. The line disappeared a short time later, and the airplane started its left-hand turn towards the first fix on the new route.

Wow, I thought, *that was incredible!* This method saves time when we can use it most, especially during busy thunderstorm sessions!

Since then, I have used it often but not to the full extent of the system. I personally prefer to issue heading and altitude changes verbally.

One exception is when I have similar sounding call signs. I had a Delta Airlines (DAL) 52 and DAL72 on my frequency simultaneously. I needed to climb one of them to a higher altitude, so I uplinked that clearance.

When I switched the first aircraft to the next frequency, I was sure to uplink it!

If an aircraft asks for a shortcut when I am somewhat busy, I generally tell them I have their request and then uplink the fix I approve. I found this technique is beneficial for when I have time to accommodate one shortcut, but I don't have time for everybody else on the frequency to start asking too.

Another time, I had an aircraft request a shortcut. If I had approved their request, they would have flown through the next sector with several aircraft they would have been in conflict with. Therefore, I told them "unable due to traffic," and they responded, saying there was no traffic! I then explained why it wouldn't work.

This tends to happen somewhat regularly. I remember one controller had a pilot say something similar to him. He asked the pilot what his visibility was, and the pilot replied that it was about 10 miles. The controller told him he could see 150 miles, and the shortcut wasn't going to work due to traffic. Thus, the pilot didn't say anything else about it!

When looking at ADS-B In, it can be deceiving. Controllers have to look at what traffic will be across the sector, sometimes ten to twenty minutes out!

ADS-B In may show no airplanes in the area you want to fly through, which is why pilots get upset and think controllers are lying to them.

Depending on winds, a good rule of thumb is that jets fly roughly 8 miles a minute! Thus, for opposite direction traffic, that is a closure rate of 16 miles per minute! As smaller airplanes have a closure rate of 2-3 miles per minute, "10 minutes ahead" is still up to 30 miles even for some light piston aircraft.

Therefore, don't get too upset if ATC tells you "unable due to traffic," even when you don't see anything.

In November 2021, I was working the Shenandoah and Wahoo Sectors combined one evening around 9:00 p.m. The last big push of airliners that night had just finished, and I only had about ten aircraft on frequency. I took the handoff on a Southwest Airlines Boeing 737-800, headed south over Pulaski (PSK) VORTAC, en route to Florida.

After the pilot checked in, he asked if I had time for a question. As I am always happy to answer questions when traffic allows, I told him to go ahead and ask.

He said that he got the CPDLC message to change frequencies. And once he switched to the new frequency, he acknowledged that he was on the new frequency through the system. However, he had to verbally check-in, which he thought was a waste of my time since he had already acknowledged through the system.

I told him the "Voiceless Check In" function was turned off at the Washington ARTCC (ZDC), as they had a technical issue they were working on. Furthermore, I told him once it was turned on for ZDC, it would still be up to each controller.

With the ERAM computer system the ARTCCs use, controllers save their preferred settings, commonly called "pref settings." Each controller can save the map, brightness, airways, sector boundaries, data block size, and intensity settings.

Macros, multiple commands saved to a button that the controller clicks on and then clicks on the aircraft to save time, are also part of a controller's pref settings. For example, I have a saved macro for Charlotte arrivals set to fly the "Descend Via" arrival. When clicked, it changes the hard altitude to Flight Level 240, removes the temporary altitude, removes the heading and speed, and initiates the handoff to Atlanta ARTCC. If the aircraft doesn't have something like an assigned airspeed or heading, it doesn't matter as it ensures it is removed if something is there. This saves A LOT of time as we would have to enter each command separately.

In the pref settings, the controller has to select the "Voiceless Check-in" as "On."

On the radar scope, when the previous controller clicks the 'triangle with the line' to the right of the call sign, it sends the frequency change instruction to the aircraft. When voiceless check-ins are activated and the pilot acknowledges they are on the new frequency, the voice communications indicator, the angled Wi-Fi to the left of the altitude, automatically turns on for the new sector.

As of the writing of this book, the Voiceless check-in is still not activated yet, so I haven't used it to know for sure what I like or dislike with the feature. However, I will likely have it turned off for the sectors where I have a lot of traffic to climb into my stratum. The reason is, when an aircraft verbally checks on, it forces me to find them and manually mark them as on-frequency. At this point, I also climb them if I can.

I speculate that voiceless check-in will have a lot more aircraft level at the altitude below my stratum, their previous clearance, because it may take some time, when I'm busy, to notice they are marked on frequency as part of my normal radar scan instead of that verbal call, forcing attention to them. We will see what the future holds.

The only slight downfall I see to CPDLC is it frees up the frequency enough, so at times, pilots don't think I am as busy as I truly am. That is when they start asking for shortcuts and making other requests.

When I worked at the TRACON, there were many more instructions given to each aircraft due to vectoring everybody on a downwind, base, and then intercepting the final approach course. At the ARTCC, it can get hectic and be complex without a lot of radio chatter.

There are two types of busy. First is when you have a bunch of aircraft all going to the same place being vectored. This is when the controller spits out one clearance after another nonstop.

The other type is when you have both volume and complexity. One day, I was working Shenandoah and Wahoo combined – and Indy ARTCC gave three aircraft shortcuts cutting eastbound in different parts of my sector! All three aircraft were at FL390 - one was going to Newark, New Jersey (KEWR), one was headed to New York's JFK International, and the other was an overflight en route to Europe.

Then, I got another aircraft from Atlanta ARTCC, which gave a short-cut to the Europe-bound airliner, headed northbound at FL350.

In addition, I got two aircraft headed westbound to Chicago-O'Hare (KORD) cutting perpendicular to the normal traffic flow, which are D.C. Metro departures, climbing southwest-bound through the overflights!

When everybody is on the preferred routes, they are generally spaced apart except for a few expected tie-points in the sector. There can be heavy traffic, but it is very manageable since the complexity is low.

However, in situations like I had with all the shortcuts given before they got to my sector, the complexity level went way up. It takes a lot more time to scan and think before issuing a clearance. These are the times when it may not sound very busy, but it is. Add CPDLC uplinks to the mix, and it may even sound like the controller is slow.

Finally, bad rides make this much worse. I had an Airbus A321 overflight, headed southwest-bound, check-in my frequency, and he kept keying up, asking about the rides at different altitudes. After his third transmission, I told him I was pretty busy so just let me know if he wants to change altitude. He didn't ask about the rides anymore, and he decided to stay at FL360. It is always nice when a pilot understands and complies.

CHAPTER 21

MISSED RESTRICTION

I was working the Mansfield Sector at Cleveland ARTCC when we had Air Force Two (AF2), a United States Air Force aircraft carrying the sitting Vice President of the United States, depart from the Detroit area headed to Columbus, Ohio. AF2 checked onto my frequency level at 16,000' msl, south-southeast-bound.

Once they were inside my airspace, I issued the clearance to cross 15 miles northwest of GUNNE at and maintain 10,000 feet, which the pilot read back correctly.

As they started to get close to GUNNE, I noticed they were still level at 16,000 feet msl. They were already well past the point where most aircraft start descending. I waited a little longer and then asked the pilots if they were going to make the crossing restriction, to which they told me they would with no problem - with a slight judgmental demeanor in the tone of his voice.

They were flying the U.S. Air Force version of the Boeing 757, designated as a C-32. FedEx flew Boeing 757s, and they would wait until the last possible minute and then dive the aircraft down. Knowing this, I knew they could physically make the restriction, but I was a little surprised they intended to make an evasive descent. Like other cargo carriers, FedEx is more concerned about flying for efficiency instead of passenger comfort. I thought this wasn't the way pilots usually fly their aircraft when they have passengers on board, especially when those include VIPs.

When they were about a minute and a half away from the crossing point, the pilot of AF2 told me they were not going to make it, and sounded quite humble. So, I cranked them left to a 080 heading and descended them to 10,000 feet msl.

The reason why I had to turn them is that, if they didn't make that restriction, they would violate the airspace for the Columbus Sector at Indianapolis ARTCC, which owned 11,000 feet and above.

I proceeded to call the Columbus Sector on the landlines to point them out. After they approved the point out, I then called Columbus TRACON to APREQ (Approval Request) AF2 descending to 10,000 feet, turning direct Appleton (APE) VOR - the next fix past GUNNE. Columbus TRACON approved my request, and I was able to get AF2 back on its way.

If a controller ever asks if you can make a restriction previously issued, you should seriously consider what is being asked. Controllers work the same airspace day-in and day-out for years. They generally know what is common for the different clearances issued. More importantly, they usually know when something isn't looking correct.

Another time at Charleston TRACON, I was providing VFR flight following to a Cessna 172. They departed Charleston airport headed westbound on a cross-country flight. The STARs system, the radar system used by TRACONs, has a limited number of fixes and airports programmed into it. For those airports programmed in, the system can draw a line from the aircraft to the fix/destination to give controllers an idea of where that specific aircraft is headed.

As the C172 was about 25 miles into their flight, it appeared on radar they were right of their intended course. Naturally, being VFR allowed them to fly how they wanted, and not necessarily in a straight line. I decided not to say anything and just keep an eye on them.

A few minutes later, it looked like they were even further off course. At that point, I asked the pilot if they were on course as I was showing them about 15 degrees right of course.

They said they were on course.

A short while later, it appeared they were back on course. I assumed they made the correction without saying anything, as so many pilots do when they don't want to admit they were wrong.

The following week, I went to my local Civil Air Patrol meeting. One of the CAP members said he had an ATC question for me... I obliged.

He said he had been flying on a cross-country, and ATC said it appeared they were right of their course. As he told me this, I started smiling and told him I was the controller who asked!

Surprised, he went on to say he was so confused by it as he and his pilot friend flying with him both double-checked everything, and it appeared they were on course the whole time.

I told him from my side it appeared they were back on course a few minutes after I asked, so I assume he made the correction. He said no, they were on the same heading the whole time.

The only thing I could think of was their position was far enough away from the radar site at CHS, and our systems now use multiple radar sites. Therefore, maybe he was in just the right location where the radar coverage overlapped, and the computer showed them on a slightly different position. I further explained this happens between radar sites, even at the ARTCCs, and that controllers will see the radar target make a slight jump when they move into different "sort boxes."

I told him I didn't observe a jump on his aircraft, but I was busy enough I may not have noticed that minor detail.

When controllers ask you about these types of situations, the controller isn't always 100% accurate, so don't blindly assume something is wrong. However, DO take it seriously, especially for altitude issues, as there may be traffic or terrain you are conflicting with. It is always worth double-checking because most of the time, the controller sees something that you do not see.

I had a Boeing 757-200 (B752) level at Flight Level 380 headed west-southwest bound over Pulaski (PSK). I had another aircraft in the handoff to me from the north, headed southbound over PSK at FL380, and both were tied over PSK. I had to move one of them, and based upon other factors in the situation, I chose to move the B752.

I told the B752's flight crew that I had to move them for traffic so descend and maintain FL360. The pilots countered, asking if, instead, they could climb to FL400.

As I had a different aircraft at their 10 o'clock position headed north-bound at FL390, I had about 2 ½ minutes to get them to FL400; other-wise, it wouldn't work. I told the pilots "if I give you higher, can you be level at flight level 400 in two minutes or less?"

They asked me to repeat my question, so I did, and they responded, "we sure can try."

I went back to them and said: "you either can or you can't, but I need to know either way!"

They said, "We're not sure but will do our best."

Controllers cannot base control decisions on if a pilot will try hard. It must be a clear "yes, they can comply" or "no, they can't comply" answer. If we give a pilot a crossing restriction such as "Climb and maintain Flight Level 400, be level in two minutes or less," then, if the pilot accepts those instructions, they must make the restriction. Otherwise, it is a pilot deviation.

A pilot deviation is much better than a midair collision, but either way, it is in everybody's best interest to maintain positive separation!

Against the pilot's wishes, I descended the B752 to FL360. Once they cleared the traffic, they could climb up to FL400 - their new requested final altitude. So yes, it did force them to burn a little extra fuel for a few minutes, but that was the only way to guarantee separation.

Be sure you can comfortably make a restriction before you accept one. Trying hard is not good enough. The best case for missing a restriction is a Pilot Deviation, which is way better than a midair collision.

Remember, if you accept a restriction and later realize you can't comply with it, **tell ATC as soon as possible**. The controller will have to make some changes, whether it is by moving an aircraft or by doing a point-out on the landlines.

Either way, you want to be very proactive in these situations.

CHAPTER 22

TCAS

For a while, I worked the Marion Sector at Cleveland ARTCC, which mainly handled Cleveland-Hopkins Airport (KCLE) departures headed westbound.

This section of airspace ranged from the vicinity of KCLE to about 30 nautical miles west, at an altitude between 13,000' msl to 16,000' msl. The Carlton Sector owned the airspace between 17,000' msl to Flight Level 230. The reason for this was to allow some room for the KCLE departures to climb while simultaneously allowing the Detroit-Metro Airport (KDTW) arrivals to start their descent, in order to make their crossing restrictions with the DTW TRACON.

Since this was a constantly congested block of airspace, there was an automated information transfer (AIT) procedure set up for these KCLE departures. As a default, the Marion Sector would climb the KCLE departure to 16,000' msl.

Then, if the aircraft was climbing well enough, the Marion Sector controller would handoff the aircraft to Carlton.

After taking the handoff, the Carlton Sector controller would enter the altitude they would allow the aircraft to climb to and handoff the aircraft back to the Marion Sector, who kept radio communications, and climbed the aircraft to the released altitude.

This procedure drastically reduced the time wasted using standard point-out procedures where the Marion controller would call the Carlton controller for every aircraft.

The technique used by the Carlton controller would vary, but I found, most of the time, if they had a DTW arrival, they would allow the CLE aircraft to climb to FL190 so they could descend the DTW arrival to FL200. Otherwise, they would release FL230 for the CLE departure.

On one particular day, I was working the Marion Sector during a departure push. I had both departure routes lined up with aircraft, mostly Embraer ERJ-145s (E145s) with a few mainline aircraft mixed in. Carlton was also busy with a DTW arrival push.

Partway through the push, I had a Continental Airlines Boeing 737-800 (B738) on the AMRST departure. The B738 climbs really well, depending on their load, especially when compared to the regional airline jets like the E145 and Canadian Regional Jet 200 (CRJ2).

The Continental B738 checked onto my frequency, leaving approximately 8,000' msl for 12,000' -the top of CLE TRACON's airspace. I acknowledged their call and climbed them to 16,000' msl. Then, per our AIT procedure, I handed the aircraft off to the Carlton Sector.

At the same time, I had a De Havilland Canada DHC-8 "Dash 8-400" (DH8D) turboprop aircraft a few miles in ahead of the B738, which I was stepping up under the B738. Since turboprops are slower than jets, we have to use altitude separation, so I was climbing them up every one or two thousand feet at a time once the B738 climbed through that altitude – a process ATC refers to as "stepping them up."

The DH8D is a very fast turboprop and can climb at 250 knots just like jets and, therefore, could keep up with the climbing jets.

The Carlton Sector entered an "Interim Altitude" of FL190 for the B738, then flashed it back to me. I took the handoff and climbed the B738 to FL190.

The ARTCCs have a couple of types of altitude entries we can make into the aircraft data block. The final requested altitude from the flight plan is entered in "hard." An "Interim" or "Temporary Altitude" is entered and shows a "T" next to the number in the data block. So, we enter T-altitudes into the data block for every altitude we issue until the aircraft reaches its final altitude. Suppose a pilot requests a different altitude for some reason, like avoiding turbulence. In that case, if we can't give it right away, we will use the T-altitude again to reflect their current assignment and then change the hard altitude to their new requested altitude.

As the B738 climbed through 16,000 msl, I saw the DTW arrival descending to FL200 and issued a traffic advisory to the B738. They responded that they were looking. After the B738 climbed through FL180, I directed the DH8D to climb to 17,000' msl.

Everything seemed to be going well.

Then, the B738 said they had a TCAS RA (Traffic Collision Avoidance System - Resolution Advisory) and were descending!

I acknowledged and then issued another traffic advisory to the B738, which was now within about three miles. They replied that they did not have the traffic in sight, so they descended!

Controllers are required to avoid giving control instructions when pilots declare they are responding to a TCAS RA.[83] The best we can do is issue the traffic warning and wait for their resolution advisory to conclude.

When I've seen TCAS RAs happen before, the descending aircraft only went down about 500'. This time, I watched and realized the other traffic was in a descent already - the B738 was going past that.

I keyed up and said, "Continental 123, additional traffic at your twelve o'clock, less than a mile climbing to 17,000."

The B738's flight crew acknowledged and begun to look.

At that point, I turned the DH8D left 40 degrees for the aircraft descending with a RA. That way, even if the B738 descended through their altitude, they wouldn't come even remotely close.

Luckily, the B738's RA ended, and they leveled off with separation maintained, - 5 miles or 1,000', - between all three aircraft.

They informed me the RA alert was over and asked what altitude I wanted them. The DTW arrival leveled at FL200 as instructed, so I climbed the B738 back up to FL190.

Anytime we had an aircraft respond to a TCAS RA, we had to file a report so it could be investigated. I saw a few RAs in the Marion/Carlton shelf even though the aircraft were altitude separated. I was told the TCAS algorithm doesn't know what the assigned altitude for each aircraft was, and it would respond as if the trajectories continued. It did seem to get better a little while after that, so I presume there was a software update that fixed this issue.

A few months later, I had an E145 tell me they had a TA. Even though I knew about TCAS, I didn't realize that TA stood for a Traffic Advisory. Nor did I know it was different than a Resolution Advisory, where the system instructed the crew to make altitude changes.

I'm sure those poor pilots wished they didn't even mention the TA, as I started asking all of the questions I needed to know in order to fill out the RA form.

Finally, they had to tell me in basic terms that they did not get a RA, nor did they have to change their altitude.

Once I understood, that was a relief. I hate doing paperwork!

CHAPTER 23

REQUESTS

At Charleston Int'l/AFB, the traffic was typically the heaviest on week-days – Monday through Friday - during the daytime. KCHS is both an active Air Force Base and a popular destination for military pilot training cross country flights (the thought being "what a nice place to get 'stuck' for the weekend").

On this particular day, I was working in the TRACON, which was already somewhat busy. Then, four Beechcraft T-6 Texan IIs were inbound on IFR flight plans. Separate aircraft, mind you, not as a formation.

KCHS has intersecting runways, and we were landing on Runways 15, the main runway, and 21. The first three aircraft requested instrument approaches, and I vectored them per their requests...

The last T-6 of the group requested the full TACAN Runway 15 with procedure turn – where they start over the airport, fly the opposite direc-tion of the inbound aircraft for roughly 8 miles, turn around and make an approach to the runway to land. As it was a busy day, I told him unable due to traffic, but I could give vectors TACAN Runway 15.

He said he didn't want vectors: he wanted the TACAN Runway 15 with the full procedure turn. I told him I was too busy to allow a procedure turn, so "say intentions."

He replied and again requested full TACAN Runway 15 with procedure turn. Sigh.

At this point, I started getting a little frustrated with him and said I could accommodate the procedure turn. That is, if they want to go into a holding pattern for a minimum of 30 to 45 minutes. By then, hopefully, traffic will die down enough to allow for it.

That is when the Instructor Pilot keyed up and said they could accept vectors to final.

If ATC is too busy to accommodate your request, be ready for a backup plan. Flying the full procedure into a medium-size or larger airport is going to be hit or miss - it just depends on traffic at the time. Generally, practice approaches can be accommodated, but doing a full procedure turn really delays other aircraft due to the extra time on the final approach course. All four T-6s flew several approaches then landed for the weekend. The JO 7110.65 says practice approaches, IFR or VFR are last priority.[84] If VFR, 500' separation is OK.[85]

One afternoon, I had an Embraer ERJ-145 (E145) check-in my frequency on the BAGGY Arrival to KCHS, leaving 12,000 feet msl for 10,000 feet msl, requesting lower. At their location at that point, they were about 10 miles outside my airspace. In order to get lower, I would have to point them out to Beaufort RAPCON.

Unless there is a reason why we need to start them down early, we generally wait until they are past the boundary lines. We try to limit the amount of landline coordination performed to only those needed. Too much coordination can be the one way to put another controller behind when busy. I told the E145 I'd have lower in a few minutes.

As they were leveling at 10,000 feet msl, the E145 came back and said they were in moderate turbulence and requested lower. I had no idea there was any turbulence in the area, as that was the first report of the day, and I didn't even take the time to respond to the E145.

I called Beaufort and pointed the E145 out descending, which they approved. Then, I descended the E145 to 5,000 feet msl and asked them what altitudes the turbulence started.

They replied it started at 14,000 feet msl. I told them that this was the first turbulence report all day so please let me know once it stopped. They said the turbulence stopped a bit later as they descended through 9,000 feet msl. I informed the ARTCC since the turbulence started in their airspace, so they could advise incoming aircraft before they encountered it.

Controllers get many requests for altitude changes and turns during a pilot's initial check-in and, generally, those aircraft are still outside the new controller's airspace. So, if you are getting bumped around, have a cloud buildup ahead, or whatever issue you may have, please say that reason with your initial request and we will do our best to help!

I gave the E145 pilots credit for asking for lower during their initial transmission instead of using the term "…with request."

When I was about halfway through my IFR pilot training, I started to notice other pilots using the term "…with request." As it seemed like a polite way to communicate with ATC, I started using it for every request I made.

Once I started working as a radar controller at Cleveland ARTCC, I had pilots using this technique, and I realized it is a giant waste of time for both the controllers and pilots!

Let's think about it further. If you as the pilot keys up the frequency and say, "Approach, Piper 12345, with request."

The controller then says, "Piper 12345, say request."

You respond by saying, "Approach, Piper 12345, requesting to climb to six thousand."

Then the controller says, "Piper 12345, climb and maintain six thousand."

The pilot reads it back, "Piper 12345, leaving four thousand for six thousand."

Finally, after five transmissions, this back-and-forth is over.

Your goal as a pilot should be to make your radio transmissions as short, clear, and concise as possible. I realize it doesn't seem like it takes that much longer. However, the extra time involved seems like an **eternity** when a controller is busy!

If you look at our hypothetical request, it has five different transmissions
Pilot: "Approach, Piper 12345, with request."
ATC: "Piper 12345, say request."
Pilot: "Approach, Piper 12345, requesting to climb to six thousand."
ATC: "Piper 12345, climb and maintain six thousand."
Pilot: "Piper 12345, leaving four thousand for six thousand."

If we get rid of the first and second transmissions, does it change what is being communicated to ATC?

No, it does not. Frankly, I believe it is more considerate and polite to ATC by skipping the first two transmissions and starting with the third to make your altitude change request.

Even though I tell people not to use the "…with request" technique, you still don't want to key up on an initial transmission to make a long request or one with multiple components – remember the airliner requesting a new route due to Thunderstorms when I was busy? In these situations, the best technique is to give a quick highlight of what you're requesting.

For example, suppose you are planning to fly multiple approaches. In that case, all you need to say is, "Approach, Cessna 12345, two zero miles northeast of Charleston at three thousand, requesting multiple practice approaches."

If you want to help ATC when you plan to fly IFR, please file an IFR flight plan!

There are a few problems with air filing, or requesting a "pop-up" clearance.

First, controllers don't ask for all the information required on the flight plan, specifically pertaining to information needed for search and rescue. Because of this, some controllers will have you contact Flight Service and file your flight plan in the air with them. Then, they will wait to receive the flight progress strip before issuing the pilot an IFR clearance. Honestly, now that electronic flight bags (EFBs) are mainstream, there is no excuse not to file unless you were VFR and unforecasted weather moved in – catching you off guard.

Second, having an IFR flight plan on file provides all the information needed to the controller. Otherwise, the controller has to type all of the information into the system. At the TRACONs, controllers can put basic information into the radar scope computer, such as if you are flying directly to your destination. However, if there are multiple legs or remarks are needed, the controller has to use a separate computer to create or amend a flight plan. When ATC is busy, that takes a lot of time and attention away from their primary duties of separating aircraft.

In addition, I would advise you to put "Practice Approaches" in the Remarks section of your flight plan. In the ARTCC, we click on the asterisk on the D-Side Computer, and we see the remarks. In the ATCTs or TRACONs, it will be printed on the strip.

Regarding multiple practice approaches, I have seen controllers use different techniques. After radar identifying the aircraft, some controllers will ask the pilot to list all of the approaches they are requesting.

Others will only ask for one approach at a time.

Some only want one at a time because they will put the type of approach being flown into the aircraft's data block on the radar scope. However, some controllers will want to write down the whole list.

At the ARTCCs, paper and pens are becoming scarcer since everything is typed into the system - unlike TRACONs, who still use paper flight progress strips. Therefore, if you have been asked multiple times what approach you requested after you already told them, this might be why.

Some other examples you could use to avoid the "...with request" dance are:

"Center, N12345, request direct Grand Forks airport."

"Center, N12345, continuous light chop at one two thousand, requesting one six thousand."

"Approach, N12345, continuous light chop with some moderate turbulence, requesting descent."

"Approach, N12345, requesting thirty degrees right deviation around a buildup."

"Center, N12345 requesting descent," (if getting close to destination but still at altitude).

"Approach, N12345 requesting direct Appleton to avoid weather."

"Approach, N12345, requesting short vectors for ILS Runway 33."

"Center, N12345 requesting shortcut."

"Approach, N12345, level ten thousand with information bravo, requesting ILS Runway 33."

I know several pilot training institutions teach "...with request" as a required technique when talking with air traffic control. I can tell you that I've spoken to other controllers about this and, at least the controllers who work at the ARTCCs (busier facilities), most of those people have agreed with me that when pilots say "... with request" is a complete waste of time!

One of my pilot friends and I have frequently discussed this very topic at length. He noted that during his advanced flight training curriculum the use of the word "request" was taught whenever asking for two or more approaches. In some instances, he recalled flight students receiving poor marks or even failures on training flights for not ending their initial contact to ATC with the word "request."

I'm sure back when this technique was created, there was a good reason for it. Maybe because the radios were extremely difficult to understand - I don't know.

However, currently, at least domestically in the U.S., the consensus is that using the phrase "... with request" is a giant waste of time.

I recall that one company used it every time they checked onto the CHS TRACON frequency, saying, "Charleston Approach, N12345, with request."

I would respond by saying, "N12345, say request."

"N12345, please confirm the arresting cables are down." Since KCHS is a military base, two arresting cables are installed on the main runway – part of a mechanical system used to rapidly decelerate an aircraft as it lands. If they happened to be up, it would create a lot of damage on the DC-9 series aircraft, including the MD-88s they often flew to KCHS.

Even asking this question could be phrased quicker and easier by using plain language initially: "Charleston Approach, N12345, please confirm the arresting cables are down."

That is a lot better than the "...with request" dance!

On a side note, at least at KCHS - I'm not sure about other military facilities - the arresting cables are controlled in the tower. Therefore, we had to tell every aircraft to ask their question again with the tower controller. If you ever fly to a runway that has cables, they are depicted on the approach plate.

In the Chart Supplement and Terminal Procedures Publication, the Airport Diagram has the symbol and the type of cable system. If you'd like, you can ask the tower to confirm they are down. However, most pilots do not ask this question.

I was working the Shenandoah and Wahoo Sectors combined at Washington ARTCC. I had a U.S. Navy Boeing P-8 Poseidon ask that, when I had time, they had a request. The last few aircraft who called me had requested long reroutes due to the thunderstorms, and I made the assumption that it would be the same request this time, so I told them to standby on their request.

I continued working for at least five minutes before I got back to them, and they wanted me to verify their route as they were only sure about their current leg, which ended at Greensboro VOR (GSO). I read their route, and they confirmed they had it correctly.

If I knew what the request was about, I would have gotten back to them a lot sooner. If they had simply stated, "Center, NAVY123, we'd like to confirm our routing when you have time," I would have confirmed their route right away.

One afternoon, I had a business jet check-in on my frequency and ask if I needed him on the arrival. In fact, his intuition was correct and I had routing to issue him via the WAALK2 arrival.

It is so much easier for everybody involved to file your route using the preferential routing. The EFBs make this so easy. Then, you can request a shortcut once you are airborne.

One trick is to ask for the shortcut leaving Flight Level 240. Most of the ARTCC low altitude sectors go up to and include FL230. If you wait until you are talking to the high sector (above FL240), they are the ones who have a better picture of the traffic and can make the decision.

I've seen so many pilots ask for a shortcut, and the controller tells them no due to whatever reason they have. Then, they switch the pilot to the next frequency. That pilot immediately checks in with the next controller, asking for the shortcut. Often, the sector you are being switched to is the controller sitting next to your previous sector and knows you were already denied the shortcut. Immediately asking again tends to upset people and make them avoid working extra hard to accommodate the request. Therefore, it is best to wait to ask again once you are two or more sectors away from when you originally asked and were denied.

Simply check-in as usual and say requesting [fix] (i.e., "Center, N12345 level, Flight Level three four zero, requesting direct GRDPA").

If you really want a shortcut, ask for the initial fix on the arrival. If you get anything further than that, eventually, you will be rerouted back onto the beginning of the arrival as usual. Even if the controller can't do that fix, they will give you something as far away as they can feasibly go.

Be sure not to sound needy. If we can accommodate your request, we will. The one excuse we get all the time is "we are running late." I'm sure it is true most of the time, but it's hard not to become cynical every time we hear it – which is most days, especially when there is bad weather!

I had a CRJ climbing out of Richmond, Virginia, who checked onto my frequency, leaving FL190. The pilot keyed up and asked for a shortcut to a fix out west due to the weather over Kansas.

I was moderately busy at the time, and giving them a shortcut wouldn't work. There are times pilots use the weather as justification for their shortcuts. Please only use this when it is true. ATC will bend over backward to make deviations possible. However, especially during bad weather, if you are merely using it as an excuse, realize there is a good chance you are increasing the workload for the controller at a time when that person is already busy.

If you are wondering about the ride conditions, simply report your current ride when you check-in. That will usually prompt the controller to advise you of what they know. If you report on saying "smooth" and the controller doesn't give you a ride report, then smooth rides will probably continue.

CHAPTER 24

RATE OF DESCENT

One afternoon in the summer of 2020, I was working the Wahoo and Shenandoah Sectors combined at Washington ARTCC. I took a handoff on a Cessna Citation coming from Florida and going to Lehigh Valley International Airport (KABE) in Allentown, Pennsylvania.

The Citation was level at Flight Level 450, and to their credit, they were on the preferred route from the south: direct COURG..SCAPE.V377. HAR.V162.DUMMR..KABE (this is the formatting the ATC computer systems use; one period is for an intersection of an airway, and two periods means direct.

This preferred route is used for several airports to and near Allentown and is probably the routing we have to issue most often in my area. The routes that take the most time to issue are some of the New England routes, as they can have a lot of individual fixes instead of airways. It is much easier for pilots to file the preferred route, so it doesn't have to be changed while they are airborne – and you can ask for a shortcut once airborne.

In my assigned sectors that day, I must get the aircraft to a certain altitude, depending on where exactly they are. If they are at Roanoke VOR-DME (ROA) or west, we can leave them at their cruise altitude. If they are over Lynchburg VOR-DME (LYH), they must be at or below FL350, and if their course takes them near Flat Rock VOR/TACAN (FAK), they must be at or below FL310. The reason is the next sector has to descend them down through all of those climbing and descending aircraft going to/from the Washington Metro airports.

This Citation was east of LYH but close enough that I could keep them at FL350 instead of forcing them down to FL310. When the time came, I instructed them to descend and maintain Flight Level 350.

The pilot immediately asked if the descent could be at the pilot's discretion, and I told him he was unable due to airspace restrictions. The pilot read the clearance back, with the tone of a man clearly upset.

In the ARTCC environment, we have to start aircraft descending from their cruise altitude for several reasons. On the east coast, there are a lot of major airports, creating heavy traffic in all phases of flight. This makes for a very complex airspace design for the instrument departures, terminal arrivals, and routes. The routes are all set up to separate the aircraft using different restrictions which means, at times, I may need to start an aircraft down before the pilot would like, just like for this Citation.

After the Citation read the descent clearance back, I started focusing on other aircraft as I was moderately busy. I continued my scan and came back across the Citation. It had been a few minutes since he was supposed to start descending, and he was currently at FL438.

I pushed the Vertical Rate Indicator (VRI) button we now have with the newish ERAM computer system, which shows an aircraft's vertical rate of climb or descent. It showed a mere 200 feet per minute (fpm) rate of descent, so I keyed up and told the Citation to say their rate of descent because I was in disbelief the VRI was correct.

The pilot said he was doing 200 fpm.

I was dumbfounded that a pilot would do this after I already told him they couldn't have "Pilot's Discretion" down and I needed to get him down.

The AIM states "Descend or climb at an optimum rate consistent with the operating characteristics of the aircraft to 1,000 feet above or below the assigned altitude, and then attempt to descend or climb at a rate of between 500 and 1,500 fpm until the assigned altitude is reached. If at anytime the pilot is unable to climb or descend at a rate of at least 500 feet a minute, advise ATC."[86]

I would guess the average jet descends 1,500-2,000 fpm, sometimes even more.

Since he had already wasted several minutes of valuable time with his extremely shallow rate of descent, I keyed back up and told him to maintain 2,500' per minute or greater all the way down. I added that, if he was unable, to advise as I would have to turn him out due to traffic I needed to get him underneath.

He accepted the clearance and, as I monitored his descent, he was precisely at 2,500 feet per minute, clearing underneath the crossing traffic and making the airspace restriction.

Let me be very clear here: Yes, I know the AIM direction is subjective and pilots can twist "optimum rate" into whatever argument they choose to make. Nevertheless, I expect jets to do an absolute minimum of 1,000 fpm, but preferably 1,500+ fpm rate of descent. I expect turboprop aircraft at the high altitudes to fly a minimum of 1,000+ fpm rate of descent. Even in the terminal environment, I expect them to do around 500-1,000 fpm minute or greater. Unless you're on approach or close to the ground, 100-200 fpm descents are not acceptable for anybody!

I realize, even with ADS-B In or TCAS, most pilots cannot see the traffic they are in conflict with. And with closure rates of 16 miles per minute, it is difficult to see the traffic 30-45 miles away - a mere 2-3 minutes. Controllers know well before pilots become aware when there is traffic for them. We issue aircraft descents for a reason, primarily for traffic or airspace restrictions. The airspace restrictions are set up not as ambiguous restrictions, but so you miss the traffic on the other routes in the next sector.

The way we typically handle pilots who try to float it down, is to issue a restriction such as "maintain 2,000 feet per minute or greater in the descent." Usually, if I have to give this type of restriction, it will be more limiting than if you made a normal descent from the beginning as I want to be absolutely sure you will be out of the way in time.

If you don't want to descend at the rates I discussed, ask ATC if you can descend at "pilot's discretion" or "make a shallow descent". There are times ATC will approve that request but if they don't - don't be that pilot trying to get away with technicalities. You will most often end up further behind than if you played the game nicely.

A few months before I left Cleveland ARTCC (ZOB), I returned to the area from a break, and the Carlton Sector was getting busy. I was told to work the D-Side, so I sat down next to a very seasoned controller who had worked a lot of traffic over his career.

To give you an idea, by the time I left in 2013, ZOB's highest traffic counts were during 2001 before the September 11th terrorist attacks. More impressive is that they didn't have RVSM (Reduced Vertical Separation Minimum) and needed 2,000' separation starting above Flight Level 280. Today, with only a few aircraft allowed to be exceptions to fly through, we only need 1,000' separation all the way up through FL410.[87] This controller worked that heavy traffic.

The Carlton Sector owned the airspace from Cleveland to Detroit over Lake Erie and mostly handled Detroit area arrivals. The sector also included the GEMNI and WEEDA standard terminal arrival routes (STARs) for Detroit Metro Airport (KDTW) and the LLEEO STAR for the satellite airports, with DTW arrivals crossing the ARTCC/TRACON boundary at 12,000' msl.

On this particular day, we had two solid lines of arrivals on both KDTW routes and a few satellites arrivals, all inbound from the south headed north/northwest. We would receive the handoffs from the high sector near Cleveland with the aircraft descending to FL240.

In addition to the arrivals, we had overflights headed westbound, which made the session more complicated.

The first crossing traffic was at FL220, a little north of Cleveland, and a second blip of crossing traffic was at 14,000' msl, a few miles before the DTW TRACON boundary. Both of these aircraft were traffic for a Boeing 737-700 inbound to DTW.

When the B737 checked on our frequency descending to FL240, the radar controller descended them to FL230. The radar controller put a 5-mile ring around the aircraft at FL220. As soon as we had 5 miles between the two aircraft, he descended the B737 down to 15,000 msl and told them to give a "good rate down," to which the B737 read back, including good rate.

When the aircraft passed AQQUA intersection, there were 36 miles before WEEDA - which we usually gave a restriction to cross WEEDA at and maintain 12,000 msl. But that day, we had two aircraft preventing us from issuing the standard crossing restriction. The B737 lost a few miles for their descent due to the traffic at FL220.

Then, we had the traffic at 14,000 crossing before the WEEDA intersection. They would have enough time to cross WEEDA at 12,000' but would have to be almost level at 15,000' by the time they passed the second aircraft.

A few minutes later, I was monitoring everything, and I told the R-Side to ask the B737 of their rate of descent because it appeared they were not going to be low enough in time. The R-Side asked, and the B737 replied they were doing 1,000 fpm.

The phrase "good rate" is not defined. This terminology is used extensively, but is not what we as controllers call "positive separation." Neither is telling a pilot to maintain a specific feet per minute rate of descent. Anytime controllers use these, we always have an "out" ready to go if it isn't going to work.

In recent years, the FAA updated the order to allow us to instruct a pilot to be level/at or above/at or below a certain altitude within so-many minutes.[88] This is becoming more popular than "good rate" because it is easy for both sides to use and understand, plus it is considered positive separation.

For example, the Citation discussed before: I instructed them to maintain 2,500 fpm or greater. If they hadn't performed properly, I was ready to turn them 90 degrees left, which would have paralleled their first traffic. They could have descended on that heading until they were clean with the other aircraft, then I could have re-cleared them on course.

This was before ZOB got ERAM, so there was no VRI button. We would either do the math (multiply times the difference in updated altitude by 5), and if it was going to be tight, we asked the pilot. With the VRI button, we ask a lot less than we used to!

The radar controller and I both knew the B737 was too high to make the crossing restriction. The bad part was a third overflight just north of the DTW TRACON boundary line prevented us from APREQ-ing the B737 to just be descending to 12,000 msl instead of crossing the fix at the boundary at 12,000 msl.

I told the controller, "I'd spin him."

He knew that would be the most straightforward play for us, so he amended his altitude to maintain 17,000 and turned him west. We were busy enough there was not another hole for them to join the arrival again until about 30 minutes later. Until then, we kept vectoring them back and forth on a west and east track.

It ended up being a lot of work for an already complex session. We could have put them into a holding pattern but didn't because it was simply better to vector them out of the way. If they had actually descended between 2,000-2,500+ fpm, which we have seen that type of aircraft do on many occasions, our original plan would have worked.

Instead, they got the scenic view of the Lake Erie shoreline for a half-hour while waiting for another open slot.

CHAPTER 25

SPECIAL INSTRUCTIONS

It was a nice VFR day with light winds, a great day to go flying, and there I was, working at Charleston TRACON (KCHS). There was a lot of VFR aircraft up because of the weather, and it was even a good day to be controlling!

I was working aircraft flying on visual approaches to Runways 3 and 33 at KCHS. I had a Cessna 172 on final for Runway 33, and I was also vectoring an MD-88 for the visual approach to Runway 3.

Of course, the MD-88 is a lot faster than the Cessna, so I slowed them to 170 KIAS and turned them onto their base leg - a flight path at right angles to the landing runway. After they rolled out onto it, I issued "square your turn to final, cleared Visual Approach Runway 03" – as we always said "Zero Three" since pilots would often somehow confuse Runway 3 with Runway 33.

The pilot read back the clearance correctly, so I moved on with my scan.

Shortly after that, I noticed the MD-88 turned towards the runway from the position where I cleared them instead of squaring their turn to the final. I asked the MD-88 to confirm they were going to square their turn to final. The pilot replied that they could turn when they wanted since they were cleared for the visual approach.

When we add restrictions like that, it is for a reason! In this case, the reason was the Cessna on final for the intersecting runway. Without the delayed turn, I would not maintain separation between the two aircraft landing on intersecting runways.

I told the MD-88, "Approach clearance canceled - turn left heading 280, climb and maintain 3,000."

When this happened, I thought the pilot was technically correct, that once cleared, they could make any turn they wanted towards the runway. In addition, I also thought it was ridiculous they would use a legal technicality to turn early when they accepted the clearance I issued.

Nevertheless, when I was doing research for this book, I wasn't able to find any publication which backed up the pilot's response. Therefore, FAR 91.123(a) prevails and the pilot should not have deviated from the ATC clearance.[89]

Even if the pilot was technically correct, what did he gain as a result of his actions? They were in a hurry to get on the ground. Instead, they delayed their arrival by probably 10 minutes as I had to sequence them back into the line.

Realistically, the controller should specify what they need, and if the pilot accepts the clearance, they should comply. It is as simple as that!

CHAPTER 26

VFR FLIGHT FOLLOWING

In June of 2001, between my freshman and sophomore years of college, I completed my final stage check, via a Part 141 flight school, for my Private Pilot certificate and became a full-fledged pilot. To continue my flight training, I decided to take summer classes.

The next flying course was mostly solo time building to prepare for the Instrument and Commercial courses. On the morning of June 8th, I planned to fly a long cross-country consisting of one leg at least 250 nautical miles long.

I decided to fly to Sioux City, Iowa because I wanted to see if there was a memorial or monument for the crash of United Airlines Flight 232.

Years earlier, on July 19, 1989, UAL232, a McDonnell Douglas DC-10, suffered an uncontained engine failure in the tail engine, which severed the hydraulic lines.[90] The flight crew, plus an off-duty DC-10 training check airman who happened to be onboard, controlled the aircraft using different engine thrust settings for the wing engines. One hundred and eighty-four people survived of the 296 onboard, and the team effort was hailed as a great example of Crew Resource Management.

On the morning of my flight, I was delayed as my first aircraft had a maintenance issue and I had to get a replacement. Finally, I loaded my gear, completed pre-flight and started the engine. I departed Grand Forks and headed south.

Grand Forks ATCT switched me to Departure Control, which was provided by the Grand Forks Air Force Base Radar Approach Control (RAPCON), the military version of approach control.

A few minutes later, I got permission from Grand Forks RAPCON to leave the frequency to call Flight Service. I opened my VFR flight plan and returned to the RAPCON frequency.

As I left the RAPCON's airspace, they terminated radar services.

I hand flew my Piper Warrior and was enjoying the flight. It was a clear day with smooth rides. It was fun to fly the long trip solo.

The longer I flew, the more I thought about calling air traffic control for flight following. I was comfortable talking with Grand Forks RAPCON and ATCT, but for some reason, I felt very intimidated by the thought of calling a different facility.

In order to keep situational awareness, I kept referencing my WAC (World Aeronautical Chart). I should have been using a Sectional, but I figured I could use one chart for a long flight instead of two. At this point, I was northeast of Sioux Falls, South Dakota, by approximately 15 miles. I was closer to the Class Delta airport than I was comfortable being without talking to ATC.

I found and selected the approach control's frequency in my Garmin GNS-430. Then, I paused because I was nervous to call a facility foreign to me. After about 30 seconds, I mustered up the courage, pressed the push-to-talk button on the yoke, and requested flight following.

The controller issued a beacon code and then radar-identified me. She then said, "Warrior 264ND, two antennas at your 12 o'clock, 15 miles, confirm you have them in sight." As she said that, I looked forward and saw a tower above the horizon!

I don't recall exactly, but I think I muttered to myself, "holy crap!" I replied, "Warrior 264ND, if it's okay, I'm going to climb."

The controller responded, "Warrior 264ND, maintain VFR."

I climbed well above the towers - which soared 3,427 and 3,445 feet msl respectively (1,984 and 1,999 feet agl). I thought, *thank goodness I called for flight following because she saved me.* I hope I would have seen the towers visually before it was too late, but I'm glad I didn't have to find out.

Eventually, ATC switched me to Sioux City TRACON. The controller alerted me to watch for a flight of four U.S. Air Force F-16s and follow them once I got them in sight. I kept searching, but I could not see the low-profile, high-speed fighter jets. Instead, the controller issued vectors to me – and I ended up being vectored way out because I never got a visual on the F-16s.

Once I returned to Grand Forks the next day, as I got stuck overnight in Aberdeen, SD due to pop-up thunderstorms, I told my flight instructor about the flight, the F-16s, and being vectored way out because I never got them in sight.

He asked me if I told ATC I was a student pilot.

No, I hadn't, nor did I think about it - plus I wasn't a student anymore! Of course, he did acknowledge that I had passed my stage check the prior week, but I was not, in fact, holding a Private Pilot certificate yet – not until my records cleared and I got issued my certificate by the FAA.

Now, as a controller, I prefer pilots tell me when they are still students. Depending on the situation, I may have made the student priority and got them in before the F-16s.

When two aircraft are tied, meaning in similar positions to their destination, neither one is first. Therefore, controllers pick which one to make first based upon several factors such as aircraft type, ground speed, location, and the like. If one of them is flown by a student pilot, I would automatically pick that aircraft to be first.

I learned a lot from that solo flight. I can understand why the 250nm leg is required for the Commercial Pilot certificate[91] because leaving your local area is essential to experience. I also learned a lot about ATC and was very thankful for that controller who told me about the antennas.

In Charleston, 17 nautical miles east of the main airport, there are two 2,000 feet tall towers. I was working an evening shift in the TRACON at dusk, and I had a pair of United States Coast Guard helicopters flying in formation, VFR at low altitude down the coast and receiving flight following.

Once they were about 20 miles away, I told them about the antennas ahead and asked if they had them in sight. The pilot sounded surprised, and they asked for a vector around them.

I turned them 30 degrees right. Once they were north of the towers, I told them they were clear and to proceed on course. The pilot said, "Thank you for the heads up," and I could tell they didn't realize they were there.

Even professional pilots make mistakes. Requesting flight following is a free service in the United States. When flying VFR, I use it every chance I get, even when I fly to the practice areas. You never know how it will help!

I am originally from Marysville, Ohio, just northwest of Columbus in the central part of the state. After I started working at Cleveland ARTCC, I went flying in northern Ohio with a local flight instructor. At that point, I had only been in that area for a short time. Therefore, we were going to fly to and do touch-and-goes at two other airports so I could learn about the local area. Since we were both qualified pilots, the CFI in the right seat would make all of our radio calls.

On this particular flight, we departed on a beautiful VFR day. As we climbed out of the uncontrolled airport, we called Cleveland TRACON for flight following. The CFI said, "N12345 with you five miles east of Medina, looking for flight following to Akron Fulton (AKR)."

We quickly approached the border leaving Cleveland's airspace and were switched to Akron-Canton TRACON. I told him to let ATC know that, after AKR, we were going to Akron-Canton Airport (CAK) - then back to Medina.

I'm not sure that he heard me, and I never followed up. Once we got close to AKR, the controller said that Akron Fulton airport was at our twelve o'clock in one-zero miles, squawk VFR, and our frequency change approved.

The CFI replied the usual way, changed our transponder, and switched our radio to the Common Traffic Advisory Frequency (CTAF)– the radio frequency commonly used at uncontrolled airfields.

Once we completed our touch-and-go, the CFI hit the flip/flop button on the radio to switch from the CTAF back to Akron-Canton TRACON and called to get flight following to our next airport.

On the way to the second airport, Approach issued a traffic alert and had us turn 40 degrees to avoid. We didn't get the traffic in sight until we finished the turn, but I think we would have collided if it wasn't for the turn ATC gave us. Once again, ATC helped me!

When you make your initial call, instead of doing the typical " Potomac Approach, N12345," say:

"Potomac Approach, Skylane 12345, eight miles west of Leesburg Airport requesting flight following to the practice area two zero miles west for maneuvers."[92]

Or similarly: "Potomac Approach, CAP1234, a Cessna 182, eight miles west of Leesburg Airport requesting flight following landing at three different airports."

By phrasing it like this, you will reduce the overall time spent on the frequency, and you will avoid the controller having to respond to you saying, "N12345, Potomac Approach, go ahead."

You prevent the whole back and forth, requiring several transmissions to get the same amount of information out. Now, the controller may not hear the whole transmission and ask you to "say again." Realistically though, time is saved overall with this technique when the controller does not ask you to repeat any component.

Everybody knows when you are flying VFR, you can do pretty much whatever you want. I believe Flight Following is a great tool to use as a pilot. Just realize that you are the lowest priority for the controller.[93] Even so, controllers do an excellent job of issuing traffic advisories. Just keep it clear and concise, so controllers get a basic understanding of what you are doing.

I was providing Flight Following for an aircraft doing photo work after Hurricane Florence. They finished in one location and were going to the next location, roughly 50 miles away. Therefore, I told them to advise before making any turns. They were flying westbound and were clear of my traffic by at least 5 miles. All of a sudden, it appeared they were turning. They didn't advise they were going to make a turn, so I wasn't expecting it. I told them I wasn't expecting a turn there and to "say intentions." They reported they were now over their next photo location, so they would be orbiting for a while.

Please give ATC a heads up when you are about to maneuver. This situation ended okay, but if there is other traffic around, the controller isn't necessarily going to tell you about it when you are straight and level. We only issue traffic when we think they will get somewhat close.

Another time, I was working as the Toledo/Pandora D-Side at Cleveland ARTCC. As I sat down to help, the traffic level was manageable at a low moderate level. A few minutes later, it started to get busier with the departure push out of Detroit Metro.

It started getting very busy, and the Radar Controller made one transmission after another. Then, a Cirrus called, requesting flight following.

The Radar Controller typed in the call sign, aircraft type (SR-22), and destination into the computer to generate a flight plan with a beacon code. He issued the code to the pilot, and then continued on to direct other aircraft.

The pilot programmed the new beacon code into the transponder and a data block for the aircraft appeared on our radar scope. The controller told the pilot, "N12345, radar contact 15 miles west of Flag City (FBC) at 11,500 feet, maintain VFR."

We were still really busy, and I was surprised the radar controller took the time to provide services to the Cirrus, but I thought it was nice that he did.

A few minutes went by, and the Cirrus keyed up, saying they were starting a descent to 5,500 feet, which would take him into Toledo TRACON's airspace for a few miles before entering Mansfield TRACON's jurisdiction.

In this situation, it takes some extra computer keyboard inputs to force the flight plan to the TRACON's computer so we can initiate an automated handoff to them.

The controller did a quick scan and didn't see any targets close to this aircraft and said, "N12345, radar services terminated, squawk VFR, frequency change approved."

I was shocked the radar controller terminated the flight following, but it is very difficult to determine how busy a controller actually is. When a controller gets busy, they can easily lighten their workload of flight following for VFR aircraft - by terminating them.

I was working at Charleston TRACON, and I was moderately busy. I had a Beechcraft King Air call in east of Charleston for VFR flight following. I told the pilot, "N12345, Charleston Approach. Remain outside the Class Charlie and standby for flight following."[94]

The King Air responded, "Oh, come on, let me go through the Charlie."

"Unable, I'll get to you in a bit," I said calmly back.

Just before another aircraft flew through the localizer, I cleared them for the approach and climbed a departing aircraft elsewhere.

I went back to the King Air and assigned him a beacon code. The data block appeared on my radar scope, and I was stunned to see he was directly north of Charleston Airport, barely outside the Class Charlie.

I was busy enough when he initially called, and I did not see his primary target - the radar target from seeing metal in the sky. He was upset I wouldn't allow him through the Class Charlie, so he must have flown within a half of a mile around it.

The Global Positioning System, or GPS, is a wonderful technology that has completely transformed how the National Airspace System (NAS) operates. It allows for new "T" and "Q" routes, which streamlines the way aircraft fly. Compared to an ILS and others, it has allowed airports without instrument approaches to get published approach procedures with little financial investment. However, new and better technologies bring new hurdles. Since pilots can pinpoint their exact location while airborne, they know when they are just outside the Class Bravo airspace. It used to be that pilots would build in buffer and stay quite a bit away from the Class Bravos. Now, they are all starting to fly just outside the boundary line.

The issue is the busier airports cannot sequence aircraft within the confines of the Class Bravo airspace during their busy times. The air traffic controllers are supposed to advise pilots within Class Bravo as to when they depart the Class Bravo[95] - when it is not apparent, such as a departure leaving the area.

Well, when the controllers are that busy trying to keep aircraft separated, it isn't exactly easy to tell pilots when they spill out of the Bravo, and then again when they enter in again.

This has been an issue for a few years now. The FAA cannot just change the Class Bravo boundary lines, as environmental impact studies are required before those changes can be made, and they take years, and millions of dollars, to complete.

Therefore, my advice is to either utilize flight following if it is close to the Class Bravo airspace, or fly far enough around it where it isn't an issue. It isn't the jets you necessarily need to worry about. Just think how many other general aviation aircraft are trying to skirt around the Bravo just like yourself. Just because it is legal, doesn't mean that it is smart.

CHAPTER 27

FIRST COME - FIRST SERVE

One night, I was working the midnight shift at Cleveland ARTCC. It was 12:30 a.m., and I was working the Briggs/Hopkins/Mansfield Sectors combined. During midnight shifts, many of the TRACONs close. Therefore, I controlled the airspace from the ground up to and including Flight Level 230. This particular night was very cloudy and IFR,[96] with an overcast ceiling around 600 feet agl.

I had two Cessna Caravans flying southbound, headed to the Akron-Canton Airport (KCAK). The first Caravan was cleared for the ILS Runway 19 but was still about 20 miles north of the airport. The second Caravan was behind them by about seven miles, whom I assigned to fly their slowest practical airspeed to create more room to allow time for the first aircraft to make their approach.

Even though the Akron-Canton TRACON closed for the midnight shift, the VFR Tower remained open. Having a tower is helpful when multiple aircraft want approaches for the same airport. The tower can call on the landline and advise landing assured, and we can clear the next aircraft for the approach. It saves time instead of waiting for the pilot to call once on the ground.

The rules for clearing aircraft for approaches controllers use at the ARTCCs are more cumbersome than at the TRACONs. When controllers are vectoring for an approach, like an ILS, they are putting you into an "Approach Gate." The Approach Gate is one mile outside the Outer

Marker. Controllers must also have the approach depicted on their radar scope to vector for that approach.[97] ARTCCs typically only have ILS approaches depicted for "busier" airports. That is why ARTCC controllers running approaches will often clear you to the Initial Approach Fix (IAF) and have you fly the whole approach instead of issuing vectors.

There are times when controllers vector aircraft too tight and accidentally vector them inside the approach gate. When I've done that, I informed the pilot I vectored them inside the gate and asked if they wanted me to turn them out to be sequenced. Not once have I had an aircraft asked to be taken around.

Pilots can request "short vectors" or "tight vectors", there is no official name, which allows the controller to vector them inside the approach gate but not past the IAF.[98]

Then, the sector south of me flashed me a handoff, a McDonnell Douglas MD-88 northbound for the Akron-Canton Airport. I ran out my "Leader Lines," which is where the computer will estimate an aircraft's future location up to 8 minutes out. It computed that both Caravans would beat the MD-88 by about 2 minutes, even though it is much faster than the Caravan; being further away made them number 3 for the approach. I took the handoff and waited for the pilots to check-in on my frequency. The MD-88 was usually much earlier in the evening arriving to KCAK. I presume they were delayed as there were a lot of thunderstorms across the country that day.

Once they checked in, I told them they were number three for the approach and asked if they wanted to make a couple of turns in the holding pattern or be vectored out. They asked to be vectored out, which, of course, is easier on the pilots. I cleared them to descend to 5,000', turn 15 degrees right, and airspeed at their discretion - allowing them to slow.

As the MD-88 was just about east of the airport, still headed north-northeast bound, they called to ask for a heading inbound.

I replied back, saying that I was still waiting for the tower to call with landing assured for the first Caravan, so it would be a few more minutes.

Shortly after that, CAK ATCT called with landing assured for the first Caravan. I then cleared the second Caravan for the ILS Runway 19 approach. Just as I was about to key up the frequency to issue a left turn heading northwest bound to the MD-88, they keyed up and said they were really getting far out there and they needed a turn towards the airport.

Smiling, I responded that I was just keying up to issue the turn and instructed them to turn left, heading 320 towards the northwest.

I still had to build in enough space for the second Caravan to complete the approach before clearing the MD-88. After they turned to the new heading, I think they realized it was not a heading for the Outer Marker. They called me and said they needed a heading a lot closer than that and were fairly argumentative on the frequency.

I responded, telling them I needed them on this heading as I was still waiting for the second Caravan to fly the approach. Furthermore, I told them I would not argue with them on the frequency (have you ever heard of liveatc.net?), but if they would like to call once on the ground, I could give them the facility phone number.

They asked for the phone number, which I provided. Shortly after that, CAK Tower called landing assured for the second Caravan. I cleared the MD-88 for the ILS Runway 19 approach then switched them to the Tower frequency.

That was the last aircraft I had for a while, so I gave my supervisor a call on the landline. I told him what had happened and let him know he may be receiving a phone call from the flight crew.

Sure enough, the captain did call the facility. He was very nice but was asking what happened as it seemed to them I had vectored them to Canada and back. My supervisor explained that he was aware of the situation and watched the video replay of the radar data. He told the captain that I had kept them as close as I could have without holding; it just took that much time for the first two Caravans to fly their approaches.

The captain was very friendly and respectful the whole time and thanked my supervisor for explaining it to him.

If you are ever confused by something ATC assigned you, you are more than welcome to call the facility to inquire about the situation. Now, don't call on every little thing, but if you have a serious concern, the facility would be more than happy to explain it to you. But - please do not ask the controller for the facility phone number if they are busy. Take note of the time of day it happened, and you can find the phone number online or through Flight Service once you land.

You will typically get a supervisor or Controller-in-Charge (CIC) when you call. If it is a CIC, they will probably give the message to the supervisor to follow up with you if they are not familiar with the situation.

I was speaking at the EAA AirVenture Oshkosh a couple years ago and, after my presentation, a pilot asked me about a Cirrus accident in Houston. He said the NTSB just published their findings and blamed the pilot for not being assertive enough when talking with ATC. I told him I remembered the accident being discussed just after it happened.

On June 9, 2016, N4252G, a Cirrus SR-20 departed the University of Oklahoma Westheimer Airport (KOUN) in Norman, Oklahoma, headed to Houston Hobby Airport (HOU).[99] Used as a hub for Southwest Airlines, HOU can be a hectic airport to fly into, depending on the time of day.

The pilot, a 46-year-old woman, along with her husband and brother-in-law as passengers, were on their way to Houston, where the passengers' father was in a Houston hospital they intended to visit.[100]

At 12:52 p.m. Central Daylight Time, the pilot was switched from HOU TRACON and contacted HOU Tower. The controller responded, "4252G, Hobby Tower, you're number two following a 737 on a three-mile final, caution wake turbulence, Runway 4, clear to land."[101]

The controller added, "Cirrus 52G, proceed direct to the numbers - you're going to be inside of a 737 intercepting a 10-mile final."

The pilot questioned it, saying, "Okay, you would like me to proceed direct to the numbers, 4252G?"

The controller responded, "N52G, what did approach tell you before?"

This is part of the controller's fundamental duties to ensure the pilot is doing what the controllers have coordinated - via landline communications, electronically via the radar scope data block, through facility Standard Operating Procedures (SOPs), or with external facilities via Letters of Agreement.[102]

For example, if I take a handoff on an aircraft climbing to Flight Level 330, but the pilot checks on saying they are only climbing to Flight Level 320, I have to investigate the situation **before** issuing any new clearances.

When this happens, I will often ask the pilot to say their assigned altitude again to be sure I heard it correctly. If the pilot says again, they were assigned FL320, I then have to get control to climb from the previous controller.

Just because the data block says FL330 doesn't mean the mistake was the previous controller typing in the wrong altitude and that controller never climbed the aircraft. There might be traffic at FL330 and if I climb the aircraft I'm talking to, I could inadvertently climb them through the other airplane. Albeit, most of the time, either the controller forgot to issue the higher altitude or issued it but the pilot made a mistake.

The bottom line is, without permission, I can't issue control instructions inside another controller's airspace, and they can't issue clearances in mine. This is one reason why making your check-in calls properly are so important.

When this happens, it takes time to coordinate so the aircraft may level in the process, causing a slight delay to their climb. If I had to guess, for me personally, a pilot checks onto my frequency reporting a different clearance than I'm expecting, maybe once every two months.

I can't tell by the audio recording or transcript if the tower controller coordinated with the TRACON, but they instructed the SR-20 "proceed direct the numbers for Runway 4, direct to Hobby."

A bit later, the controller instructed, "Cirrus 52G, maintain maximum forward speed if able and ah, proceed direct the numbers ah 737 on a nine-mile final following you with an 80 knot overtake."[103]

To me, it appears the approach controller vectored the Boeing 737 behind the SR-20 too tight, not leaving enough space for compression due to the speed differences between the jet airliner and the slower Cirrus SR-20.

Later, the controller said, "Cirrus 52G... Yeah, I've got traffic behind you, just go around and ah fly runway heading now, ah maintain VFR, we'll put you back in the downwind for Runway 35. Ah, the winds are 090 at 13, gusts 18. Can you accept Runway 35?"

In my opinion, the tower tried to help the Cirrus by keeping her in the traffic pattern instead of vectoring her out to be re-sequenced by the TRACON, which usually would take several more minutes.

She responded, "we'll go-around and line up for Runway 35 downwind."

"52G, fly runway heading Runway 4 for right now," the controller directed. This was the first go-around, which was initiated by air traffic control. The controller then instructed the pilot to enter the right downwind for Runway 35, and said he would call her base turn.

The controller issued a traffic alert to the Cirrus for a B737 on final for Runway 4, and instructed the pilot to turn base behind the B737, and cleared her to land Runway 35.

The pilot replied, "we'll make a right base following them, 4252G, for 35."

The controller advised the 737 of the Cirrus and then said, "Cirrus 52G, make turn left heading 30 degrees," to which the pilot acknowledged.

Then, the controller said, "52G, did you want to follow the 737 to Runway 4?"

The pilot agreed: "yes, that would be great, 4252G," and the controller again cleared the Cirrus to land on Runway 4.

But the pilot replied, "so am I turning a right base now, 4252G"?

"52G, roger," the controller replied. "Just ah, maneuver back for the straight-in. I don't know which way you're going now, so just turn back around to Runway 35."

The pilot said, "turning to 35, I'm so sorry for the confusion, 4252G."

This is a perfect example of asking to clarify if you are confused. I can understand how a low-time pilot would be confused, and I think the pilot did an excellent job by asking for clarification.

ATC decided to put her back onto Runway 35. If the pilot preferred Runway 4, which would have been better based upon the winds, this was an opportunity for her to have been more assertive. Instead of accepting the new clearance, she could have said, "N4252G, I prefer to land behind the 737 on Runway 4. I can turn right base now to follow. Does that work?"

Of course, I am able to say this with the benefit of hindsight.

A bit later, the controller said, "Okay, yeah, that's fine, 52G, ah just make it, ah, so you're in a right turn, keep it tight, I need you to make it tight."

"Keeping turn tight, 4252G," the pilot replied.

The controller then said, "52G, I need you to, okay, there you go, straight into Runway 35, cleared to land."

"Straight-in to 35, cleared to land, and I don't believe I'm lined up for that, 4252G," the pilot reported.

This was the pilot's second landing attempt, and due to the confusion and aircraft position, ATC told her to climb and placed her on a heading before she was lined up for the runway. The controller replied, "Okay, 52G, roger. Turn to the right and climb and maintain one thousand six hundred, right turn."

The pilot said, "one thousand six hundred, right turn, 4252G."

"52G, yes ma'am, heading about 040," reminded the controller.

"040, 4252G," the pilot echoed.

Then, the controller said, "Okay, 52G, let's do this. Can you do a right turn back to join the straight-in to 35, could you do it like that?"

The pilot said, "yes, right turn back to 35, 4252G."

"N52G, Okay, so you're just going to make a right turn all the way around to Runway 35, and now you're cleared to land," the controller stated.

A bit later, on reflection, the controller continued, "N52G, ah, if you don't want to land, if that's too high, we can put you back around on the downwind, don't force it if you can't."

The pilot said, "Okay, we'll see, thank you, 4252G."

This was the pilot's third attempt. She was over the runway, but she was again too high. As discussed earlier, controllers are very good at noticing when something appears abnormal. The controller told the pilot, "I think you're too high, Cirrus, ah, 52G. You might be too high."

"Okay, we'll go around then, 4252G," the pilot acknowledged.

"Cirrus 52G, roger," the controller stated. "Just ah, okay, just - you're just going to make a right traffic now for Runway 35, we'll come back around, and we got it this time."

"Sounds perfect, right traffic for Runway 35, 4252G," the pilot said.

"N52G, make right downwind to Runway 35, and you are cleared to land. They'll be no other traffic for Runway 4, so this one will be easy," the controller advised, hoping for the pilot's successful landing.

"Making right traffic for downwind for Runway 35, 4252G," the pilot noted.

They had a few more transmissions each: The controller cautioned her for wake turbulence due to a B737 landing in front of her on Runway 4 and cleared her to land. The pilot responded, "35, cleared to land, trying to get down again, 4252G."

As she said, "trying to get down again," she made what I would call a nervous chuckle.

A little over a minute later, the pilot said, "4252G, going around, third time will be a charm."

The controller said, "Okay, uh, Cirrus 52G, just go ahead and make the left turn now to enter the ah downwind, midfield downwind for Runway 4. If you can, just keep me a nice low-tight pattern. I'm going to have traffic four miles behind you, so I need you to just kind of keep it in tight if you could."

"Okay, this time, I'll be Runway 4, turning left for 4252G."

The controller continued, "yeah, and actually, I might end up sequencing you behind that traffic. He's going four miles a minute, um, it is going to be a little bit tight with the one behind it, so, uh, when you get on that downwind, stay on the downwind. Advise me when you have that 737 in sight. We'll either do 4 or we might swing you around to 35…"

Watching from the tower, the controller saw the Cirrus do the unthinkable. "Uh, uh ma'am, ma'am, uh, straighten up, straighten up!"

The SR-20 crashed into a parked car, a few feet from a hardware store's front entrance. All three people on board the aircraft perished, although, thankfully, nobody on the ground was injured.

When a pilot is in trouble, controllers cannot get into their cockpit to help. The only thing we can do is talk and listen. When I've listened to frequency audio recordings when pilots have been struggling, the one thing I've noticed is the controllers tend to speak to them more, trying to keep the pilot calm. It is natural to talk more to the pilot in these situations. This is the controller's calm, steady voice that pilots usually appreciate under challenging conditions.

After ATC instructed the first go-around, the spacing for arrivals never included a hole for the Cirrus. Therefore, all the attempts were going to be tight, but appeared to be possible since the Cirrus was in the traffic pattern.

In my mind, the controllers were only responsible for the first go-around of the four attempts.

When the accident happened, I remember some initial speculation wondering if the SR-20 ran out of fuel. However, the investigation revealed a different story.

The NTSB found as an accident cause that the aircraft's Angle of Attack Capability was exceeded, airspeed was not maintained, and the pilot made the incorrect action. In basic terms, the pilot didn't keep her airspeed high enough, which caused the aircraft's wings to stall. At that low altitude, there is not enough room to recover.

The NTSB also found contributing factors were the pilot's motivation and response to pressure, along with ATC personnel's decision making and judgment and unnecessary action.

When I was twelve years old, taking flying lessons from my local airport, we decided to fly to Port Columbus Airport - now named John Glenn International (KCMH). We called approach control, and they gave us radar vectors. One vector would have turned us into a cloud, so my flight instructor told them, "Unable due to clouds."[104] It shocked me that we could even say no to ATC.

Currently, the last time I remember telling ATC unable is when I was flying at CHS, and the controller vectored me eastbound, heading over the ocean. I told him I could only accept that heading for about a mile, then we needed to be turned back towards land - so we remained within gliding distance since we didn't have any water survival equipment on board[105]. The controller then gave me a vector north up the coast. It may have delayed me a couple of minutes, but I wasn't comfortable with the original clearance.

Aircraft are handled on a first-come, first-serve basis,[106] and this should be true in all situations. However, the reality is if you plan to fly into a Class Bravo airport when it is busy, being the slow general aviation aircraft, you will probably be delayed. Controllers are also required to be efficient.[107] Therefore, an argument could be made that it is more efficient to delay one GA aircraft instead of five jets.

I love flying into major airports, but I stay away unless I know it is not busy. I've flown into Minneapolis–Saint Paul International Airport (KMSP) after midnight. Similar to pilot currency, it is completely legal to fly VFR into a Class Bravo airport at peak traffic times of the day, but is it smart?

The pilot-in-command is the ultimate authority, the one who is really in control, regarding their aircraft. The pilot should have told ATC what she needed to complete the flight safely. It is perfectly acceptable for pilots to say "unable." In fact, professional flight crews do this regularly. They have SOPs which dictate most of those decisions, where the GA pilot must make their own decisions – similar to creating their own weather minimums. Some will be obvious, like cloud avoidance, and others will be gray areas.

One of my pilot friends told me he is never in a hurry to do things because it always seems like ATC is all about having pilots hurry up, then the next sector has them slow down. I told him it is because each controller has their own area of responsibility, and it is all about the most efficient use of time to get everybody on their way without delay. Once they are out of that sector, it is a brand-new scenario.

Remember the old adage: Aviate, Navigate **and then** Communicate. It can be hard to remember when you are in the situation, but it can literally be the difference in life and, sadly in some cases such as this SR-20 accident, death.

The pilot could have been more assertive instead of saying they were not lined up for that runway and would prefer to follow the 737 and land Runway 4.

The approach controller probably made the mistake of not leaving enough room between the SR-20 and the B737. Realistically, this happens regularly every day across the NAS.

The local controller could have sent her back to the TRACON to be re-sequenced, but the maneuvers given to her were standard. Controllers expect pilots to tell them if they can't do something. We have guidelines, but those cannot cover all situations.

The NTSB listed ATC as a contributing factor in the accident, but the probable cause was attributed to the pilot. It is obvious to me the tower controllers were trying to help. The controllers could have been a little better in some aspects, so I understand why the NTSB listed them as a factor - but I fully believe ATC did not cause this accident.

I can imagine being in the aircraft and how easy it would be to get frustrated when things were not going well. Nobody knows exactly how she reacted during the time even though her radio calls sounded calm, with slight frustration or nervousness when she said trying to get down.

Flying into Class Bravo airport can be thrilling. However, I would challenge you to know your own limitations. Just because it is legal to fly into a Class Bravo airport VFR as a private pilot, that doesn't necessarily make it smart. It is the same as currency. If you only fly three touch-and-goes every ninety days, you would be legal to take passengers flying, but are you proficient enough to fly with passengers or even by yourself?

On the IFR side, Part 91 allows instrument-rated pilots to depart in zero/zero conditions,[108] meaning both the cloud ceiling at zero feet agl and visibility is zero, but is that smart? If you needed to divert and land at the same airport you departed from, you wouldn't be legal to continue the approach past the decision height on an ILS - unless you declare an emergency.

I discussed this accident at length with my friend, Tom Henery, a former naval aviator. He made an interesting point, saying, "At the end of the day, Air Traffic Controllers and pilots are on the same team, but we have to know which problem is whose, and who can control what. The 737 behind me is Air Traffic Control's problem, not mine, nor can I control that aircraft. Pilots need to know their rights. Once the pilot is cleared for landing, the pilot owns the runway unless ATC revokes the clearance."

Tom is an experienced pilot with a wide array of experience. As he and I reviewed this accident, we benefit from hindsight and not being in a stressful situation. We are both saddened by this loss of life.

CHAPTER 28

UNCONTROLLED AIRPORTS

On April 15, 2017, a 1948 Cessna 170 departed Williston Municipal Airport (X60) in Williston, Florida, where the pilot, his wife, and two of their three kids made a fuel stop.[109] The Cessna 170 departed on Runway 5 on that Saturday afternoon at approximately 3:23 p.m. Eastern Daylight Time.

The weather was VFR with winds from 080 at 8 knots, gusting to 17 knots. The Cessna climbed to approximately 280 feet above ground level, then entered a stall and spun, crashing merely 543 feet from the Runway 5 centerline.

All four on the plane perished in the accident. The pilot was a Certified Flight Instructor for both Single Engine and Multi-Engine Aircraft and was a Certified Flight Instrument Instructor for airplanes. He was also an air traffic controller who worked at Atlanta TRACON.[110] News of this accident spread quickly through the FAA, and his loss was felt by many.

During the daily accident meeting on the following Monday morning, I was horrified to learn the aircraft wasn't discovered until the day after the crash. I asked if the Emergency Locator Transmitter (ELT) was working properly or if its antenna might have been damaged in the accident. Of course, the investigation was ongoing, and we were only discussing the facts as we knew them at that point.

I asked that question because it has been my experience that the airlines do an excellent job at monitoring the 121.5MHz VHF "Guard" radio frequency, but I have not experienced the same with general aviation (GA). The AIM states, "Pilots are encouraged to monitor 121.5 MHz and/or 243.0 MHz while inflight to assist in identifying possible emergency ELT transmissions."[111]

According to the FAA's Mandatory Occurrence Report from Jacksonville ARTCC, they started receiving ELT reports the day after the accident starting at 1:03 p.m. EDT, only 2 hours and 20 minutes shy of the 24-hour mark after the accident.

On the day of the accident, according to the NTSB's accident report: "The airport hosted a fly-in barbecue event from 12:30 to 3 p.m.… The vintage plane wasn't noticed by more than 20 pilots who flew out of the same airport later that day…"[112] So even though the aircraft crashed during a busy weekend in the daytime, the wreckage wasn't spotted until more than 21 hours after the accident!

Monitoring Guard is an excellent habit to develop. Every facility is required to monitor Guard - so if you ever can't get ahold of ATC, you can contact us using it. If you ever go NORDO - what ATC calls "no radio" or, in other words, "we cannot reach you," we will first try to raise you on the Guard frequency.

More importantly, the ELT reports at lower altitudes help us narrow the search area to find the beacon. Usually, we get initial reports from the airlines flying in the flight levels. Then, we ask GA aircraft in different locations to tune in 121.5 and let us know if they hear the beacon. This is why I know GA aircraft, in general, do not monitor because when they tune it in, they can hear the beacon!

The NTSB's final report stated the accident Cessna 170 did have an ELT, which aided in the search for the aircraft.

Looking at a picture of the wreckage, the airplane was bent up somewhat but, overall, was still in the original shape with the nose stuck into the ground and the undamaged tail sticking almost straight up in the air. It should have been easy to spot![113]

The pilot did not file a flight plan for this flight. Even if he did, they didn't make it far enough into the flight to activate it, which is one risk of flying VFR.

If the Cessna's pilot had received an IFR clearance prior to departure, ATC would have started looking for them the same way as for IFR arrivals if a pilot waits to cancel IFR until after they land safely.

Even when flying VFR, I am a big proponent of using air traffic services to the maximum extent possible. Granted, flight following does not afford the same protection as when flying IFR, but it is better than nothing.

According to the Air Force Rescue Coordination Center, in 2017, approximately 98% of ELT activations were not real emergencies.[114] However, that leaves about 2% that were real and, therefore, all should be treated as such. As a pilot, I used to never monitor Guard as I was flying either. However, now that I see its importance for both ELT reports, and as a second way for ATC to get in touch with me, I pretty much monitor it all the time - even when not talking to ATC, which is rare!

Even to this day, FAA employees who never knew the pilot, remember this accident. It was a very sad day to hear we lost one of our own.

Imagine you are on an IFR flight plan getting ready to fly an approach into an uncontrolled airfield. It is eleven o'clock at night – dark, and likely there is nobody at the airport.

You are being vectored by Approach for the visual approach and then instructed to advise the airport in sight.

A few minutes later, you get the airport in sight and advise the controller. The controller clears you for the visual approach and then tells you to cancel IFR in the air on this frequency or if on the ground, they will give a phone number so advise ready to copy.

Of course, copying down a phone number, then making the phone call once on the ground, assuming you don't forget, sounds like a lot of work when you could simply cancel right now.

And so, you tell the controller you'd like to cancel with them now.

The controller states, "cancellation of IFR received. Squawk VFR, change to advisory frequency approved."

You read back the instructions, then change your comm frequency to CTAF and make your radio calls while configuring for landing in a stabilized approach. You cross the runway threshold and, shortly thereafter, begin your flare. Out of nowhere, a large whitetail deer enters your field of vision, and within a split second, you strike the large, 12-point whitetail buck!

You veer off the runway and go down into the ravine, and your plane flips over. Inverted in the metal tube, you are now trapped! You grapple for your cell phone but it's out of reach. You try to transmit through your radio but your antennas, mounted atop the aircraft, are now buried in mud or broken off altogether.

How long will you be trapped before somebody comes looking for you?

Will it be the airport day shift who doesn't arrive until 8:00 a.m. the next morning?

Will you have a loved one drive to the airport, down the taxiways and runway, and hopefully see your aircraft inverted in the ravine?

Keeping your IFR flight plan active until after you shut down the aircraft is the best insurance policy you can get, and the best part is: IT IS FREE!

If we don't receive your IFR cancellation, we cannot let any other IFR aircraft fly into or out of the airport for 60 minutes after your scheduled arrival. We can allow them to fly within 30 minutes if we notify them you haven't canceled and they agree to operate within that timeframe.[115]

However, the important part is that we must start looking for you 30 minutes after your scheduled arrival - or sooner if we have reason to think we should.[116] When one is open, the first call is usually to an airport Fixed Base Operator (FBO) – the business at the airport who usually sells fuel and does maintenance. If not, we would call the police or sheriff and have them drive to the airport to find your aircraft. If they are unable, we contact the airport manager and have them look into it.

If nobody finds your aircraft, we will issue an Alert Notice (ALNOT)[117] so, system-wide, people will be looking for you. Eventually, search and rescue will be dispatched. Sometimes, we may have a military aircraft on the frequency and can have them start looking for you.

During the daily accident meetings, one of the items that I noticed as it came up often enough was, upon landing, an aircraft hitting an animal such as a deer.

Once I started taking notice, I started to ask the time of day in which the animal strike accidents occurred. All but one happened after dark.

The FAA has a Wildlife Strike Database,[118] which reporting to is voluntary so the numbers are probably higher than reported.

Since the start of the database in 1990 through 2021, there have been 1,319 accidents and incidents involving animals classified as "Deer", "Mule deer" and "White-tailed deer". That averages out to 3.5 deer strikes per month.

According to the FAA's website, "Wildlife strikes with aircraft are increasing in the United States and elsewhere. The number of wildlife strikes reported per year to the FAA increased steadily from about 1,800 in 1990 to 16,000 in 2018."

On a side note, the 406 MHz emergency locator transmitter is the newer version ELT which is digital. When activated, the U.S. Air Force Rescue Coordination Center or U.S. Coast Guard Rescue Coordination Center gets encoded information which allows them to promptly start their search by calling the aircraft owner.[119]

The older ELTs, which only broadcast on 121.5 and 243.0 MHz, have a high rate of false alerts. Due to this, the rescue coordination centers wait for confirmation of an overdue aircraft or other information before launching search and rescue efforts.

Further, in 2009, the satellite system used to monitor ELTs stopped monitoring the older versions. 406 MHz ELTs are not required in the United States, but are strongly encouraged! If you haven't upgraded yours, you may want to seriously consider it.

CHAPTER 29

WRONG SURFACE OPERATIONS

A few years ago, at DuPage Airport (KDPA) in West Chicago, Illinois, a student pilot flying solo went out to practice maneuvers in the local area. As he was returning from the northeast of the airport, he called up the Class Delta tower, and the controller told him to enter on left base for Runway 20L. The student pilot repeated the controller's transmission and continued inbound.

A short time later, the controller instructed him, "Runway 20 left, clear to land."

And so - the student pilot repeated what he heard as the clearance: "Runway 20 right, clear to land." The controller did not catch the read-back error saying the right runway instead of the left.

The student pilot, flying on left base, continued across final for Runway 20L, and turned final for Runway 20R. The controller only noticed the student was on the wrong runway when he was executing his landing flare. Thankfully, there was no traffic on 20R, so the controller decided it was safer to allow the student pilot to land on the wrong runway instead of having him go around when he was in the flare.

I don't think the pilot told ATC that he was a student pilot as, any-time controllers hear "student pilot" during an initial call[120], they generally pay close attention to that aircraft. Therefore, I always recommend student pilots identify themselves. Likewise, it is perfectly acceptable to let ATC know if you are a "low time" (non-student) pilot or if you are an "unfamiliar pilot" visiting a new airport for the first time.

This is just one example of a wrong surface operation, and I have seen many of them involving general aviation and professional pilots alike. I've reviewed reports of aircraft departing or landing using the wrong intersecting runway, off up to 60 degrees. I have also seen aircraft that have attempted an intersection departure and turned in the wrong direction.

Most of the time, when the controller notices the aircraft lined up for the wrong runway, they instruct the pilot to go around.

That afternoon, I spoke with the psychologist who worked in our office and told her about the student pilot reading back Runway 20 Right and the controller missing it.

She told me the human brain doesn't work that way: working to catch minor changes the person is not expecting. She added that controllers do better than most since they practice listening for wrong read-backs every day.

Therefore, if you are ever given a clearance similar to this scenario where you were told to expect one thing, but then you thought you heard something different, please don't just read back the clearance! Ask about it in a manner that will highlight the change. For this example, you could ask, "Confirm you want us to change to runway 20 Right?"

Controllers are required to say "change to runway" if they make a runway assignment change.[121] Therefore, if you don't hear that, be sure to ask them in a clear and concise manner.

The FAA's August 2018 published data shows 85% of wrong surface landings involve GA aircraft, with 15% involving commercial aircraft (defined as "For Hire" and does not necessarily mean airlines).[122]

On the night of November 20, 2013, at 9:20 p.m. Central Standard Time, a Boeing Dreamlifter, a highly-modified 747-400 Large Cargo Freighter used for unusual cargo operations like transporting Boeing 787 parts internationally, intended to land at McConnell Air Force Base (KIAB) in Wichita, Kansas.[123] Instead, they landed at Colonel James Jabara Airport (KAAO), eight nautical miles north of KIAB.

The runways at both airports are in similar directions; KIAB has parallel runways - 1L/19R and 1R/19L. KAAO has a single runway - 18/36. However, one runway at KIAB was closed that night, so the crew would have been looking for a single runway airport.

The Dreamlifter's crew was cleared for a visual approach and to land on Runway 19L. Using their flight deck instruments, the crew backed the approach up with RNAV/GPS Runway 19L. But once they had an airport in sight, they never crosschecked after that point. After the aircraft touched down on the wrong runway, the crew realized their error.

Additionally, the ATC computer did not alert the controller of the aircraft's low altitude as the system assumed the aircraft was landing at KAAO, which, of course, it did.

Luckily, everybody was okay, and there was no damage.[124] The ground crew had to drive a towing tug, with a police escort, from the main airport to KAAO to turn the Dreamlifter around. Also, weight was removed from the aircraft so that a new flight crew could fly it out of the small airport the following afternoon.

Only a couple of months later, on January 12, 2014, at 6:08 p.m. CST, a Southwest Airlines (SWA) Boeing 737-700, flying as Flight 4013, was inbound to Missouri's Branson Airport (KBBG).[125] It was dark outside, and the crew reported the field in sight. They were cleared for a visual approach for Runway 14 at KBBG. The controllers switched the flight crew to BBG's tower frequency, and the BBG controllers further cleared the SWA flight to land on Runway 14.

Instead, they landed six miles away at the M. Graham Clark Downtown Airport (KPLK) on Runway 12. They used maximum braking and were able to stop the large aircraft on the 3,738-foot runway, which has an enormous drop-off immediately after!

Thankfully, there were no injuries to the 124 passengers and seven crew members, nor was there any damage to the aircraft.

In both of these instances, the crews were seasoned pilots: the captain and first officer on the Dreamlifter had an estimated 20,000- hours and 11,861- hours total time respectively, and the SWA captain and first officer had 15,700- and 20,538-hours total time.

Landing at the wrong airport hasn't only happened to civilian pilots. In 2012, a United States Air Force C-17, a heavy cargo aircraft, was concluding a twelve-hour-long flight from Rome, Italy. Instead of landing at its intended destination of MacDill Air Force Base (KMCF) near Tampa, Florida, it ended up touching down at Peter O Knight Airport (KTPF) - which are only five nautical miles apart with runways in similar directions. The resulting investigation determined fatigue was to blame.[126]

In the wake of these incidents, on January 31, 2014, the FAA sent a memo to controllers reviewing the requirement to advise pilots of airports close to their destination airport which may be confusing.[127] In March 2014, the NTSB issued a Safety Alert.[128]

Perhaps the most noteworthy recent incident which narrowly avoided hundreds, if not thousands, of deaths, happened on Friday, July 7, 2017[129]at 11:56 p.m. Pacific Daylight Time at the San Francisco International Airport (KSFO) in California.

At the time, the airport was undergoing construction on one of the east/west parallel runways, Runway 10R/28L, where the runway surface was being repaved and lights replaced. The construction was being done nightly during the overnight shifts, so when they closed the runway, they turned off the approach and runway lights and, in addition, placed an illuminated flashing white "X" at each end of the runway.

Ten minutes before the incident occurred, Air Canada (ACA) Flight 759, an Airbus A320, was cleared for the FMS Bridge Visual Approach to Runway 28R. The FMS approach is coded with GPS coordinates and is included in the Flight Management System's (FMS) database for approved operators, like Air Canada.

Generally, visual approaches are easier for both the pilots and controllers. Except for when the aircraft's route already has them lined up for the runway, visual approaches allow aircraft to remain closer to the airport instead of being vectored further out for an instrument approach. And so, when the weather is good enough to support them, they are the go-to approach for controllers to assign to aircraft.

A few minutes later, ACA759 was switched to SFO tower and was cleared to land on Runway 28R. Then, the flight crew lowered the A320's landing gear and turned off the autopilot and flight director so the plane's captain could hand fly the aircraft down to landing.

Per the procedure, after they passed the final visual checkpoint on the approach, the captain initiated the right turn to line up with Runway 28R. But instead, he mistakenly lined up with Taxiway C, the parallel taxiway to the right of Runway 28R.

At the same time, the first officer was busy setting the heading bug to runway heading and programming the FMS for a possible go-around. These tasks had him focused inside the flight deck on the system and charts - instead of looking outside the aircraft.

As the aircraft was descending through 300 feet of altitude, the captain asked the first officer to confirm the runway was clear. The first officer looked outside the aircraft and keyed up the frequency, saying: "Just want to confirm, this is ACA759, we see some lights on the runway there, across the runway. Can you confirm we're cleared to land?"

The controller on duty checked his Airport Surface Surveillance Capability (ASSC) display, a radar system which detects aircraft and vehicles on the ground plus airborne aircraft close to the airport, and rescanned the runway. In reply, he said, "Air Canada 759, confirmed, cleared to land Runway 28R. There's no one on runway 28R but you."

The first officer continued, "Okay, Air Canada 759."[130] The ASSC showed ACA759 slightly right of runway centerline – a condition that the controller later told the NTSB that it was normal for aircraft while on the FMS Bridge approach to that runway.

Taxiway C had four aircraft holding short and waiting to depart at the approach end of the runway: a United Airlines (UAL) Boeing 787, a Philippine Airlines (PAL) Airbus A340, another UAL Boeing 787, and a UAL Boeing 737. Of course, being dark outside and per basic procedures, the three widebody-heavy and one narrow-body-large aircraft on the taxiway had most of their lights off.

A mere second after the ACA759 said "Okay" on frequency, the first UAL B787 waiting for departure keyed up and said, "Where is that guy going?" As the UAL said that, ACA759 was only an estimated 150 feet high and lined up for Taxiway C.

Four seconds later, as ACA759 overflew the first UAL B787 by 100 feet, the United Captain keyed up again and announced, "He's on the taxiway!"

At the same time, the PAL A340's pilots turned on their landing gear and nose lights illuminating the taxiway and the UAL B787 in front of them.

Two seconds later, as ACA759 was at 89 feet, the pilot advanced the throttles to execute a go-around. As they passed over PAL115, the radar data showed they were at an altitude of 60 feet above ground level.

Finally, three seconds after advancing the throttles, ACA759 began to climb back into the night sky. About this time, the controller noticed the aircraft was in a strange position and instructed ACA759 to go around. The pilot responded, "in the go-around, Air Canada 759,"[131] as it passed over the third aircraft in line at 200 feet agl and the fourth aircraft at 250 feet.

I spoke to Bob Hendrickson, who was the FAA Air Safety Investigator on call that weekend. He told me "The FAA Washington Operations Center (WOC) called me that night saying an aircraft abandoned their approach, went around, and subsequently landed safely."

"That's not the sort of thing which typically concerns us," he remarked. "We weren't going to go out there to investigate because they landed."

As a long-term project, Bob had been tasked with looking into wrong runway landings as they were trying to figure out how to stop them from happening.

"The next morning, I came in and was doing the stack [of accidents and incidents]," Bob continued. "I looked it up, and ACA759 went around, but it said they were lined up on the taxiway, and there were planes on there. I didn't know how bad it was... but decided maybe we better go out there and look at it."

After a short discussion with FAA management, they "launched" Bob as the agency's Investigator-in-Charge (IIC). "I went out there, and every time I peeled back a layer, it got more and more gross," he added.

Approximately 24 hours after the incident, Bob flew as a passenger in a California Highway Patrol (CHP) helicopter on the FMS Bridge Visual Approach Runway 28R. This is a common technique that investigators use to gain insights into what the accident/incident flight crew experienced.

During the helicopter flight, Bob was able to picture what the airport looked like to the crew the night before. "The moon was the same, the sky was the same, and it was the same time of night," Bob noted. "There were some planes on the parallel taxiway, which they didn't normally have. They put the airport lights on at the same settings. They did everything humanly possible to make it look exactly the same; it was pretty impressive."

At the Monday morning roundup meeting following the incident, Bob presented the information he had up to that point to the group via speakerphone. I was in attendance and there was a long discussion about this event.

During that discussion, one piece of information which I found interesting was that a Delta Airlines flight, a Boeing 737 arrived approximately 4 minutes before the ACA incident. The Delta crew of Flight 521 also had issues identifying Runway 28R, but they were able to correct since they backed up the visual approach with lateral navigation (LNAV).

Later that week, the FAA's Office of Accident Investigation and Prevention (AVP) held a special meeting discussing this incident. During this time, a video was shown - a simulation created using radar data.

I knew what most people quickly realized when the facts of the situation were revealed: how close this incident was to becoming the largest aviation disaster in history - even larger than the two Boeing 747s that struck at Tenerife in 1977.[132] As I sat there in the meeting, I knew the disaster was averted, and everybody was safe, but watching that simulation was unnerving!

According to Bob, his team completed most of their investigation a few months after the incident.

"Air Canada's Airbus aircraft had two different configurations for their flight management system," he explained, FMS being an onboard computer system handling navigation.

"The FMS on this aircraft flew the instrument portion of the Visual Approach. Once the aircraft reached the point where they were required to navigate visually, 4.4 miles from the runway – approximately only 4 nautical miles to touchdown, they would have to clear out the system and reprogram in the Missed Approach procedures in case they had to go-around."

"Due to this, the first officer was busy programming the FMS for the next phase of flight as the Captain was essentially flying the aircraft by himself, without lateral guidance from the instruments or from a second set of eyes confirming everything was correct."

Bob didn't like this approach, saying: "This was a tough approach; it isn't as easy as it sounds."

The investigators scheduled a meeting with Air Canada. In the room were around a dozen people, including the pilots, the airline's chief pilots, union representatives, and Airbus representatives.

Knowing they were dealing with pilots from a foreign country, Bob told the investigation team, including both FAA and NTSB, that, "we're not going to get anything out of these guys, they're not going to open up to us unless we give them all of our stuff." Everybody agreed and they prepared their briefing.

At the start of the meeting, Bob had the picture of the airport he took from the helicopter displayed on the overhead projector. Whenever they would use the projector for something, they would immediately return to that picture again, similar to seeing a computer desktop background every time you close a window.

At the end of the two-hour briefing, Bob said to everybody except the pilots, "Hold up your hand if you think you don't understand why it is they couldn't see those airplanes on the runway."

About half of the group raised their hands.

"You've been sitting here for two hours and that picture has been up on the board," Bob continued. "Let me ask you, how many planes are in that picture?"

Describing the photo, Bob noted: "the photo is taken on a one-mile final, about 20-25 seconds from touchdown, or 10-15 seconds from contact with the second airplane waiting for takeoff."[133] They all started looking closely at the photo and studied it. One person walked up to the picture and found the red and green wingtip lights.

However, nobody guessed at the number of aircraft.

"These pilots are coming in at 3:00 in the morning according to their circadian clock, as they were on reserve in the Eastern time zone. They're going maybe 150-160 knots," Bob told the group. "They've got 20 seconds to pick up the runway, make a decision, and head in for it. They have about 10 seconds to make the decision to go around."

"During this time, the pilot had to overcome the expectation bias from 'knowing' he was lined up for the correct runway, admitting there was a problem during 'severe clear' weather, and making the decision to go-around, which he did. That's a good pilot."

"You've had ten times that long, and you can't see that there are two airplanes on that runway, 500 people between them!" That's when the group realized the two pilots encountered a difficult situation in unforgiving conditions.

The investigators then interviewed both pilots, who opened up and discussed the event - especially the first officer. Neither pilot saw any of the four aircraft on the taxiway.

The first officer said he didn't feel comfortable continuing the approach and called for the go-around while, at the same time, the captain was debating it.[134]

Both pilots told investigators they went around at 400 feet msl when they initiated the go-around but the data showed otherwise. "By the time the pilots made the decision, configured the aircraft for the go-around and started their climb, it would be easy to believe that when they saw the altimeter, it showed 400 feet msl and climbing." Bob concluded.

According to Bob, the investigators used different methodologies to determine the number of feet the A320 missed the second aircraft in line on the taxiway. Their calculations ranged from 6-20 feet separation. Ultimately, the NTSB decided to use one method for their final report, which concluded **ACA759 narrowly avoided the PAL A340 by a mere 13 ½ feet!**

The investigators calculated the descent rate of 700 feet and decided that if the crew had waited one second longer, they would have collided with the PAL A340, the second aircraft in line on Taxiway C.[135]

Bob explained that the FMS Bridge Visual was a horrible approach, and air traffic controllers stopped using it the next day as part of their mitigation plan.

On August 18, 2017, the FAA issued a Safety Alert for Operators discussing the ACA759 incident and best practices to avoid a similar situation.[136] In July 2018, the FAA also published a training video named *Wrong Surface Landing*.[137]

During the investigation, Bob attended a stakeholder's meeting at the FAA Regional Office in Seattle. Somebody presented an idea: adjust the software on ASDE-X from only detecting surface vehicles to also detecting aircraft lined up for a wrong surface. The "Airport Surface Detection Equipment — Model X," or ASDE-X, is a runway-safety tool that enables air traffic controllers to detect potential runway conflicts by providing detailed coverage of movement on runways and taxiways. By collecting data from a variety of sources, ASDE-X is able to track vehicles and aircraft on airport surfaces and obtain identification information from aircraft transponders.

Bob worked tirelessly for two years convincing different groups involved this system change would enhance safety and, therefore, was worth upgrading. It took over three years to design, develop and certify the adjusted system which has, according to Bob, been installed at all the major airports. When the system detects a possible wrong surface landing, a loud, audible alarm warns the controllers.

Furthermore, Bob said, **"100% of wrong runway landings happen when the pilots are proceeding visually. They do not happen on instruments."**

Please be vigilant when you are flying, especially in a complex environment. Wrong surface operations have become a big issue that happens more often than we would like. If you hear something different than you were told to expect, like this student pilot landing at DuPage, be sure to clarify the clearance.

Simply reading back what you heard is not enough. Controllers will correct those wrong read-backs most of the time, but it is too easy to miss those types of read-backs. If a controller changes your runway, they are supposed to say, "Change to Runway, 20 Right, clear to land." If you don't hear that, be sure to ask for clarification.

If you are cleared for a visual approach, especially at night, tune in the instrument approach as a backup. Doing this helped the DAL521 crew land in the otherwise confusing situation.

If professional flight crews can easily make a mistake, it obviously needs to be taken seriously for all pilots, especially recreational pilots. Some techniques used to avoid using the wrong way are to check your heading once you line up on the runway centerline for departure. If flying a visual approach, back it up with a precision approach such as an ILS, GPS (LPV), or a non-precision approach as a last resort.

I would like to note that the ACA759 crew did make the right call and initiate the go-around. Even though this was an extremely close call, they did avoid disaster.

_____

CHAPTER 30

NOTAMs

In 2014, Laura – who is now my wife - and I spent a lot of time on my Sea Ray Sundancer cabin cruiser powerboat, which I had docked at the Cedar Point Marina in Sandusky, Ohio. As we drove to the boat, we passed the closed Sandusky Municipal Airport (KSKY). The city had closed the airport the December before, intending to sell the land to developers who would turn it into a sports center.

When it was open and operating, KSKY was a great little airport. It had two intersecting runways, a co-located VOR (SKY), and the best part was it sat on the Lake Erie shoreline. King Air service was provided as a means to travel to the islands - one of the state's best kept secrets!

One of the Standard Instrument Departures (SIDs) out of Cleveland used the SKY VOR, so I saw it on the URET screens often. And anytime we drove past, I always paid special attention - as I do when I pass any airport.

One day in June, I was driving past and saw a Cessna on the ramp at Sandusky! The grass was all overgrown, and not a single vehicle was present. Nevertheless, there were two people walking towards the hangar. I couldn't help wonder how they missed the NOTAM (Then "Notice to Airmen," but now called "Notice to Air Missions") stating the airport as closed.

A couple of weeks later, I was driving by again, and there were two airplanes on the ramp, parked somewhat close to each other. Between the airplanes were three people standing and talking to each other.

Again, I wondered how those pilots missed that the airport was closed, as I presume the airport had painted a large "X" at the end of each runway. The grass was left unkept and overgrown - not only in the yard areas but through the cracks in the concrete all over the place. The airport completely looked like what it was: abandoned!

During the rest of that summer, I saw airplanes at the airport a few more times, and I thought it had to be out-of-area pilots because word spread quickly through the local aviation community about the closure. Surely, pilots would check NOTAMs before they flew?!

Later, in 2016, I was working in Washington, D.C. in Air Traffic Safety Oversight as part of a class where they went step-by-step through the audit process using an actual audit that was in progress.

This particular audit looked into chart issues, where items that were no longer there were still depicted on sectionals, along with newly built obstacles that had not yet been reflected on the charts.

I came to learn that the FAA is at the mercy of outside agencies reporting the information to them before they can add them to the publications. There can sometimes be a sizeable gap before these updates are reported.

The cartographer in our office was leading the effort. Once the class was finished, I opened the sectional for northern Ohio. Almost three years later, the Sandusky Municipal Airport was still depicted.

I walked across the office to his cubicle and told him about SKY closing and that it is still on the VFR Sectional chart. He asked if I still had it pulled up on my computer, to which I said yes, and we both walked back to my computer to take a look.

As I showed it to him, he told me it was actually correct because they had the name crosshatched. I have to admit, I had not seen that before. As I looked to see if the airport was still depicted on the Sectional, I didn't read the information associated with the airport icon. I hope I would have noticed it if I was planning a flight there, but either way, I enjoyed learning something new.

★ ★ ★

When I was in college in June of 2001, I enrolled in the next pilot course, mainly for VFR solo flying to build experience and time. I would accomplish two cross-country lessons for this flight by flying to the Twin Cities of Minneapolis & Saint Paul, Minnesota, spend the night with friends who went home for the summer, then fly back to Grand Forks, North Dakota.

I have always enjoyed flying at night, as there is something so peaceful and majestic about it. I absolutely love it!

I had my flight planning complete for both lessons. I arrived at the airport and turned in my slip to the SOF (the University's student Supervisor of Flight) to get an aircraft assigned. He looked at my plan and asked me what time I would arrive at the Flying Cloud Airport (FCM), to which I answered around 11:30 p.m.

He asked why so late. I told him I wanted to get some night-flying logged. He then asked if the lesson required nighttime flying, to which the answer was no; I just wanted to because it had been a while since I've flown at night, and I liked it.

He told me that he had to deny my request because the Flight Operations office closes at 11:00 p.m., and since the lesson did not require night flying, I needed to change my plan to arrive before they closed.

I went to the flight planning room and debated some options. I originally planned a longer flight than I needed, as I was just going to have fun with it. Knowing my time crunch, I found two airports closer to my flight path. I decided to fly KGFK..KMKT..KFBL..KFCM. I crunched numbers using my calculator, and I determined I could make it before Flight Operations closed. I called the Flight Service Station and filed my new VFR flight plan.

I went back to the desk and advised the SOF of my new plan, which he approved, giving me the aircraft book. I picked up my suitcase and flight bag and headed towards Charlie Ramp.

I got airborne in a Piper Warrior and enjoyed my evening flight. As I got close to Mankato, I checked the weather and tuned in to the CTAF, making standard radio calls. I entered the downwind for the northwest runway. I started descending, and I was now on short final, configured properly, the airspeed was on point. I was happy with my approach.

As I was less than a half-mile from the runway threshold, a yellow, high wing tricycle airplane taxied onto the runway and started their departure roll. I couldn't believe it!

I immediately applied full power to execute a go-around and announced on the radio frequency that I was going around due to the aircraft taking off in front of me! As pictures of low-wing aircraft landing on top of high-wing aircraft ran through my mind, I offset to the right so we wouldn't collide.

I kept them in sight the whole time and continued to make my radio calls. I entered the airport's traffic pattern and ultimately landed safely.

I taxied to the ramp to get fuel. After parking, I walked into the fixed base operator (FBO) building – where I noticed several signs posted for the CTAF frequency change. That is when it hit me: I didn't call Flight Service to check NOTAMs for the new airports – and I was broadcasting on the wrong frequency the whole time!

On December 1, 2016, I arrived at my cubicle in Washington, D.C. early in the morning. As part of my morning routine, I read the Administrator's Daily Alert Bulletin (ADAB) and the Air Traffic Organization's Report (ATO Report), both of which summarize accidents and operational incidents from the day or weekend before. That day, only one event stuck out to me.

According to the reports, the night before, at 8:37 p.m. CST, a Beechjet (BE40) was cleared for takeoff on Runway 15L at the Houston George Bush Intercontinental Airport (KIAH) in Texas.

Instead, the BE40 departed Taxiway WA, the parallel taxiway the pilots were supposed to cross on their way to the runway. At that time, Taxiway WA had been NOTAM-ed closed for two years due to construction. As the aircraft departed from the closed taxiway, it struck two barricades, both of which were illuminated in the darkness.

Airport Operations examined the damage and found tire marks on both barricades, with one being completely destroyed. And when this all occurred, construction crews were working approximately 2,500 feet past those barricades. Luckily, there were no reports of any injuries.

The local controller, on the radio called "Tower", was looking through the windows, scanning his area of jurisdiction. The tower was located approximately two miles away from the runway threshold, making it difficult due to "slant range visibility issues."

Due to this problem, the ATCT issued a Letter to Airmen earlier that year notifying pilots of several locations, including the taxiways near the departure end of Runway 15L, that were not visible from the tower cab.[138] They warned that controllers would issue clearances based upon "known traffic" and not from what they could see.

During my two-plus years at FAA Headquarters, there were numerous reports of pilots landing on NOTAM-closed runways. The NOTAM system has long been problematic, with both pilots and controllers missing them.

A former FSDO inspector told me the pilots are still responsible for knowing and adhering to the NOTAMs, even if ATC cleared them to land on a closed runway. I'm sure that is true. However, controllers also have to jump through hoops when it happens in hopes that it never happens again.

In the wake of the Air Canada incident at SFO, the NTSB recommended to the FAA to fix the NOTAM system issues. NTSB Chair Robert Sumwalt underscored the problem with NOTAMs even further, calling them "just a bunch of garbage that nobody pays any attention to."[139]

NTSB Vice Chair Bruce Landsberg said in the Air Canada 759 Incident Report statement that, in the current NOTAM and preflight information system, "lays an impossibly heavy burden on individual pilots, crews and dispatchers to sort through literally dozens of irrelevant items to find the critical or merely important ones. When one is invariably missed, and a violation or incident occurs, the pilot is blamed for not finding the needle in the haystack!"[140]

Unless stated in an ATIS, controllers are now required to issue NOTAMs to the pilot which may restrict an approach or landing, even if the pilot received them during their preflight briefing.[141]

En route controllers are no longer allowed to have pilots contact FSS to satisfy this requirement.

CHAPTER 31

DRONES

When I was working at Headquarters, one of the most important topics we talked about was "drones." At the time, drones, or the new official name: Unmanned Aircraft Systems (UASs), had new regulations being developed and implemented due to the popularity of the new systems.

UASs have become very cheap for people to buy, and you see them often. Shopping malls regularly fly demonstration models to improve sales. Today, UASs are even being used by law enforcement and fire departments to assist in their efforts.

When appropriately used, UASs can be a lot of fun for personal use or to provide a significant number of benefits for commercial and government service.

The FAA has implemented new regulations under Parts 89 and 107. These rules require UAS pilots to see-and-avoid manned aircraft, maintain line-of-sight with their drone, remain within 400 feet above ground level, or within 400 feet of an obstacle, such as when taking photographs of a skyscraper, among many other rules.[142]

To date, there has been one documented midair collision between a UAS and a manned aircraft. On September 21, 2017, an Army Blackhawk Helicopter collided with a UAS just east of Staten Island, NY. There was a Temporary Flight Restriction (TFR) as the U.S. President was visiting the area, and the Army Blackhawk was doing TFR patrol at 300 feet northbound along the shoreline.

The helicopter struck the quadcopter drone but, initially, the crew didn't know what happened. The lead helicopter's wingman crew saw the drone just before the collision. Even though the Blackhawk sustained hundreds of thousands of dollars in damage, they made it back to their base and landed safely.

Upon post-flight inspection, parts of the drone were found lodged in an engine intake of the Blackhawk. The NTSB tracked down the drone operator using the serial numbers printed on drone parts they recovered.

Once they contacted the drone operator, he was very cooperative with the investigation. He owned five drones and flew them often. That day, he had been operating the drone beyond line-of-sight, approximately 2.5 miles away, using his iPad to navigate. He lost connection with the drone, so he hit the "return home" button a few times - but the drone never returned. He thought it must have dropped into the ocean and was a loss, so he packed up and went home. He was completely unaware it collided with the Blackhawk and was also unaware of the TFR.

If a recreational pilot who operates several UASs regularly does not know the recommendations/regulations, do you think most UAS owners operate in the same manner?

Hopefully, in the years since this accident, more operators have become aware of the regulations.

In 2018, The University of Dayton Research Institute performed a test to see how an aircraft wing would do when a drone hit it in flight.[143]

They used a Mooney M20 wing and a DJI Phantom 2 quadcopter, which weighed 2.1 pounds. They fired the quadcopter from a tube into the wing at 238 miles per hour (207 knots).

They published a video of their test showing the collision in real-time and again at extreme slow motion. The drone crashed into the wing's leading edge, penetrating into and damaging the wing spar.

The drone's manufacturer, DJI Technology Inc., responded to the test as being unrealistic[144] and said the test was, "at a higher speed than the combined maximum speed of the drone and airplane." They further argued the aircraft would be lower and slower for a likely collision.

There are many reports of Near-Midair Collisions between manned aircraft and drones. Furthermore, several pilot reports of midair collisions with a drone have been filed, but when the FAA conducted a swab DNA test on the aircraft's surface, it has always shown it was actually the result of a bird strike.

I have also seen many pilot reports of near-misses with drones at altitudes up to the mid-FL200s. What are the chances drones are on top of the mind for those pilots and that is why they 'see' them so high? I don't know, and there is no way to prove them otherwise.

I like the video of the collision test. While I agree the speeds are high, it appears that the wing would still be flyable and hopefully allow for a safe landing. If the speeds were lower, there should be less damage.

If you ever collide with or have a near-midair, definitely report it to ATC or the FSDO as soon as practical. It helps to add them to the database, and if there is a specific area in which it is often happening, they will try to find the operators.

CHAPTER 32

ATC ZERO

On March 21, 2020, in the early days of the COVID-19 pandemic, I was working at Washington ARTCC. As I returned from break, the Shenandoah (SHD) and Wahoo (WAH) Sectors, which are side-by-side sectors owning Flight Levels 340 through 600, were getting busy. I offered the SHD Radar Controller a break, but she passed, so I relieved the SHD D-Side. As I was plugging in, I was told New York ARTCC just went "ATC Zero" and to stop all incoming aircraft from the adjacent sectors.

"ATC Zero" is when a facility is unable to provide air traffic services or "zero services." Every facility has contingency plans for if/when these situations happen. One of the first steps is to shut the adjacent sectors/facilities off. This puts them into a "No-Notice Hold," meaning the other sectors can hold their airplanes or do whatever they want, but they cannot accept any handoffs allowing any aircraft into the affected airspace.

After receiving a briefing and assuming the SHD D-Side position, I called the three sectors around us and put them into a hold.

A couple of minutes later, the Baden Sector in Atlanta ARTCC called and shut us off: they couldn't take any more aircraft due to the number already inside their airspace! At that time, I had three aircraft in handoff status to them. While I had them on the line, I asked if they could take the one aircraft at FL410, heading southbound direct to Pulaski (PSK).

I asked about that particular aircraft because we had another aircraft headed northbound at FL410 plus an aircraft headed westbound underneath them at FL400, all in the same general area. I knew the aircraft I asked him about was a Boeing 737-800 with a maximum certified altitude was FL410. That means I couldn't climb them to put them into a holding pattern. We would need to be spot-on with vectoring to avoid Atlanta ARTCC's airspace while maintaining separation from our traffic. Luckily, the Atlanta controller agreed to take them, and they continued on their route.

I switched off the landline and told the radar controller what I had just coordinated. Most of the aircraft in our sector were headed southwest-bound towards Atlanta ARTCC. In a No-Notice Hold situation, the highest priority is the aircraft closest to the boundary to that sector.

When a controller is put into a No-Notice Hold, it raises our workload significantly. We have to issue holding instructions to all of the aircraft affected, which takes time. Once all the holding instructions have been issued, and the aircraft have entered the holding patterns, our workload goes down significantly, usually lower than before the hold. Once aircraft are established in the hold, it is relatively easy to peel them out in an orderly fashion.

The radar controller started putting aircraft in "Present Position Holds." The first two aircraft took their holding instructions and entered their holding patterns. The radar controller told the next aircraft, "I have holding instructions, advise ready to copy."

This aircraft departed the Washington D.C. metro area and was flying to Texas. The pilot responded by asking if we actually meant the holding instructions for them. The radar controller told them, "Affirmative. New York Center just went ATC Zero and, due to saturation, I have to put you into the hold. Advise ready to copy."

Instead of taking the holding instructions, the pilot said, "we are currently 839 miles from our destination, and New York Center is behind us. Why do we have to hold?"

Now, I have to admit, this is one of my pet peeves! I completely understand when a pilot asks us to confirm what they heard was correct. However, the minute pilots start arguing after we have confirmed the clearance or statement, that is when it becomes frustrating.

And this happens most often with holding patterns! I have never seen a pilot talk a controller out of putting them into the hold. Therefore, any argument is a waste of time. Whenever we, as controllers, get put into the hold by another sector or facility, we usually have to issue holding instructions to several aircraft. Thus, we do not have the time to waste with a back-and-forth about why they are going into the hold after we've stated the reason.

If you need to declare an emergency, or need to divert for some reason, then, by all means, please tell us! If you have a special circumstance, such as being low on fuel, just make a simple statement as you read back your holding instructions stating you only have about so-many minutes (i.e., 15 minutes) to hold before you will need to divert. That type of information is valuable as we can sometimes work out an exception for that particular aircraft. Otherwise, please take the holding instructions and wait for things to slow down on frequency. Once they slow, feel free to ask your questions.

The radar controller responded to the pilots, saying that yes, New York Center is ATC Zero, but the next sector put us into a No-Notice Hold due to saturation from the backup of traffic, and added that the aircraft needed to advise when ready to copy holding instructions.

The pilot came back and said, "OK, hold on." I was mystified that they didn't even grab a pen during the back-and-forth. Eventually, they received their holding instructions and entered the hold.

Whenever a sector gets "shut off" and the controller has to put aircraft into holding patterns, they drastically reduce the number of aircraft they can safely run through their airspace. Even though there are mathematical formulas for the size of holding patterns, the truth is, we don't know precisely where a holding aircraft will end up. Typically, we specify the inbound leg between ten and twenty-five miles at higher altitudes.

However, we don't know how wide the radius of the turns will be, as the winds aloft can make a huge difference. Therefore, even though ARTCC standard separation is 5 miles laterally, we generally don't let any aircraft close to the lateral confines of the holding pattern. This severely limits the number of aircraft we can run through our airspace, which is why the Baden Sector put us into the hold.

Flying throughout the COVID-19 pandemic has proven that changes can happen rapidly. When this happened, two areas in Indianapolis ARTCC (ZID) were shut down due to a positive test result for COVID-19. One of their affected sectors is adjacent to the SHD Sector. Therefore, we had a lot of aircraft routed around ZID's airspace, flying through ours. The SHD Sector was psychotically busy several times during those days. I know the traffic in the United States overall started going down, but the traffic through the SHD Sector went way up.

After we finally got all our aircraft into holding patterns, I was relieved from the position for the day. Later that afternoon, I looked online and discovered everybody was delayed less than an hour and found only two areas within the New York ARTCC that went ATC Zero. Somehow, the Traffic Management Unit (TMU) implemented plans that opened up all the major NYC airports. However, oceanic traffic was still restricted.

Chicago Midway Airport (KMDW) was the first tower to go ATC Zero due to COVID-19. Similar to towers that close at night, they NOTAM-ed three of the four runways closed - or 6 of 8 runways if you want to be extremely technical!

The next day, several GA aircraft were performing touch and goes at the uncontrolled field. This put a strain on the incoming IFR traffic - even though Southwest Airlines canceled all their flights. The FAA published an additional NOTAM prohibiting Touch-and-Goes.

On April 21, Washington ARTCC had a positive COVID-19 case: a contractor whose duties took them throughout the building. Due to this, Washington ARTCC went ATC Zero during the midnight shift so cleaning crews could perform a deep cleanse throughout the facility. They planned the ATC Zero a few hours in advance, which should have helped with a smooth transition (I wasn't working). The facility was opened up early the following day, resuming normal operations.

During the pandemic, I would guess most facilities, if not all of them went ATC-Zero. The ARTCCs would shut down during the midnight shifts for a couple hours between the evening crew and midnight shift change for deep cleaning. Of course, COVID-19 is not the only reason an ATC facility can go ATC-Zero. The question is: what actions do you take in preparation for the ATC facility you are communicating, or planning to communicate with, goes ATC Zero?

When towers are shut down, they typically announce on the frequency that they are shutting down and what the pilots should do. They should also place a statement onto the ATIS, stating it will be an uncontrolled airfield and whom to contact for IFR clearances. The good news: any traffic in the pattern is usually aware of their traffic. During your flight planning, take note of other airfields that could serve as alternates. If you are talking to a tower, it should convert to uncontrolled, and you should still be able to land. However, it never hurts to know a close alternate airport if the airport authority decides to close the airport.

If a radar facility becomes ATC Zero, the process is more complex. Typically, another radar facility will assume the affected airspace. However, this could take several minutes to several hours. Once they are set up, they will need everybody to change their frequency and start identifying every aircraft. During this time, be extra vigilant of your TCAS or ADS-B In. If you are receiving VFR Flight Following, then you should be able to continue VFR with minimal issues. If you are VFR in Class Bravo airspace, I would exit the Class Bravo as soon as practical.

However, if a facility goes ATC Zero without being able to make a statement on frequency about what is happening and who else to contact, then you should follow IFR communication failure procedures. If you can fly VFR and land, do it.

As most pilots realize, when aircraft are issued an IFR clearance, the clearance itself does not provide traffic separation services. Realistically, it is a route in case of lost communications. Controllers separate traffic on a sector-by-sector basis. Before a controller takes a handoff, they do a traffic scan and usually fix any issues before taking the new aircraft. They may turn or change altitude for the aircraft already on their frequency, or they may call the other controller and have them move their aircraft before taking the handoff. This is why you may get a turn or change in altitude long after being on the frequency with a controller.

In my opinion, the longer you keep flying on your flight plan without communicating with ATC, the riskier your flight becomes. You may want to think about requiring your passengers to remain seated with their seatbelts on in case of any evasive maneuvers you may have to make.

As I've said before, a good technique is to monitor the Guard frequency of 121.5. Every ATC facility is still required to monitor it at all times. This is an excellent tool to use if you are lost, can't find a frequency, or if something abnormal happens where you cannot communicate normally. Somebody monitoring Guard should get you a frequency to contact the assuming facility. If you are not in range, broadcast on 121.5 in the blind for an aircraft at a higher altitude to relay your message to ATC.

To view operational issues across the country, visit the ATC Command Center's Operation webpage at fly.faa.gov.

Also, please do not argue about receiving holding instructions. Controllers are generally excellent about keeping pilots in the loop when they get new information. Remember, getting you out of the hold and on your way helps the controller too; it gets you out of their sector!

At the end of the day, remember three things. First, ATC issues clearances in an effort to make the situation most efficient for everybody involved. If you are not comfortable with an instruction, tell ATC "unable" and they will make adjustments as needed.

Second, if you are going to do anything abnormal such as a shallow descent rate, a step climb, start orbiting when on a VFR cross country, or more, tell ATC before it becomes an issue.

Finally, If you even consider declaring an emergency, please do it, we are here to help!

Never forget that you, as the pilot-in-command, are the final authority and the one who is in control! I hope to talk to you on frequency. Have a great flight!

– "XI"

APPENDIX A: PHRASEOLOGY

I got my instrument rating while I was in college. Being an ATC major and an instrument-rated pilot, I thought I had a decent understanding of good phraseology.

When I finally made it to Cleveland ARTCC, I was initially assigned to the training department - as one would expect. The first task is to learn your maps.

We had to memorize all of the VORs within Cleveland ARTCC's air-space plus the first one outside the airspace on airways. Then, we got to move on to our area-specific map – where we had to memorize the low altitude en route chart - including all VORs, airway names, airway degrees from VORs and waypoints, the high altitude en route chart, all of the airports in the area, along with the approaches into each airport.

Since I was assigned to Area 8, it had six low altitude sectors (at that time), which meant there was A LOT for me to learn. I remember we counted them out, and I had to memorize 2,098 items for the one map test, which we only had a month to study for!

Once we passed our various tests, we started training in the simulator. There were only a limited number of positions able to be worked at any given time, so, out of the five time slots, we'd individually be assigned two or three scenarios each day. The other time slots we were assigned to be "Ghost Pilots," acting as the pilots talking on the simulated frequency.

One of the first scenarios when I was working as a Ghost Pilot, I decided I would talk on the simulated frequency the same way I would when in the airplane. I figured it would be more realistic for the trainee if I acted like an actual pilot.

I said things like:
- OK, we're climbing to ten, Piper 12345
- Beechjet 12345, we'll hustle up to twenty-three
- Citation 345 leaving six-point-two for ten

I continued using actual "pilot phraseology" until one of the older instructors got annoyed. Retired controllers often work as contractors in the training department, and this particular guy was one everybody enjoyed working with. He enjoyed mentoring students and was calming when otherwise tensions would be high from the simulated traffic.

This was the first time I worked as Ghost Pilot with him as the instructor and, after I made the first transmission, he turned around and said, "what did you just say?"

I repeated my radio call the same way I initially said it, and claimed I was phrasing it the way I do when I fly. He became visibly upset, which I had never seen with him before, and replied that I am to use standard phraseology - especially as the controller working the scenario deserves for it to be done correctly as it is his job on the line if things don't go well.

I never thought of it from that point of view before; the controller working the scenario's job was indeed on the line as we were all on probation, and employment was contingent upon us passing training. Plus, because I upset one of the nicest guys of the bunch, I was genuinely embarrassed.

From that point forward, I tried my best to use exact phraseology.

Once I made it into the ATC operation and became certified, I have mostly worked with professional pilots ever since. Even though some are absolutely horrible with how they talk on frequency, the vast majority of them make clear transmissions. Over the years, I have come to appreciate it when a pilot uses good phraseology, and I wished I would have learned and utilized it as a pilot from the start.

Therefore, I will give some phraseology examples that you can use to have clear and concise communication with air traffic control. I have a few of the following examples in previous chapters, but I wanted to put them all into one place.

Basics

First off, the one thing controllers absolutely hate is a long-winded transmission!

I call this "thinking on frequency," or when a person keys up the frequency and starts talking without knowing what they want to say beforehand. There are often long pauses and a lot of extra and unnecessary verbiage.

Typically, air traffic trainees start to do this when they begin training, and their instructors work it out of them fairly quickly. However, it happens on both sides of the frequency. Some GA pilots, who have no reason to practice or improve their radio skills, can be the worst. It always seems to happen when I am busy as a controller and then a pilot keys up to make a 20 second - or longer - transmission purely to say they are looking for flight following. It feels like an eternity!

When a pilot does this to me, it actually makes them my lowest priority. If I'm busy enough where I'm concerned, after every transmission, a pilot will ramble on the frequency - wasting precious time - I will limit the transmissions or deny service altogether. Remember that VFR flight following is an additional service when a controller has time. If you "think on frequency," I will need more time to deal with you. Therefore, it is in your best interest to practice your radio calls and know what you want to say before pushing the push-to-talk (PTT) button.

Try to keep your radio calls simple, to the point, and streamlined. If you want to be friendly, it is fine to say "Good morning/afternoon/evening" when you check-in and a "Good day/night" as you are leaving - and vice versa. Anything more than that becomes unnecessary.

If you have a question about something, it is nice to ask, "Center, N12345, do you have time for a question?" If the controller is really busy, they may not even acknowledge your call. If they didn't hear it from being on a landline, which is the case 95% of the time, or some other reason, wait for a few minutes for another lull in the radio chatter and ask again. If the controller doesn't answer you after the second time, don't ask again unless it is absolutely needed. And a shortcut request does NOT qualify as "needed!"

Controllers get criticized a lot for talking too fast on the frequency and, at times, I have been guilty of this too. However, some pilots also talk too fast. The amount of time it takes to ask the other person to repeat takes a lot longer than just making the transmission at a slow pace.

I recall this one time when a pilot started talking before his PTT button was fully pressed, and his call sign was mostly cut-off because of it. After the second time, I said his callsign was cut-off every time, and that I didn't get it. I asked if it was the aircraft, as I thought it could be. He then repeated his callsign twice and, on the second time in that transmission, I finally confirmed who it was. But then, he talked so fast that I honestly couldn't understand him! I had to ask four times before I finally understood what he was trying to say. So, you will be further ahead if you avoid talking too fast on the radio.

Remember, "roger" is simply an acknowledgment, "affirmative" means yes, "negative" means no and "wilco" means will comply. Many pilots use "roger" as "affirmative," but that is wrong.

Finally, one of the most important things is if you are not sure about something, please just ask ATC to repeat the clearance.[145] If you readback what you thought you heard, especially saying a different number, there is a good chance the controller won't catch the readback error unless you high-light it somehow. I discuss this in Chapter 29 about changing runways. You can say "confirm changing runways" to highlight your confusion. This applies to altitudes, headings, frequencies, etc. However, in most situations it is easier to simply ask ATC to repeat the clearance.

Frequencies

Even though the correct way to read a frequency back is to say it exactly as the controller says (i.e., "one-two-eight point eight"), I personally like it when pilots use group form. So, when I say, "N12345, contact Washington

Center one-three-three point zero two," I think it is better confirmation when the pilot says, "N12345, Washington Center one thirty-three point zero two." The way some of the radios sound, hearing the "three-three" sounds often enough like "two-three."

When using group form, I also suggest saying "point" when the last number would be zero, which ATC will not say. For example, if given a radio frequency of 128.8, I would respond "twenty-eight point eight." That will make it much clearer for the controller to hear.

If you feel the need not to repeat the facility, that is OK but please, ALWAYS read back frequencies.

When switching to a new frequency, wait a few seconds to ensure there is no transmission underway[146], such as a pilot reading back a new route. Taking a brief moment to listen to the new frequency can help improve your own situational awareness of the conditions, controller workload, and other traffic on the frequency.

Altitudes

When a controller tells you, "N12345, climb and maintain three-thousand," the absolute best response is to say, "N12345, leaving two thousand for three thousand." This is preferable because, when you say "leaving" an altitude for a different one, both for climbing and descending, you allow options for the air traffic controller.

Once a pilot reports leaving an altitude, the controller can assign a similar type aircraft that altitude without waiting for your aircraft to be above the next 1,000-foot mark - or 2,000 feet if above Flight Level 410 or Non-RVSM above FL280.[147]

Now, there are many clearances when you do not need to repeat everything the controller says. For example, you do not need to read back the winds when getting a takeoff clearance. **The rule of thumb should be to read back everything that is an important number – be it a frequency or code - or has to do where the aircraft is going or not to go** such as headings, altitudes, taxi, hold short, cross runway, line up and wait or takeoff clearances.

Simply repeat the exact clearance when you are instructed to do something important. For example, "N12345, climb and maintain five thousand, be at or above four thousand in two minutes or less for traffic." Now, you don't need to say "for traffic," but everything else has to be restated.

I've had many pilots who will reply with something like, "N12345, hurry through four thousand maintain five thousand." This is a red flag for controllers, and they will have to take extra time to confirm the clearance properly. There can be no ambiguity for restrictions!

Therefore, simply say, "N12345, leaving three thousand for five thousand and be at or above four thousand in two minutes." This clearance is a crossing restriction and, therefore, must be read back accordingly.

When issued a classic crossing restriction such as "cross 15 miles northwest of the GUNNE at and maintain one zero thousand," don't forget to advise when you start your descent: "N12345 leaving one six thousand to cross one-five miles northwest of GUNNE at and maintain one zero thousand."

Headings

Say the whole instruction back, reading the numbers individually, not in group form. Use the anchor word(s) "turn left/right," or "heading," as part of the readback as headings, speeds, and altitudes can be confused if they are not said properly.

Speeds

Be sure to use the word "speed," "slow to" or "speed up to," as part of your readback to avoid confusion with headings or speeds.

If you are unable to fly a speed assigned, be sure to offer what you can do. For example, if the controller assigns you 300 knots, you could reply, "unable, we can do a max of 290 knots."

Using this technique will save two transmissions because the controller will automatically ask you what speed you can do if you tell them "unable."

Altimeter Settings

Controllers are required to advise pilots of the altimeter setting at least once while they are in their control jurisdiction. Controllers typically accomplish this task during the pilot's initial check-in, or when first descending out of the flight levels.

When I fly VFR, I must admit that I mostly respond to the transferring controllers' altimeter setting call with a "Roger," and my call sign. It is far more critical to ensure the correct setting in the IFR setting, so I read back the number.

In the TRACON environment, the altimeter setting read to the pilot is more up to date than the one reported hourly on the ATIS. The TRACONs have the current pressure displayed at the sector, which is a real-time display.

In the ARTCCs, the altimeter settings are updated into the system hourly, if not sooner due to a rapid change.

Realistically, in all settings, it is probably easier and quicker to just say the four digits back, like "two niner niner two," although I never read back the altimeter location.

Routes

When you are issued a new route in flight, it can be a demanding task to accomplish. There tend to be many more reroutes issued during bad weather days. Due to this, it can be challenging to find the time to issue the new route.

Controllers use different personal techniques, but when I issue a new route, I try to only issue the route without any other control instructions. Sometimes, I issue a heading to get them pointed in the correct direction, and I also issue and spell out the whole route.

The RNAV routes often have many more fixes than when using the airways, so it can take A LOT of time to issue. When reading them back, you don't need to worry about spelling the fixes unless you need to clarify something for yourself – again, make it clear you are questioning the clearance. If you miss a fix or two, you don't need to ask for the whole route to be reread. You can read back what you have, then when you get to the fix you missed, say "I missed this fix" and continue reading the remainder of the route.

Simply read the route back by stating each fix, pronouncing them the best you can. I sometimes have pilots who spell out the whole route and, while I'm confirming what they say, it feels like it takes forever as there are other things I need to do. You will know if you have a wrong spelling once you program the new route into your navigation system. If you do, you can ask about the wrong fix once you realize the problem.

Other times, I read a route and tell them "standby" on their readback so I can issue some additional clearances - then get back to them. If a controller does that, that is a clear sign they are busy!

The Part 121 & 135 operators will have dispatchers try to get more direct routes for their aircraft, especially when there are weather reroutes which they received on the ground before departure. If you are requesting a new route (more typical in the ARTCC environment), it is best to say

- "Center, N12345, requesting routing through the A.R.s (Atlantic Routes)."
- "Center, N12345, we have a route request with several fixes west around the thunderstorms."

At the ARTCCs, most sectors no longer have pen and paper at the ready. Therefore, the controller needs to either get pen and paper - or be ready to type into the system for reference - which some controllers type into the D-Side position when working solo for quick reference until they figure out if the requested route will work or not.

Holding

Read back the holding clearance completely. As mentioned in Chapter 32, please do not argue about the hold. You can say your time restriction as you are replying to the controller.

- Typically, ATC will tell you they have holding instructions and advise "ready to copy."
  - o A good response is, "N12345, be advised, we only have enough fuel to hold for 15 minutes, ready to copy holding instructions."
  - o "N12345, cleared to Gordonsville to hold west on the 272-degree radial, 10-mile legs, expect further clearance 1350, and be advised, we can only hold for 30 minutes due to fuel restraints."

Beacon Codes

A small percentage of pilots do not read back new transponder codes. A long time ago, I remember a flight instructor telling me that there is no reason to read back a transponder code assignment as it only wastes everybody's time, including the controller's, as the controller will see the change on the radar scope – bad idea!

At the ARTCC, our long-range radars only update once every twelve seconds. I don't have the time to wait for you to change your beacon code, then watch for the change once it updates. In the ARTCC environment, when a beacon code change is required, the computer system shows the 4-digit code the aircraft is currently squawking. It changes from the wrong code to the ground speed every few seconds. Therefore, it is not the most straightforward change to see right away – so it is so much easier for everybody involved to simply respond verbally.

I have pilots not acknowledge my instructions probably, on average, once a month. When pilots don't respond verbally, it makes us think you didn't hear our transmission, so we issue it again. You would be surprised how many times pilots don't hear us on the first transmission!

One afternoon, I was busy with deviations due to thunderstorms, and I instructed an Embraer ERJ-175 (E175) to reset their beacon code. I waited for a response but instead, I had another aircraft ask for a deviation.

I issued that deviation, then went back and repeated the E175 to reset their transponder. The pilot got snippy on the frequency and said he already did.

If he would have simply said, "N12345, squawk zero zero four seven," that would have been the end of it!

Flight Following

When you make your initial call, instead of doing the typical "Potomac Approach, N12345" say
- "Potomac Approach, Skylane 12345, eight miles west of Leesburg Airport requesting flight following to the practice area two zero miles west for maneuvers."

- "Potomac Approach, CAP1234, a Cessna 182, eight miles west of Leesburg Airport requesting flight following landing at three different airports."

By phrasing it like this, you will reduce the overall time spent on the frequency and avoid the controller having to respond to you saying, "N12345, Potomac Approach, go ahead," – cutting down on the whole back and forth, requiring several transmissions to get the same amount of information out.

Now, the controller may not hear the whole transmission and ask you to "say again." However, in the grand scheme, using this technique saves time overall.

Airborne IFR Pickup

This will let the controller know to look for your flight plan instead of creating something into the system.
- "Columbus Approach, N12345 eight miles northeast of Marysville airport requesting IFR clearance on file to Medina."

For Practice Approaches:
- "Columbus Approach, N12345 four miles east of Marysville, requesting multiple practice approaches starting with ILS Runway 9 right to the Ohio State Airport with Information X-Ray."
- "Columbus Approach, N12345 four miles east of Marysville, requesting multiple practice approaches, if you have time, starting with ILS Runway 28 right to the Port Columbus Airport, with Information India."

I like to ask when trying to fly to the main airport for the area by stating, "if you have time." This will tell the controller your intentions without reading a laundry list of approaches that they may not be ready to copy down yet. Let ATC ask you the remaining approaches. You want to keep it simple by not giving too much information at once. In other words, try to figure out what is truly needed for your next segment of flight.

Requests

As mentioned in Chapter 23, please avoid saying "with request." Think of the most streamlined way to make your request in one transmission such as:

- "Center, N12345, requesting direct Grand Forks airport."
- "Center, N12345, we have continuous light chop at one two thousand, requesting one six thousand."
- "Approach, N12345, we have continuous light chop with some moderate turbulence, requesting descent."
- "Approach, N12345, requesting thirty degrees right deviation around a buildup."
- "Center, N12345 requesting descent," (if getting close to destination but still at altitude)
- "Approach, N12345 requesting direct Appleton to avoid weather."
- "Approach, N12345, requesting short vectors for ILS Runway 33."
- "Center, N12345 requesting shortcut."
- "Approach, N12345, level ten thousand with information bravo, requesting ILS Runway 33."

Missing Restrictions

If you are going to miss a restriction that you initially accepted, be sure to **tell ATC as soon as possible**. There is a reason why ATC issued the restriction so give them plenty of time to move other traffic or coordinate with another controller. You can use plain language for this

"Center, N12345, unable to cross fifteen north of GUNNE at 10,000' msl."

Emergencies

In my opinion, emergency calls should be muscle memory. Go through your aircraft's abnormal and emergency checklist and practice calls for all of them.

- "Mayday, Mayday, Mayday, N12345, engine failure, we are going to land on the highway below us."
- "Pan-Pan, Pan-Pan, Pan-Pan, N12345, we have a high oil temperature warning, we are diverting to Cleveland-Hopkins airport, please have emergency equipment standing by."
- Or after the third go-around after ATC consistently asking to keep it tight: "Tower, N12345 declaring emergency as we need a normal pattern/be vectored for a normal landing."

- "Center, N12345, declaring emergency, we lost our alternator. We've shut off all non-essential electrical equipment but not sure how long before we lose our radio. We intend to land at our destination. Can we get a landing clearance now?"
- "Center, N12345, declaring emergency due to flap failure, requesting delay vectors (or a holding pattern) so we can run checklists."

ATC will always ask number of people on board, remaining fuel in hours and minutes (except certain places like a U.S. Air Force base and they want the number of gallons or pounds).[149] Instead of saying the list of items, if you have time wait for ATC to ask for them. If you don't have time, go ahead and say it all. ATC may take a few extra minutes, but they can review the frequency recordings to get the info. Remember to Aviation, Navigate, *and then* Communicate.

If you have the time to change frequencies as instructed:

Check-in saying "N12345, emergency aircraft, level eight thousand" or "N12345 requesting to stay on this frequency to the ground or only one change."

The most common type of emergency I've worked on are medical emergencies.

"Approach, N12345, medical emergency, a 60-year-old male with shortness of breath, we are diverting to Marysville Airport. Please have an ambulance meet us on the ramp."

"Center, N12345 declaring emergency, we have a seventy-two-year-old female unconscious, requesting visual approach to Port Columbus Airport with emergency equipment standing by."

For medical emergencies, ATC is going to ask about the patient. Remember, the radio frequencies are open for anybody to monitor. Therefore, do not give any personal information. They want to know their age, gender, and nature of illness and if you have given any first aid (i.e., are they on oxygen? Is there a doctor or nurse on board giving treatment? Etc).

Medevac Flights

A recent change with the JO 7110.65 now requires any pilot requesting priority as a medical evacuation must use the term "Medevac" as part of their call sign during radio transmissions.[150]

- "Approach, Medevac N12345, level eight thousand."
- "Center, Medevac N12345 requesting direct destination."

You can always request whichever shortcut you'd like to have.

It helps when you file your flight plan to add "L" at the beginning of your aircraft registration number (e.g. LN12345). Or, if you have an approved call sign, you can input "Medevac" in the Remarks section of your flight plan. According to the new change, doing either of these will not automatically get you priority handling. However, I still suggest doing it because many controllers will work on getting you a shortcut before you even reach their airspace.

Turbulence

If you are curious about the rides, the best way to inquire is to report your current ride conditions during your initial check-in. ATC will generally give you a ride report during their response. If they don't, and you are currently experiencing smooth rides, smooth rides probably prevail.

PIREPs

Controllers generally welcome PIREPs. When giving one, just use plain language.

- "Center, N12345 had moderate turbulence from eight thousand to one zero thousand."
- "Approach, N12345 had light rime icing between two thousand to five thousand and the temperature was -2." *We always need the outside air temperature with icing reports.*
- "Center, N12345 we had a pocket of severe turbulence, we have no injuries and no aircraft damage." *ATC is required to ask about injuries and damage.*
- "Approach, N12345, the tops are two thousand two hundred."

Remarks

Even though a flight plan's Remarks section is not officially "phraseology," I think this is an important topic to include here.

Remarks are seen by controllers in one of two ways. In the ARTCC, there is a toggle button which will switch between the route of flight and remarks. Otherwise, it is printed on the bottom of the flight progress strip at ATCTs and TRACONs/RAPCONs.

Remarks I recommend using are:

- If your aircraft is equipped with a Satellite Phone, please include "Sat Phone" with the phone number. This is a fantastic backup in case we lose communication with you!
- If you are a medevac flight, add "MEDEVAC" to the Remarks section (unless you added a "L" to your call sign).
- If you have an approved call sign which is not widely used, or you are leaving your normal operating area, add the three-letter identifier and the telephony (i.e., "NDU- SIOUX" or "GLF- GULFSTREAM TEST" – our system only uses capital letters)
- Enter "NO OVER WATER" if you are not able to fly over the Great Lakes, ocean, or any large body of water where you wouldn't necessarily be within gliding distance to the shore.
- "NO DESCEND VIA"
- "NO RNAV SIDS/STARS"
- If you are on a Maintenance Flight, use "MX FLIGHT" or "TEST FLIGHT"
- "DVRSN" if you are requesting priority due to a diversion from the original destination.[151]
- Some companies put their minimum RVR (runway visual range) requirements.
- Anything else you think could aid the controller; anything valuable, such as "PRACTICE APPROACHES" when performing instrument training.

Always Do

- Always tell ATC when you plan to fly multiple legs for Flight Following
- Always use your complete call sign until ATC abbreviates.
- Always read back all control instructions – Altitude, Heading, Speeds, Beacon Codes, Taxi Instructions (including crossing or holding short of a runway).

- Always monitor a Guard frequency (121.5 or 243.0)
- Always say your altitude leaving and newly assigned altitude (i.e. "leaving four thousand for two thousand.")
- Always read back a different runway saying "Change To" Runway 20R, clear to land."

Always Avoid

- Avoid asking for a specific heading for a deviation, especially with the ARTCC. Winds aloft can be high (I've seen as high as 155 knots), so we have no clue what heading you are on - please just say if you need right or left deviations (i.e., "ten degrees right" or "thirty degrees left"). The exception to this rule is if you need a significant turn, then use 360, 090, 180, or 270 headings to communicate.
- Avoid "air filing" IFR: some controllers will have you contact the Flight Service Station (FSS) as we don't get all flight plan info such as the color of aircraft, point of contact, fuel, etc. Electronic flight bags make it so easy the only reason to air file is if the weather changes and you now need to go IFR to get in.
- Avoid "thinking on frequency" – the long-winded babble that takes forever for somebody to say and which blocks the frequency from everybody else to use during these long transmissions.
- Avoid talking too fast (although controllers do this too).
- Avoid "playing" on Guard (i.e., saying "on Guard," "I'm bored", etc.) – we have to monitor, and this can be distracting when we are busy.
- Avoid switching frequencies immediately after receiving the new frequency without a chance for ATC to understand and correct your readback.
- Avoid tuning in to a new frequency and immediately keying up to talk without waiting enough time to see if there is currently a pilot/controller interaction (i.e., ATC issued a new route and you key up during the two seconds it took the pilot to read back the new clearance).
- Unless you want to follow ICAO standards for international flights, avoid saying "CPDLC equipped" during check-in. If you are equipped and logged in, the ARTCC system shows a solid white box next to your call sign, so we see that before you checked onto the frequency. If you suspect an issue, simply ask in plain language.

Never Do

- Never say "with request." (see Chapter 23 if you missed it)
- Never use "no delay," "hurry through," "we'll hustle," or similar – unless this is how ATC phrased it. Never use these when you've been issued a crossing restriction such as "N12345, be at or above four thousand in two minutes or less, climb and maintain five thousand."
- Never argue on frequency - you can always call on the phone post-flight.
- Never turn the volume all the way down so you don't have to listen to the ATC frequency when you are supposed to be talking to ATC– I've heard flight instructors doing this so they could teach without background noise. If we can't reach you, we have to try different techniques to get you back. Simply tell us you'll be off frequency for 5 minutes if you need that. Note that this does not apply in an emergency; you fly the airplane first in that situation!
- Never argue about being put into a holding pattern - you can ask why and for how long is to be expected, but most of the time, the controllers don't know how long either!
- Never say "We've got the traffic on the box/fish finder/TCAS."
- When you are cruising at higher altitudes (8,000-10,000' msl or higher), never file direct to an airport which has preferred routing. If you do, you will have one or more reroutes while airborne. It is much easier to file the preferred route, then ask for a shortcut.
- Never read back the controller stated reason (i.e., "… radar vectors for traffic").
- Never keep asking for the same information over and over again (i.e., asking about the moderate chop in several locations when ATC is busy and has already given you the info) – one needy pilot can put a controller behind the 8-ball quickly!

APPENDIX B: ODDS & ENDS

I have several small topics I wanted to include which always seem to interest people when I am talking to them.

"Roger" is Simply an Acknowledgement

I know this is getting pretty technical - aviation in itself is technical though, isn't it? But please remember the following:

"Roger" is simply an acknowledgment.

"Affirmative" means yes.

"Negative" means no.

This became an issue a while back when the FAA was cracking down on controllers for how they implemented visual separation. Controllers had to call the traffic and ask the pilot if they could maintain visual separation from the traffic.

If the pilot said "affirmative," then the controller would issue the visual separation clearance.

If the pilot responded to the questions by saying "roger," then that was not good enough, and the controller would not issue the clearance.

I know it sounds petty and, in a way, it really is. However, it could be the difference between getting a clearance that helps you or not.

Equipment Identifiers

A change that happened within the previous ten years is the FAA flight plans started to use the ICAO format.

One of the significant differences between the two formats is the Equipment Suffix. The original FAA version used a chart: /A (DME, Transponder with Mode C), /G (GNSS, Transponder with Mode C), and many more. The ICAO format has the filer check a box indicating each type of equipment on board.

The ARTCCs system converts the ICAO version into the FAA format, and is indicated to the controller with the aircraft type section both in the flight plan and on the radar scope data block.

ARTCC controllers appear to have an understanding of the system now. But during the transition, there would be an error in the system requiring the controller to update the Equipment Type, and they would ask the pilot for the information. The pilots would come back with a laundry list of types, which confused many controllers as they were simply looking for the /L or /G. Those situations usually ended up with the controller getting frustrated and making up the code they thought best as the pilots no longer had the old form to tell the code.

TRACONs are still using the old system. When you are a VFR popup, the system automatically assigns /A unless otherwise specified. It is not too important to know if a VFR aircraft has GNSS.

With IFR flights, the most essential parts for ARTCC controllers to know is whether you have en route GPS and if you are RVSM capable.

I think it is a good idea to know off the top of your head which FAA identifier your aircraft would be. That way, if you get a controller looking for that code, you will be ready.

You Don't Have TCAS in your Cessna 172 (but that would be Nice!)

This one is purely my own idiosyncrasy, but that doesn't mean I haven't heard other people complaining too. You don't have TCAS (traffic collision avoidance system) in your Cessna 172, Piper Cherokee, or Beechcraft Bonanza.

Last time I checked, a TCAS II system on a new jet was approximately a $350,000 upgrade. You have ADS-B In, which is a great tool and I avoid flying without it. However, it doesn't give you Resolution Advisories ("Traffic, Pull-Up!"). I love ADS-B In when flying. When we make traffic calls to you, it really doesn't matter to us if you see the traffic on your iPad or GPS. All we care about is if you have the traffic in sight, not if you see it on your "Fish Finder."

Even if you do have TCAS in your aircraft, it doesn't help us when you say you have the traffic on TCAS. Simply say, "looking for traffic."

Believing Canceling IFR Upsets Us... Not at all

I have had several professional pilots tell me that when they get upset with ATC for some reason, they just cancel IFR as they know that makes us angry.

Well, as I've told each of them, as a controller, we are happy when you cancel IFR because we no longer need to worry about providing a service to you.

The one exception to this is when I had an aircraft at Charleston TRACON that wanted a shortcut. The problem with that shortcut was that it would put them right in the middle of a swarm of traffic. I denied them the turn.

They canceled IFR and then proceeded as they wished. Well, of course, I knew which radar target they were, so I ended up having to move several other airplanes out of their way, when I was already busy. Even though they were VFR, and it was up to them to see and avoid, I'm not going to let them get too close to another aircraft I'm communicating with if I can help it.

The other thing I've had pilots tell me that they think will upset controllers is when they don't think the controller is doing something right, they can ask for a "Time Check."

I don't know if prior controllers understood that as being code for an upset pilot, but I could see it making it easy to write down the exact time to call in a complaint to ATC management as a reference for them to pull the tapes (although tapes are now digital storage, the terminology remains).

Today, it is extremely easy for management to find the times a flight went through a certain sector, then listen to the audio recordings. The audio systems will even drop all of the "dead air" time, which really speeds up the search.

The Famous "I'm a Cool Pilot" Voice

Any time you have a group of people, there is always a certain percentage that are explained as being "that guy/gal". Aviation, in particular, has people with some fairly large egos on both sides of the frequency – I think that is obvious.

Controllers are a sharp bunch of people who tend to make jokes about things we consider to be idiotic. The biggest one I know is what I refer to as the "I'm a Cool Pilot Voice." It sounds absolutely ridiculous and usually extremely difficult to understand. "Uhh...yeah... Center... this is... ahh... N... ahh... 12345, at ahh niner thousand climbing one-two thousand" in the deepest voice they can muster - which sounds horrible, by the way.

Don't be that pilot, because yes, we will be laughing at how ridiculous you sound!

Frequency Changes

When ATC starts to issue frequency change but stops – it's usually because something changed in the middle, like new traffic or a controller calling on the landline.

Yes, we are on landlines more than pilots think!

IAFDOF (Inappropriate Altitude for Direction of Flight)

There is a reason why the even and odd altitudes are set up based upon the cardinal direction of flight.[152] There are some exceptions ATC uses to separate the oddball traffic from their normal flows but, in general, everybody should be trying to be at the proper altitude for the direction of flight.

There are a lot of business jets which ask for FL450 to save fuel when they are headed westbound as it is the aircraft's ceiling. I've seen issues arise often enough that I don't know that doing this is worth the fuel savings.

Lasers

Boy, is this an issue!!! In the United States, there were 9,723 laser strikes reported on aircraft in 2021![153]

A reported 6,852 laser strikes in 2020 even though traffic counts were low due to COVID and 6,136 reports in 2019, as reported by the FAA. 5,663 total events were reported by the FAA for 2018.

If you get lased, do your best to get away from the laser. It is almost impossible to keep a laser pointed at a moving aircraft. There has been no evidence of long-term damage to the eyes.

Gravelly Point – Wake Turb

One of our favorite family hangouts is at Gravelly Point, a part of the National Park Service's George Washington Memorial Parkway in Arlington County, Virginia. The area is located at the approach end of Runway 19 at Ronald Reagan-Washington National Airport (KDCA).

When the airport is on South Flow (Runway 19 is active), you can hear wake turbulence whistling and feel it blowing as the aircraft fly over around 100' agl on short final for Runway 19. I've tried to capture the sounds from the wake turbulence on video but the videos don't really capture it well.

If you have a chance to visit, it is a unique and very cool experience!

"Expect" Clearances

If a controller instructs you to, "expect to descend via. For now, descend at pilot's discretion, maintain Flight Level 340," make sure you start your descent in a timely manner in order to meet the expected clearance.

Altitude Reports

I had a Learjet who checked onto the Shenandoah Sector's frequency from Atlanta ARTCC, headed northbound. They said Flight Level 320 for 350, but I showed FL327. I asked them to say altitude leaving again.

The pilot again said 320, and I replied I was showing 327 so is that correct?

He got upset and said he was leaving FL329, 330, 331. I said, "Roger, since you are coming from a different facility, I have to confirm your mode C is within 300' of your reported altitude."[154] Please stick to the AIM radio technique procedure when calling a new facility.

ATC Frequency Stumbles

Flight 1248 checked onto my frequency without a handoff. Most often, these happen when they are switched to the wrong sector.

The pilot was talking fast so I had to ask three times to get the call sign correct.

As I was typing it into the system to find them, the controller working the sector owning the airspace below mine said, "Sorry, here is the handoff."

Sometimes, when we can't find the call sign in the system, we may ask for your beacon code and look it up that way. It saves us a lot of time and grief!

"Next Sector Request"

I initiated a handoff to the next sector for an aircraft headed northeast bound. That sector called me on the landline instructing me to assign the aircraft a heading of 110°. I said "wilco, XI" - my operating initials which is how we conclude all landline calls.

I keyed up the frequency and said "N12345, turn right heading 110°, next sector's request due to traffic."

The pilot didn't respond which annoyed me because this was the third time since he checked on my frequency where I issued a clearance and he didn't respond.

Emphasizing the callsign, I said "N12345, turn right heading 110°."

The pilot answered but instead of taking the heading, the pilot said "what is the reason for the turn?"

Frustrated because this pilot had been a "problem" since he entered my sector, I said "N12345, due to traffic, turn right heading 110°."

He then told me I didn't need to be short with him, and I responded that I had to make multiple transmissions every time I've called him and he needs to listen better!

I never have a problem stating the reason for instructions I've issued, but please take the clearance and ask during your readback. If the controller made a mistake, they can change it then. However, if they issue a clearance, it is for a reason and it is better to start the turn so they don't have to turn you even further, which the next sector did since this pilot took so long to start his turn!

APPENDIX C: DEFINITIONS

The following definitions come from the Pilot/Controller Glossary. Although not a full list, these are definitions that are referenced in the stories throughout this book.

AERONAUTICAL INFORMATION MANUAL (AIM) – A primary FAA publication whose purpose is to instruct airmen about operating in the National Airspace System of the U.S. It provides basic flight information, ATC Procedures and general instructional information concerning health, medical facts, factors affecting flight safety, accident and hazard reporting, and types of aeronautical charts and their use.

AFFIRMATIVE– Yes.

AIR ROUTE TRAFFIC CONTROL CENTER (ARTCC) – A facility established to provide air traffic control service to aircraft operating on IFR flight plans within controlled airspace and principally during the en route phase of flight. When equipment capabilities and controller workload permit, certain advisory/assistance services may be provided to VFR aircraft.

AIR TRAFFIC CLEARANCE– An authorization by air traffic control for the purpose of preventing collision between known aircraft, for an aircraft to proceed under specified traffic conditions within controlled airspace. The pilot-in-command of an aircraft may not deviate from the provisions of a visual flight rules (VFR) or instrument flight rules (IFR) air traffic clearance except in an emergency or unless an amended clearance has been obtained. Additionally, the pilot may request a different clearance from that which has been issued by air traffic control (ATC) if information available to the pilot makes another course of action more practicable or if aircraft equipment limitations or company procedures forbid compliance with the clearance issued. Pilots may also request clarification or amendment, as appropriate, any time a clearance is not fully understood, or considered unacceptable because of safety of flight. Controllers should, in such instances and to the extent of operational practicality and safety, honor the pilot's request. 14 CFR Part 91.3(a) states: "The pilot in command of an aircraft is directly responsible for, and is the final authority as to, the operation of that aircraft." THE PILOT IS RESPONSIBLE TO REQUEST AN AMENDED CLEARANCE if ATC issues a clearance that would cause a pilot to deviate from a rule or regulation, or in the pilot's opinion, would place the aircraft in jeopardy.

AIR TRAFFIC CONTROL SYSTEM COMMAND CENTER (ATCSCC)– An Air Traffic Tactical Operations facility responsible for monitoring and managing the flow of air traffic throughout the NAS, producing a safe, orderly, and expeditious flow of traffic while minimizing delays. The following functions are located at the ATCSCC:
  a. Central Altitude Reservation Function (CARF). Responsible for coordinating, planning, and approving special user requirements under the Altitude Reservation (ALTRV) concept.
  (See ALTITUDE RESERVATION)
  b. Airport Reservation Office (ARO). Monitors the operation and allocation of reservations for unscheduled operations at airports designated by the Administrator as High Density Airports. These airports are generally known as slot controlled airports. The ARO allocates reservations on a first come, first served basis determined by the time the request is received at the ARO.
  (Refer to 14 CFR Part 93)

(See CHART SUPPLEMENT U.S.)

c. U.S. Notice to Airmen (NOTAM) Office. Responsible for collecting, maintaining, and distributing NOTAMs for the U.S. civilian and military, as well as international aviation communities. (See NOTICE TO AIRMEN)

d. Weather Unit. Monitor all aspects of weather for the U.S. that might affect aviation including cloud cover, visibility, winds, precipitation, thunderstorms, icing, turbulence, and more. Provide forecasts based on observations and on discussions with meteorologists from various National Weather Service offices, FAA facilities, airlines, and private weather services.

AIR TRAFFIC SERVICE– A generic term meaning:
a. Flight Information Service.
b. Alerting Service.
c. Air Traffic Advisory Service.
d. Air Traffic Control Service:
    1. Area Control Service,
    2. Approach Control Service, or
    3. Airport Control Service.

ALERT NOTICE (ALNOT)– A request originated by a flight service station (FSS) or an air route traffic control center (ARTCC) for an extensive communication search for overdue, unreported, or missing aircraft.

APPROACH GATE– An imaginary point used within ATC as a basis for vectoring aircraft to the final approach course. The gate will be established along the final approach course 1 mile from the final approach fix on the side away from the airport and will be no closer than 5 miles from the landing threshold.

AREA NAVIGATION (RNAV)– A method of navigation which permits aircraft operation on any desired flight path within the coverage of ground- or space-based navigation aids or within the limits of the capability of self-contained aids, or a combination of these.

Note: Area navigation includes performance-based navigation as well as other operations that do not meet the definition of performance-based navigation.

BLOCKED– Phraseology used to indicate that a radio transmission has been distorted or interrupted due to multiple simultaneous radio transmissions.

CEILING– The heights above the earth's surface of the lowest layer of clouds or obscuring phenomena that is reported as "broken," "overcast," or "obscuration," and not classified as "thin" or "partial."

CHOP– A form of turbulence.
a. Light Chop– Turbulence that causes slight, rapid and somewhat rhythmic bumpiness without appreciable changes in altitude or attitude.
b. Moderate Chop– Turbulence similar to Light Chop but of greater intensity. It causes rapid bumps or jolts without appreciable changes in aircraft altitude or attitude.

CLIMB VIA– An abbreviated ATC clearance that requires compliance with the procedure lateral path, associated speed restrictions, and altitude restrictions along the cleared route or procedure.

CONFLICT ALERT– A function of certain air traffic control automated systems designed to alert radar controllers to existing or pending situations between tracked targets (known IFR or VFR aircraft) that require his/her immediate attention/action.

CONTROLLED AIRSPACE– An airspace of defined dimensions within which air traffic control service is provided to IFR flights and to VFR flights in accordance with the airspace classification.
a. Controlled airspace is a generic term that covers Class A, Class B, Class C, Class D, and Class E airspace.

b. Controlled airspace is also that airspace within which all aircraft operators are subject to certain pilot qualifications, operating rules, and equipment requirements in 14 CFR Part 91 (for specific operating requirements, please refer to 14 CFR Part 91). For IFR operations in any class of controlled airspace, a pilot must file an IFR flight plan and receive an appropriate ATC clearance. Each Class B, Class C, and Class D airspace area designated for an airport contains at least one primary airport around which the airspace is designated (for specific designations and descriptions of the airspace classes, please refer to 14 CFR Part 71).

c. Controlled airspace in the United States is designated as follows:

1. CLASS A– Generally, that airspace from 18,000 feet msl up to and including FL600, including the airspace overlying the waters within 12 nautical miles of the coast of the 48 contiguous States and Alaska. Unless otherwise authorized, all persons must operate their aircraft under IFR.

2. CLASS B– Generally, that airspace from the surface to 10,000 feet msl surrounding the nation's busiest airports in terms of airport operations or passenger enplanements. The configuration of each Class B airspace area is individually tailored and consists of a surface area and two or more layers (some Class B airspace areas resemble upside-down wedding cakes), and is designed to contain all published instrument procedures once an aircraft enters the airspace. An ATC clearance is required for all aircraft to operate in the area, and all aircraft that are so cleared receive separation services within the airspace. The cloud clearance requirement for VFR operations is "clear of clouds."

3. CLASS C– Generally, that airspace from the surface to 4,000 feet above the airport elevation (charted in msl) surrounding those airports that have an operational control tower, are serviced by a radar approach control, and that have a certain number of IFR operations or passenger enplanements. Although the configuration of each Class C area is individually tailored, the airspace usually consists of a surface area with a 5 NM radius, a circle with a 10 NM radius that extends no lower than 1,200 feet up to 4,000 feet above the airport elevation, and an outer area that is not charted. Each person must establish two-way radio commu-

nications with the ATC facility providing air traffic services prior to entering the airspace and thereafter maintain those communications while within the airspace. VFR aircraft are only separated from IFR aircraft within the airspace.
(See OUTER AREA)

4. CLASS D– Generally, that airspace from the surface to 2,500 feet above the airport elevation (charted in msl) surrounding those airports that have an operational control tower. The configuration of each Class D airspace area is individually tailored and when instrument procedures are published, the airspace will normally be designed to contain the procedures. Arrival extensions for instrument approach procedures may be Class D or Class E airspace. Unless otherwise authorized, each person must establish two-way radio communications with the ATC facility providing air traffic services prior to entering the airspace and thereafter maintain those communications while in the airspace. No separation services are provided to VFR aircraft.

5. CLASS E– Generally, if the airspace is not Class A, Class B, Class C, or Class D, and it is controlled airspace, it is Class E airspace. Class E airspace extends upward from either the surface or a designated altitude to the overlying or adjacent controlled airspace. When designated as a surface area, the airspace will be configured to contain all instrument procedures. Also in this class are Federal airways, airspace beginning at either 700 or 1,200 feet agl used to transition to/from the terminal or en route environment, en route domestic, and offshore airspace areas designated below 18,000 feet msl. Unless designated at a lower altitude, Class E airspace begins at 14,500 msl over the United States, including that airspace overlying the waters within 12 nautical miles of the coast of the 48 contiguous States and Alaska, up to, but not including 18,000 feet msl, and the airspace above FL600.

CONTROLLER PILOT DATA LINK COMMUNICATIONS (CPDLC) – A two-way digital communications system that conveys textual air traffic control messages between controllers and pilots using ground or satellite-based radio relay stations.

DESCEND VIA– An abbreviated ATC clearance that requires compliance with a published procedure lateral path and associated speed restrictions and provides a pilot-discretion descent to comply with published altitude restrictions.

EMERGENCY– A distress or an urgency condition.

EN ROUTE DECISION SUPPORT TOOL (EDST)– An automated tool provided at each Radar Associate position in selected En Route facilities. This tool utilizes flight and radar data to determine present and future trajectories for all active and proposal aircraft and provides enhanced automated flight data management.

EN ROUTE MINIMUM SAFE ALTITUDE WARNING (E-MSAW)– A function of the EAS that aids the controller by providing an alert when a tracked aircraft is below or predicted by the computer to go below a predetermined minimum IFR altitude (MIA).

EXPEDITE– Used by ATC when prompt compliance is required to avoid the development of an imminent situation. Expedite climb/descent normally indicates to a pilot that the approximate best rate of climb/descent should be used without requiring an exceptional change in aircraft handling characteristics.

FILED– Normally used in conjunction with flight plans, meaning a flight plan has been submitted to ATC.

FLIGHT LEVEL– A level of constant atmospheric pressure related to a reference datum of 29.92 inches of mercury. Each is stated in three digits that represent hundreds of feet. For example, Flight Level (FL) 250 represents a barometric altimeter indication of 25,000 feet; FL255, an indication of 25,500 feet.

FLIGHT MANAGEMENT SYSTEMS– A computer system that uses a large data base to allow routes to be preprogrammed and fed into the system by means of a data loader. The system is constantly updated with respect to position accuracy by reference to conventional navigation aids. The sophisticated program and its associated data base ensures that the most appropriate aids are automatically selected during the information update cycle.

FLIGHT PLAN– Specified information relating to the intended flight of an aircraft that is filed electronically, orally, or in writing with an FSS, third-party vendor, or an ATC facility.

FLIGHT STANDARDS DISTRICT OFFICE– An FAA field office serving an assigned geographical area and staffed with Flight Standards personnel who serve the aviation industry and the general public on matters relating to the certification and operation of air carrier and general aviation aircraft. Activities include general surveillance of operational safety, certification of airmen and aircraft, accident prevention, investigation, enforcement, etc.

FUSION [STARS]- the combination of all available surveillance sources (airport surveillance radar [ASR], air route surveillance radar [ARSR], ADS-B, etc.) into the display of a single tracked target for air traffic control separation services. FUSION is the equivalent of the current single-sensor radar display. FUSION performance is characteristic of a single-sensor radar display system. Terminal areas use mono-pulse secondary surveillance radar (ASR 9, Mode S or ASR 11, MSSR).

GENERAL AVIATION– That portion of civil aviation that does not include scheduled or unscheduled air carriers or commercial space operations.

GO AROUND– Instructions for a pilot to abandon his/her approach to landing. Additional instructions may follow. Unless otherwise advised by ATC, a VFR aircraft or an aircraft conducting visual approach should overfly the runway while climbing to traffic pattern altitude and enter the traffic pattern via the crosswind leg. A pilot on an IFR flight plan making an instrument approach should execute the published missed approach procedure or proceed as instructed by ATC; e.g., "Go around" (additional instructions if required).

GROUND DELAY PROGRAM (GDP)– A traffic management process administered by the ATCSCC, when aircraft are held on the ground. The purpose of the program is to support the TM mission and limit airborne holding. It is a flexible program and may be implemented in various forms depending upon the needs of the AT system. Ground delay programs provide for equitable assignment of delays to all system users.

HANDOFF– An action taken to transfer the radar identification of an aircraft from one controller to another if the aircraft will enter the receiving controller's airspace and radio communications with the aircraft will be transferred.

HOLD FOR RELEASE– Used by ATC to delay an aircraft for traffic management reasons; i.e., weather, traffic volume, etc. Hold for release instructions (including departure delay information) are used to inform a pilot or a controller (either directly or through an authorized relay) that an IFR departure clearance is not valid until a release time or additional instructions have been received.

HOLD PROCEDURE– A predetermined maneuver which keeps aircraft within a specified airspace while awaiting further clearance from air traffic control. Also used during ground operations to keep aircraft within a specified area or at a specified point while awaiting further clearance from air traffic control.

IFR AIRCRAFT– An aircraft conducting flight in accordance with instrument flight rules.

IMMEDIATELY– Used by ATC or pilots when such action compliance is required to avoid an imminent situation.

INSTRUMENT APPROACH PROCEDURE– A series of predetermined maneuvers for the orderly transfer of an aircraft under instrument flight conditions from the beginning of the initial approach to a landing or to a point from which a landing may be made visually. It is prescribed and approved for a specific airport by competent authority.
(See SEGMENTS OF AN INSTRUMENT APPROACH PROCEDURE) (Refer to 14 CFR Part 91) (Refer to AIM)
  a. U.S. civil standard instrument approach procedures are approved by the FAA as prescribed under 14 CFR Part 97 and are available for public use.
  b. U.S. military standard instrument approach procedures are approved and published by the Department of Defense.
  c. Special instrument approach procedures are approved by the FAA for individual operators but are not published in 14 CFR Part 97 for public use.

JET ROUTE– A route designed to serve aircraft operations from 18,000 feet msl up to and including Flight Level 450. The routes are referred to as "J" routes with numbering to identify the designated route; e.g., J105.

LOST COMMUNICATIONS– Loss of the ability to communicate by radio. Aircraft are sometimes referred to as NORDO (No Radio). Standard pilot procedures are specified in 14 CFR Part 91. Radar controllers issue procedures for pilots to follow in the event of lost communications during a radar approach when weather reports indicate that an aircraft will likely encounter IFR weather conditions during the approach.

LOW ALTITUDE AIRWAY STRUCTURE– The network of airways

serving aircraft operations up to but not including 18,000 feet msl.

MAYDAY– The international radiotelephony distress signal. When repeated three times, it indicates imminent and grave danger and that immediate assistance is requested.

MINIMUM IFR ALTITUDES (MIA)– Minimum altitudes for IFR operations as prescribed in 14 CFR Part 91. These altitudes are published on aeronautical charts and prescribed in 14 CFR Part 95 for airways and routes, and in 14 CFR Part 97 for standard instrument approach procedures. If no applicable minimum altitude is prescribed in 14 CFR Part 95 or 14 CFR Part 97, the following minimum IFR altitude applies:

In designated mountainous areas, 2,000 feet above the highest obstacle within a horizontal distance of 4 nautical miles from the course to be flown; or

b. Other than mountainous areas, 1,000 feet above the highest obstacle within a horizontal distance of 4 nautical miles from the course to be flown; or

c. As otherwise authorized by the Administrator or assigned by ATC.

MILES-IN-TRAIL– A specified distance between aircraft, normally, in the same stratum associated with the same destination or route of flight.

MINIMUM SAFE ALTITUDE WARNING (MSAW)– A function of the EAS and STARS computer that aids the controller by alerting him/her when a tracked Mode C equipped aircraft is below or is predicted by the computer to go below a predetermined minimum safe altitude.

MINIMUM VECTORING ALTITUDE (MVA)– The lowest msl altitude at which an IFR aircraft will be vectored by a radar controller, except as otherwise authorized for radar approaches, departures, and missed approaches. The altitude meets IFR obstacle clearance criteria. It may be lower than the published MEA along an airway or J-route segment. It may be utilized for radar vectoring only upon the controller's determination that an adequate radar return is being received from the aircraft being controlled. Charts depicting minimum vectoring altitudes are normally available only to the controllers and not to pilots.

NEGATIVE– "No," or "permission not granted," or "that is not correct."

NONRADAR– Precedes other terms and generally means without the use of radar, such as:
  a. Nonradar Approach. Used to describe instrument approaches for which course guidance on final approach is not provided by ground-based precision or surveillance radar. Radar vectors to the final approach course may or may not be provided by ATC. Examples of nonradar approaches are VOR, NDB, TACAN, ILS, RNAV, and GLS approaches.
  b. Nonradar Approach Control. An ATC facility providing approach control service without the use of radar.
  c. Nonradar Arrival. An aircraft arriving at an airport without radar service or at an airport served by a radar facility and radar contact has not been established or has been terminated due to a lack of radar service to the airport.
  d. Nonradar Route. A flight path or route over which the pilot is performing his/her own navigation. The pilot may be receiving radar separation, radar monitoring, or other ATC services while on a nonradar route.
  e. Nonradar Separation. The spacing of aircraft in accordance with established minima without the use of radar; e.g., vertical, lateral, or longitudinal separation.

NORDO (No Radio)– Aircraft that cannot or do not communicate by radio when radio communication is required are referred to as "NORDO."

NOTICE TO AIR MISSIONS (NOTAM)– A notice containing information (not known sufficiently in advance to publicize by other means) concerning the establishment, condition, or change in any component (facility, service, or procedure of, or hazard in the National Airspace

System) the timely knowledge of which is essential to personnel concerned with flight operations.

OBSTACLE– An existing object, object of natural growth, or terrain at a fixed geographical location or which may be expected at a fixed location within a prescribed area with reference to which vertical clearance is or must be provided during flight operation.

PAN-PAN– The international radio-telephony urgency signal. When repeated three times, indicates uncertainty or alert followed by the nature of the urgency.

PILOT IN COMMAND– The pilot responsible for the operation and safety of an aircraft during flight time.

PILOT'S DISCRETION– When used in conjunction with altitude assignments, means that ATC has offered the pilot the option of starting climb or descent whenever he/she wishes and conducting the climb or descent at any rate he/she wishes. He/she may temporarily level off at any intermediate altitude. However, once he/she has vacated an altitude, he/she may not return to that altitude.

POSITIVE CONTROL– The separation of all air traffic within designated airspace by air traffic control.

PRACTICE INSTRUMENT APPROACH– An instrument approach procedure conducted by a VFR or an IFR aircraft for the purpose of pilot training or proficiency demonstrations.

PREARRANGED COORDINATION– A standardized procedure which permits an air traffic controller to enter the airspace assigned to another air traffic controller without verbal coordination. The procedures are defined in a facility directive which ensures approved separation between aircraft.

PREARRANGED COORDINATION PROCEDURES– A facility's standardized procedure that describes the process by which one controller shall allow an aircraft to penetrate or transit another controller's airspace in a manner that assures approved separation without individual coordination for each aircraft.

PREFERENTIAL ROUTES– Preferential routes (PDRs, PARs, and PDARs) are adapted in ARTCC computers to accomplish inter/intrafacility controller coordination and to assure that flight data is posted at the proper control positions. Locations having a need for these specific inbound and outbound routes normally publish such routes in local facility bulletins, and their use by pilots minimizes flight plan route amendments. When the workload or traffic situation permits, controllers normally provide radar vectors or assign requested routes to minimize circuitous routing. Preferential routes are usually confined to one ARTCC's area and are referred to by the following names or acronyms:

a. Preferential Departure Route (PDR). A specific departure route from an airport or terminal area to an en route point where there is no further need for flow control. It may be included in an Instrument Departure Procedure (DP) or a Preferred IFR Route.

b. Preferential Arrival Route (PAR). A specific arrival route from an appropriate en route point to an airport or terminal area. It may be included in a Standard Terminal Arrival (STAR) or a Preferred IFR Route. The abbreviation "PAR" is used primarily within the ARTCC and should not be confused with the abbreviation for Precision Approach Radar.

c. Preferential Departure and Arrival Route (PDAR). A route between two terminals which are within or immediately adjacent to one ARTCC's area. PDARs are not synonymous with Preferred IFR Routes but may be listed as such as they do accomplish essentially the same purpose.

PRIMARY RADAR TARGET– An analog or digital target, exclusive of a secondary radar target, presented on a radar display.

PROCEDURE TURN– The maneuver prescribed when it is necessary to reverse direction to establish an aircraft on the intermediate approach segment or final approach course. The outbound course, direction of turn, distance within which the turn must be completed, and minimum altitude are specified in the procedure. However, unless otherwise restricted, the point at which the turn may be commenced and the type and rate of turn are left to the discretion of the pilot.

PUBLISHED INSTRUMENT APPROACH PROCEDURE VISUAL SEGMENT– A segment on an IAP chart annotated as "Fly Visual to Airport" or "Fly Visual." A dashed arrow will indicate the visual flight path on the profile and plan view with an associated note on the approximate heading and distance. The visual segment should be flown as a dead reckoning course while maintaining visual conditions.

Q ROUTE– 'Q' is the designator assigned to published RNAV routes used by the United States.

QUICK LOOK– A feature of the EAS and STARS which provides the controller the capability to display full data blocks of tracked aircraft from other control positions.

RADAR– A device that provides information on range, azimuth, and/or elevation of objects by measuring the time interval between transmission and reception of directional radio pulses and correlating the angular orientation of the radiated antenna beam or beams in azimuth and/or elevation.
  a. Primary Radar– A radar system in which a minute portion of a radio pulse transmitted from a site is reflected by an object and then received back at that site for processing and display at an air traffic control facility.
  b. Secondary Radar/Radar Beacon (ATCRBS)– A radar system in which the object to be detected is fitted with cooperative equipment in the form of a radio receiver/transmitter (transponder). Radar pulses transmitted from the searching transmitter/receiver (interrogator)

site are received in the cooperative equipment and used to trigger a distinctive transmission from the transponder. This reply transmission, rather than a reflected signal, is then received back at the transmitter/receiver site for processing and display at an air traffic control facility.

RADAR APPROACH CONTROL FACILITY– A terminal ATC facility that uses radar and nonradar capabilities to provide approach control services to aircraft arriving, departing, or transiting airspace controlled by the facility.

    a. Provides radar ATC services to aircraft operating in the vicinity of one or more civil and/or military airports in a terminal area. The facility may provide services of a ground controlled approach (GCA); i.e., ASR and PAR approaches. A radar approach control facility may be operated by FAA, USAF, US Army, USN, USMC, or jointly by FAA and a military service. Specific facility nomenclatures are used for administrative purposes only and are related to the physical location of the facility and the operating service generally as follows:

        1. Army Radar Approach Control (ARAC) (US Army).

        2. Radar Air Traffic Control Facility (RATCF) (USN/FAA and USMC/FAA).

        3. Radar Approach Control (RAPCON) (USAF/FAA, USN/FAA, and USMC/FAA).

        4. Terminal Radar Approach Control (TRACON) (FAA).

        5. Airport Traffic Control Tower (ATCT) (FAA). (Only those towers delegated approach control authority)

RADAR CONTACT–

    a. Used by ATC to inform an aircraft that it is identified using an approved ATC surveillance source on an air traffic controller's display and that radar flight following will be provided until radar service is terminated. Radar service may also be provided within the limits of necessity and capability. When a pilot is informed of "radar contact," he/she automatically discontinues reporting over compulsory reporting points.

    b. The term used to inform the controller that the aircraft is identified and approval is granted for the aircraft to enter the receiving controllers airspace.

RADAR FLIGHT FOLLOWING– The observation of the progress of radar-identified aircraft, whose primary navigation is being provided by the pilot, wherein the controller retains and correlates the aircraft identity with the appropriate target or target symbol displayed on the radar scope.

RADAR IDENTIFICATION– The process of ascertaining that an observed radar target is the radar return from a particular aircraft.

RADAR POINT OUT– An action taken by a controller to transfer the radar identification of an aircraft to another controller if the aircraft will or may enter the airspace or protected airspace of another controller and radio communications will not be transferred.

RADAR SERVICE– A term which encompasses one or more of the following services based on the use of radar which can be provided by a controller to a pilot of a radar identified aircraft.
   a. Radar Monitoring– The radar flight-following of aircraft, whose primary navigation is being performed by the pilot, to observe and note deviations from its authorized flight path, airway, or route. When being applied specifically to radar monitoring of instrument approaches; i.e., with precision approach radar (PAR) or radar monitoring of simultaneous ILS,RNAV and GLS approaches, it includes advice and instructions whenever an aircraft nears or exceeds the prescribed PAR safety limit or simultaneous ILS RNAV and GLS no transgression zone.
   b. Radar Navigational Guidance– Vectoring aircraft to provide course guidance.
   c. Radar Separation– Radar spacing of aircraft in accordance with established minima.

RADAR SERVICE TERMINATED– Used by ATC to inform a pilot that he/she will no longer be provided any of the services that could be received while in radar contact. Radar service is automatically terminated, and the pilot is not advised in the following cases:

a. An aircraft cancels its IFR flight plan, except within Class B airspace, Class C airspace, a TRSA, or where Basic Radar service is provided.

b. An aircraft conducting an instrument, visual, or contact approach has landed or has been instructed to change to advisory frequency.

c. An arriving VFR aircraft, receiving radar service to a tower-controlled airport within Class B airspace, Class C airspace, a TRSA, or where sequencing service is provided, has landed; or to all other airports, is instructed to change to tower or advisory frequency.

d. An aircraft completes a radar approach.

RADAR TRAFFIC ADVISORIES– Advisories issued to alert pilots to known or observed radar traffic which may affect the intended route of flight of their aircraft.

REMOTE COMMUNICATIONS OUTLET (RCO)– An unmanned communications facility remotely controlled by air traffic personnel. RCOs serve FSSs. Remote Transmitter/Receivers (RTR) serve terminal ATC facilities. An RCO or RTR may be UHF or VHF and will extend the communication range of the air traffic facility. There are several classes of RCOs and RTRs. The class is determined by the number of transmitters or receivers. Classes A through G are used primarily for air/ground purposes. RCO and RTR class O facilities are nonprotected outlets subject to undetected and prolonged outages. RCO (O's) and RTR (O's) were established for the express purpose of providing ground-to-ground communications between air traffic control specialists and pilots located at a satellite airport for delivering en route clearances, issuing departure authorizations, and acknowledging instrument flight rules cancellations or departure/landing times. As a secondary function, they may be used for advisory purposes whenever the aircraft is below the coverage of the primary air/ground frequency.

ROGER– I have received all of your last transmission. It should not be used to answer a question requiring a yes or a no answer.

RNAV– (See AREA NAVIGATION (RNAV))

RUNWAY USE PROGRAM– A noise abatement runway selection plan designed to enhance noise abatement efforts with regard to airport communities for arriving and departing aircraft. These plans are developed into runway use programs and apply to all turbojet aircraft 12,500 pounds or heavier; turbojet aircraft less than 12,500 pounds are included only if the airport proprietor determines that the aircraft creates a noise problem. Runway use programs are coordinated with FAA offices, and safety criteria used in these programs are developed by the Office of Flight Operations. Runway use programs are administered by the Air Traffic Service as "Formal" or "Informal" programs.

    a. Formal Runway Use Program– An approved noise abatement program which is defined and acknowledged in a Letter of Understanding between Flight Operations, Air Traffic Service, the airport proprietor, and the users. Once established, participation in the program is mandatory for aircraft operators and pilots as provided for in 14 CFR Section 91.129.

    b. Informal Runway Use Program– An approved noise abatement program which does not require a Letter of Understanding, and participation in the program is voluntary for aircraft operators/pilots.

SAFETY ALERT– A safety alert issued by ATC to aircraft under their control if ATC is aware the aircraft is at an altitude which, in the controller's judgment, places the aircraft in unsafe proximity to terrain, obstructions, or other aircraft. The controller may discontinue the issuance of further alerts if the pilot advises he/she is taking action to correct the situation or has the other aircraft in sight.

    a. Terrain/Obstruction Alert– A safety alert issued by ATC to aircraft under their control if ATC is aware the aircraft is at an altitude which, in the controller's judgment, places the aircraft in unsafe proximity to terrain/obstructions; e.g., "Low Altitude Alert, check your altitude immediately."

    b. Aircraft Conflict Alert– A safety alert issued by ATC to aircraft under their control if ATC is aware of an aircraft that is not under their control at an altitude which, in the controller's judgment, places both aircraft in unsafe proximity to each other. With the alert, ATC will offer the pilot an alternate course of action when feasible; e.g., "Traffic Alert, advise you turn right heading zero niner zero or climb to eight thousand immediately."

Note: The issuance of a safety alert is contingent upon the capability of the controller to have an awareness of an unsafe condition. The course of action provided will be predicated on other traffic under ATC control. Once the alert is issued, it is solely the pilot's prerogative to determine what course of action, if any, he/she will take.

SEVERE WEATHER AVOIDANCE PLAN (SWAP)– An approved plan to minimize the affect of severe weather on traffic flows in impacted terminal and/or ARTCC areas. A SWAP is normally implemented to provide the least disruption to the ATC system when flight through portions of airspace is difficult or impossible due to severe weather.

SMALL UNMANNED AIRCRAFT SYSTEM (sUAS)– An unmanned aircraft weighing less than 55 pounds on takeoff, including everything that is on board or otherwise attached to the aircraft.

SQUAWK (Mode, Code, Function) – Used by ATC to instruct a pilot to activate the aircraft transponder and ADS–B Out with altitude reporting enabled, or (military) to activate only specific modes, codes, or functions. Examples: "Squawk five seven zero seven;" "Squawk three/alpha, two one zero five."

TAILWIND– Any wind more than 90 degrees to the longitudinal axis of the runway. The magnetic direction of the runway shall be used as the basis for determining the longitudinal axis.

TRACK OF INTEREST (TOI)– Displayed data representing an airborne object that threatens or has the potential to threaten North America or National Security. Indicators may include, but are not limited to: noncompliance with air traffic control instructions or aviation regulations; extended loss of communications; unusual transmissions or unusual flight behavior; unauthorized intrusion into controlled airspace or an ADIZ; noncompliance with issued flight restrictions/security procedures; or unlawful interference with airborne flight crews, up to and including hijack. In certain circumstances, an object may become a TOI based on specific and credible intelligence pertaining to that particular aircraft/ object, its passengers, or its cargo.

TRAFFIC ADVISORIES– Advisories issued to alert pilots to other known or observed air traffic which may be in such proximity to the position or intended route of flight of their aircraft to warrant their attention. Such advisories may be based on:

a. Visual observation.
b. Observation of radar identified and nonidentified aircraft targets on an ATC radar display, or
c. Verbal reports from pilots or other facilities.

Note 1: The word "traffic" followed by additional information, if known, is used to provide such advisories; e.g., "Traffic, 2 o'clock, one zero miles, southbound, eight thousand."

Note 2: Traffic advisory service will be provided to the extent possible depending on higher priority duties of the controller or other limitations; e.g., radar limitations, volume of traffic, frequency congestion, or controller workload. Radar/ nonradar traffic advisories do not relieve the pilot of his/her responsibility to see and avoid other aircraft. Pilots are cautioned that there are many times when the controller is not able to give traffic advisories concerning all traffic in the aircraft's proximity; in other words, when a pilot requests or is receiving traffic advisories, he/she should not assume that all traffic will be issued.

TRAFFIC ALERT AND COLLISION AVOIDANCE SYSTEM (TCAS)– An airborne collision avoidance system based on radar beacon signals which operates independent of ground-based equipment. TCAS-I generates traffic advisories only. TCAS-II generates traffic advisories, and resolution (collision avoidance) advisories in the vertical plane.

TRAFFIC INFORMATION SERVICE–BROADCAST (TIS–B)– The broadcast of ATC derived traffic information to ADS–B equipped (1090ES or UAT) aircraft. The source of this traffic information is derived from ground–based air traffic surveillance sensors, typically from radar targets. TIS–B service will be available throughout the NAS where there are both adequate surveillance coverage (radar) and adequate broadcast coverage from ADS–B ground stations. Loss of TIS–B will occur when an aircraft enters an area not covered by the GBT network. If this occurs in an area with adequate surveillance coverage (radar), nearby aircraft that remain within the adequate broadcast coverage (ADS–B) area will view the first aircraft. TIS–B may continue when an aircraft enters an area with inadequate surveillance coverage (radar); nearby aircraft that remain within the adequate broadcast coverage (ADS–B) area will not view the first aircraft.

TRAFFIC MANAGEMENT UNIT– The entity in ARTCCs and designated terminals directly involved in the active management of facility traffic. Usually under the direct supervision of an assistant manager for traffic management.

TRANSFERRING CONTROLLER– A controller/ facility transferring control of an aircraft to another controller/facility.

TRANSMITTING IN THE BLIND– A transmission from one station to other stations in circumstances where two-way communication cannot be established, but where it is believed that the called stations may be able to receive the transmission.

TRANSPONDER– The airborne radar beacon receiver/transmitter portion of the Air Traffic Control Radar Beacon System (ATCRBS) which automatically receives radio signals from interrogators on the ground, and selectively replies with a specific reply pulse or pulse group only to those interrogations being received on the mode to which it is set to respond.

TURBULENCE– An atmospheric phenomenon that causes changes in aircraft altitude, attitude, and/or airspeed with aircraft reaction depending on intensity. Pilots report turbulence intensity according to aircraft's reaction as follows:

a. Light– Causes slight, erratic changes in altitude and or attitude (pitch, roll, or yaw).

b. Moderate– Similar to Light but of greater intensity. Changes in altitude and or attitude occur but the aircraft remains in positive control at all times. It usually causes variations in indicated airspeed.

c. Severe– Causes large, abrupt changes in altitude and or attitude. It usually causes large variations in indicated airspeed. Aircraft may be momentarily out of control.

d. Extreme– The aircraft is violently tossed about and is practically impossible to control. It may cause structural damage.

UNMANNED AIRCRAFT SYSTEM (UAS)- An unmanned aircraft and its associated elements related to safe operations, which may include control stations (ground, ship, or air based), control links, support equipment, payloads, flight termination systems, and launch/recovery equipment. It consists of three elements: unmanned aircraft, control station, and data link.

VECTOR– A heading issued to an aircraft to provide navigational guidance by radar.

VFR CONDITIONS– Weather conditions equal to or better than the minimum for flight under visual flight rules. The term may be used as an ATC clearance/instruction only when:

a. An IFR aircraft requests a climb/descent in VFR conditions.

b. The clearance will result in noise abatement benefits where part of the IFR departure route does not conform to an FAA approved noise abatement route or altitude.

c. A pilot has requested a practice instrument approach and is not on an IFR flight plan.

Note: All pilots receiving this authorization must comply with the VFR visibility and distance from cloud criteria in 14 CFR Part 91. Use of the term does not relieve controllers of their responsibility to separate aircraft in Class B and Class C airspace or TRSAs as required by FAA Order JO 7110.65. When used as an ATC clearance/instruction, the term may be abbreviated "VFR;" e.g., "MAINTAIN VFR," "CLIMB/DESCEND VFR," etc.

VIDEO MAP– An electronically displayed map on the radar display that may depict data such as airports, heliports, runway centerline extensions, hospital emergency landing areas, NAVAIDs and fixes, reporting points, airway/route centerlines, boundaries, handoff points, special use tracks, obstructions, prominent geographic features, map alignment indicators, range accuracy marks, and/or minimum vectoring altitudes.

VISUAL APPROACH– An approach conducted on an instrument flight rules (IFR) flight plan which authorizes the pilot to proceed visually and clear of clouds to the airport. The pilot must, at all times, have either the airport or the preceding aircraft in sight. This approach must be authorized and under the control of the appropriate air traffic control facility. Reported weather at the airport must be: ceiling at or above 1,000 feet, and visibility of 3 miles or greater.

VISUAL FLIGHT RULES– Rules that govern the procedures for conducting flight under visual conditions. The term "VFR" is also used in the United States to indicate weather conditions that are equal to or greater than minimum VFR requirements. In addition, it is used by pilots and controllers to indicate type of flight plan.

WAKE TURBULENCE– A phenomenon that occurs when an aircraft develops lift and forms a pair of counter–rotating vortices.

WILCO– I have received your message, understand it, and will comply with it.

APPENDIX D: ARTCC DATA BLOCKS

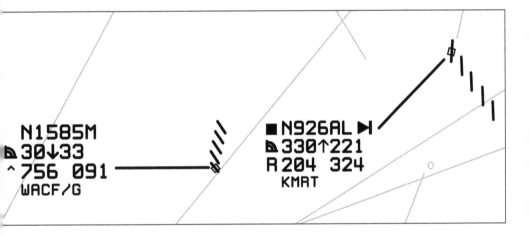

I was able to get pictures in the simulator at Washington ARTCC to use for the book cover. The data blocks at the ARTCC have several parts which all have meanings.

The top row is the aircraft call sign.

The second row is the assigned altitude on the left and on the right is the current altitude (if they differ).

The third row starts with the Computer Identification Number (CID), which is the number we use to type in all the clearances into the computer. On the right side is the aircraft's ground speed.

The fourth line is programmable by the individual controller. Most controllers have the aircraft's destination, but some have aircraft type. On the cover, I have one of each (KMRT for Marysville Airport in Ohio and WACF/G is a Waco YMF-5 with GPS).

The N926AL data block also has the new CPDLC buttons. On the left side, the solid white box shows the aircraft is logged into the CPDLC system, and my sector has control to send messages.

The angled "Wi-Fi" symbol is the voice indicator. We manually toggle it on and off to indicate when an aircraft is on our frequency. With voice-less check-ins through CPDLC, this will automatically appear when the aircraft confirms that they made the frequency change through the system.

The "R" means the next sector has taken the handoff.

On the right side of the N926AL data block, the arrow with the line is a button we can click to send a frequency change message through CPDLC to the pilots.

The "\" or "/" with the box over it is the radar target (aircraft). The ones in the trail are the histories – the previous targets.

NOTES

[1] Federal Aviation Administration (FAA). (2020, August). *Air Traffic By The Numbers*. U.S. Department of Transportation (USDOT). (March 16, 2022). https://www.faa.gov/air_traffic/by_the_numbers/media/Air_Traffic_by_the_Numbers_2020.pdf

[2] FAA. (2021, June 17). *Air Traffic Control* (FAA Job Order [JO] 7110.65Z). ¶2-3-5 Aircraft Identity and Table 2-3-8 President and Family. USDOT. (January 26, 2022).

[3] FAA. (2021, June 17). *Facility Operation and Administration* (FAA JO 7210.3CC). ¶5-1-2 The President, Vice President, and EXEC1F Aircraft Monitoring. USDOT. (January 26, 2022).

[4] FAA. (2021, June 17). *Air Traffic Control* (FAA JO 7110.65Z). ¶2-1-4. Operational Priority. USDOT. (January 26, 2022).

[5] FAA. (2021, June 17). *Air Traffic Control* (FAA JO 7110.65Z). ¶4-3-4. Departure Release, Hold for Release, Release Times, Departure Restrictions, and Clearance Void Times. USDOT. (January 26, 2022).

FAA. (2021, June 17). *Aeronautical Information Manual* (*AIM*). ¶5-2-7 Departure Restrictions, Clearance Void Times, Hold for Release, and Release Times. USDOT. (January 26, 2022).

[6] FAA. (2021, June 17). *Air Traffic Control* (FAA JO 7110.65Z). ¶10-4-3. Traffic Resumption. USDOT. (January 26, 2022).

[7] FAA. (2021, June 17). *Air Traffic Control* (FAA JO 7110.65Z). ¶10-3-1(a)1. Overdue Aircraft/Other Situations. USDOT. (January 26, 2022).

[8] FAA. (2021, June 17). *Air Traffic Control* (FAA JO 7110.65Z). ¶4-3-1. Departure Terminology. USDOT. (January 26, 2022).

[9] Responsibility and authority of the pilot in command, 14 C.F.R. § 91.3 (2022).

[10] FAA. (2021, June 17). *Facility Operation and Administration* (FAA JO 7210.3CC). ¶2-3-3 (b). Currency. USDOT. (January 26, 2022).

[11] FAA. (2021, June 17). *AIM*. ¶4-4-1(a). Clearance. (January 26, 2022).

[12] Compliance with ATC clearances and instructions, 14 C.F.R. § 91.123(a) (2022).

[13] FAA. (2021, June 17). *Air Traffic Control* (FAA JO 7110.65Z). ¶4-2-8(d)1-4. IFR-VFR and VFR-IFR Flights. USDOT. (January 26, 2022).
FAA. (2021, June 17). *AIM*. ¶4-4-9 VFR/IFR Flights. USDOT. (January 26, 2022).

[14] FAA. (2017, September 14). *Instrument Procedures Handbook*. Chapter 1. Departure Procedures and Categories of Departure Procedures. USDOT. (January 26, 2022). https://www.faa.gov/regulations_policies/handbooks_manuals/aviation/instrument_procedures_handbook/media/FAA-H-8083-16B.pdf

[15] FAA. (2021, June 17). *AIM*. ¶4-1-6. Pilot Visits to Air Traffic Facilities. USDOT. (January 26, 2022).

[16] National Transportation Safety Board (NTSB). (2018, October 10). *Aviation Accident Final Report* (Accident Number: WPR17FA057). (January 26, 2022).

[17] Cessna Aircraft Company (2004). *Information Manual Skyhawk SP* (Rev. 5). Section 4, Page 5. (January 26, 2022).

[18] FAA. (1982, November 9). *National Safety and Operational Criteria For Runway Use Programs* (FAA Order 8400.9). USDOT. (January 26, 2022).

[19] FAA. (2021, June 17). *AIM*. ¶4-4-7(c). Pilot Responsibility upon Clearance Issuance. USDOT. (January 26, 2022).

[20] FAA. (2021, June 17). *Air Traffic Control* (FAA JO 7110.65Z). ¶2-1-1(a)1. ATC Service. USDOT. (January 26, 2022).

[21] FAA. (2021, June 17). *Air Traffic Control* (FAA JO 7110.65Z). ¶5-7-3(c)1.b. Speed Assignments. USDOT. (January 26, 2022).

[22] Supplemental oxygen, 14 C.F.R. § 91.211(a)1 (2022).

[23] NTSB. (2018, September 4). *Aviation Accident Final Report* (Accident Number: CEN17FA168). (January 26, 2022).

[24] FAA. (2021, June 17). *AIM*. ¶7-1-7(a)1. Categorical Outlooks. USDOT. (January 26, 2022).

[25] FAA. (2021, June 17). *Air Traffic Control* (FAA JO 7110.65Z). ¶3-9-3(b)2. Departure Control Instructions. USDOT. (January 26, 2022).

[26] FAA. Spatial Disorientation [Brochure]. https://www.faa.gov/pilots/safety/pilotsafety-brochures/media/spatiald.pdf (March 1, 2022).

[27] FAA. (2021, June 17). *Air Traffic Control* (FAA JO 7110.65Z). ¶4-2-5(a)3. Route or Altitude Amendments. USDOT. (January 26, 2022).

[28] FAA. (2021, June 17). *Air Traffic Control* (FAA JO 7110.65Z). ¶2-4-15(c). Emphasis For Clarity. USDOT. (January 26, 2022).

[29] FAA. (2021, June 17). *Air Traffic Control* (FAA JO 7110.65Z). ¶2-4-9. Abbreviated Transmissions. USDOT. (January 26, 2022).

[30] FAA. (2021, June 17). *AIM*. ¶4-2-4(a)2. Aircraft Call Signs. USDOT. (January 26, 2022).

[31] FAA. (2021, June 17). *AIM*. ¶4-2-4(a)1. Aircraft Call Signs. USDOT. (January 26, 2022).

[32] FAA. (2021, June 17). *Air Traffic Control* (FAA JO 7110.65Z). ¶13-1-9(f). Acknowledgement of Automated Notification. USDOT. (January 26, 2022).

[33] FAA. (2021, June 17). *Air Traffic Control* (FAA JO 7110.65Z). ¶5-5-4(d). Minima. USDOT. (January 26, 2022).

[34] FAA. (2021, June 17). *Air Traffic Control* (FAA JO 7110.65Z). ¶4-5-1. Vertical Separation Minima. USDOT. (January 26, 2022).

[35] FAA. (2021, June 17). *Air Traffic Control* (FAA JO 7110.65Z). ¶5-5-4(d)3.(a)(3). Minima. USDOT. (January 26, 2022).

[36] FAA. (2021, June 17). *Air Traffic Control* (FAA JO 7110.65Z). ¶5-4-5(h)1. Transferring Controller Handoff. USDOT. (January 26, 2022).

[37] FAA. (2021, June 17). *Air Traffic Control* (FAA JO 7110.65Z). ¶5-2-18(c)1. Validation of Mode C Readout. USDOT. (January 26, 2022).

[38] FAA. (2021, June 17). *AIM*. ¶4-4-10(a). Adherence to Clearance. USDOT. (January 26, 2022).

FAA. (2021, June 17). *AIM*. ¶4-2-3(e). Compliance with Frequency Changes. USDOT. (January 26, 2022).

[39] FAA. (2021, June 17). *Air Traffic Control* (FAA JO 7110.65Z). ¶10-4-4(e). Communications Failure. USDOT. (January 26, 2022).

[40] FAA. (2021, June 17). *AIM*. ¶5-6-13. Interception Procedures. USDOT. (January 26, 2022).

[41] FAA. (2021, June 17). *Air Traffic Control* (FAA JO 7110.65Z). ¶2-1-27. Pilot Deviation Notification. USDOT. (January 26, 2022).

FAA. (2021, March). *Air Traffic Procedures Bulletin* [Fact Sheet]. https://www.faa.gov/air_traffic/publications/media/atb_march_2021.pdf (March 1, 2022).

[42] FAA. (2021, June 17). *Air Traffic Control* (FAA JO 7110.65Z). ¶10-2-1. Information

Requirements. USDOT. (January 26, 2022).

[43] FAA. (2021, June 17). *AIM*. ¶6-3-2. Obtaining Emergency Assistance. USDOT. (January 26, 2022).

[44] FAA. (2021, June 17). *Air Traffic Control* (FAA JO 7110.65Z). ¶10-1-1(c). Emergency Determinations. USDOT. (January 26, 2022).

[45] FAA. (2021, June 17). *Air Traffic Control* (FAA JO 7110.65Z). ¶10-2-5(a)2. Emergency Situations. USDOT. (January 26, 2022).

[46] Responsibility and authority of the pilot in command, 14 C.F.R. § 91.3(c) (2022).

[47] NTSB. (2002, February 19). *Flight Path Study- American Airlines Flight 77*. (January 26, 2022). https://www.ntsb.gov/about/Documents/Flight_Path_Study_AA77.pdf

[48] National Archives and Records Administration (NARA). (2004, May 6). *Memorandum for the Record*. (January 26, 2022). https://www.archives.gov/files/declassification/iscap/pdf/2011-048-doc22.pdf

[49] cjnewson88. (2012, August 10). *9/11 Pentagon Attack Flight 77 RADAR and ATC Recording - Reagan National* [Video]. YouTube. https://youtu.be/P0GI-1gja5Q

[50] FAA. (2021, June 17). *Air Traffic Control* (FAA JO 7110.65Z). ¶2-1-4(e). Operational Priority. USDOT. (January 26, 2022).

[51] FAA. (2021, June 17). *AIM*. ¶5-6-12. Emergency Security Control of Air Traffic (ESCAT). USDOT. (January 26, 2022).

FAA. (2021, June 17). *AIM*. ¶5-6-13. Intercept Procedures. USDOT. (January 26, 2022).

FAA. (2021, June 17). *AIM*. ¶ 5-6-14. Law Enforcement Operations by Civil and Military Organizations. USDOT. (January 26, 2022).

FAA. (2021, June 17). *AIM*. ¶6-2-3. Intercept and Escort. USDOT. (January 26, 2022).

[52] FAA. (2021, June 17). *AIM*. ¶5-6-13. Intercept Procedures. USDOT. (January 26, 2022).

FAA. (2021, June 17). *AIM*. Table 5-6-1. Intercepting Signals. USDOT. (January 26, 2022).

[53] FAA. (2021, June 17). *AIM*. ¶5-6-13(a)2. Interception Procedures. USDOT. (January 26, 2022).

[54] Aviation Safety Network. ASN Wikibase Occurrence #169583. (March 12, 2022). https://aviation-safety.net/wikibase/169583

[55] Responsibility and authority of the pilot in command, 14 C.F.R. § 91.3(b) (2022).

[56] NTSB. (2000, November 28). *Aircraft Accident Brief* (Accident Number: DCA00MA005). (January 26, 2022).

57 FAA. (2008, July 26). KFS66 Radar & Audio Recording [Video]. USDOT. (July 15, 2021).

58 FAA. (2008, July 26). UAL355 Radar & Audio Recording [Video]. USDOT. (July 15, 2021).

59 NTSB. (1986, January 31). *Aircraft Accident Report* (Accident Number: AAR-86/02). (January 26, 2022).

60 FAA. (2021, June 17). *Air Traffic Control* (FAA JO 7110.65Z). ¶10-1-3. Providing Assistance. USDOT. (January 26, 2022).

61 FAA. (2009, June 23). *Fighting Fires Caused By Lithium Type Batteries in Portable Electronic Devices* (Safety Alert for Operators [SAFO] 09013). USDOT. (January 26,2022). https://www.faa.gov/other_visit/aviation_industry/airline_operators/airline_safety/safo/all_safos/media/2009/SAFO09013.pdf

62 FAA. (2022, February 25). *Events with Smoke, Fire, Extreme Heat or Explosion Involving Lithium Batteries* [Data Set]. USDOT. (March 9, 2022). https://www.faa.gov/hazmat/resources/lithium_batteries/media/Battery_incident_chart.pdf

63 FAA. (2021, June 17). *AIM*. ¶4-4-20(a). Adherence to Clearance. USDOT. (January 26, 2022).

64 NTSB. (2015, November 15). *Aviation Accident Final Report* (Accident Number: ERA15MA259A). (January 26, 2022).

65 NTSB. (2016, November 21). *Midair Accidents*. [Video Playlist]. YouTube. https://youtube.com/playlist?list=PL5aVmmm4Qt9H9XDVaSTJawGLHP7ZVpdp6

66 Compliance with ATC clearances and instructions, 14 C.F.R. § 91.123(a) (2022).

67 FAA. (2021, June 17). *Air Traffic Control* (FAA JO 7110.65Z). ¶2-1-4. Operational Priority. USDOT. (January 26, 2022).

68 FAA. (2021, June 17). *Air Traffic Control* (FAA JO 7110.65Z). ¶2-1-29(a)1. RVSM Operations. USDOT. (January 26, 2022).
FAA. (2021, June 17). *AIM*. ¶4-6-1(c). RVSM Authorization. USDOT. (January 26, 2022).

69 FAA. (2021, June 17). *Air Traffic Control* (FAA JO 7110.65Z). ¶4-5-1(b). Vertical Separation Minima. USDOT. (January 26, 2022).

70 FAA. (2021, June 17). *Air Traffic Control* (FAA JO 7110.65Z). ¶5-4-10(f). En Route Fourth Line Data Block Usage. USDOT. (January 26, 2022).

71 FAA. (2008, July 26). N8045Y Radar & Audio Recording [Video]. USDOT. (July 15, 2021).

72 NTSB. (2011, December 19). *Aviation Accident Final Report* (Accident Number:

ERA11FA036). (January 26, 2022).

[73] FAA. (2021, June 17). *Air Traffic Control* (FAA JO 7110.65Z). ¶2-6-4(a). Issuing Weather and Chaff Areas. USDOT. (January 26, 2022).

[74] NTSB. (2011, December 19). *Aviation Accident Final Report* (Accident Number: ERA11FA036). (January 26, 2022).

[75] *Knous v. United States*, 183 F. Supp. 3d 1279 (N.D. Ga. 2016). https://casetext.com/case/knous-v-united-states-3

[76] Responsibility and authority of the pilot in command, 14 C.F.R. § 91.3(a) (2022).

[77] FAA. (2021, June 17). *Air Traffic Control* (FAA JO 7110.65Z). ¶2-1-6. Safety Alert. USDOT. (January 26, 2022).

[78] *Knous v. United States*, No. 16-11968 (11th Cir. Mar. 31, 2017). https://casetext.com/case/knous-v-united-states-1?

[79] FAA. (2021, June 17). *AIM.* ¶7-1-21(b) & Table 7-1-9. PIREPs Relating to Turbulence. USDOT. (January 26, 2022).

[80] FAA. (2021, June 17). *AIM.* ¶4-2-2(a). Radio Technique. USDOT. (January 26, 2022).

[81] FAA. (2021, June 17). *Air Traffic Control* (FAA JO 7110.65Z). ¶5-4-5(b). Transferring Controller Handoff. USDOT. (January 26, 2022).

[82] FAA. (2021, June 17). *Air Traffic Control* (FAA JO 7110.65Z). ¶5-2-18. Validation of Mode C Readout. USDOT. (January 26, 2022).

[83] FAA. (2021, June 17). *Air Traffic Control* (FAA JO 7110.65Z). ¶2-1-28(a). TCAS Resolution Advisories. USDOT. (January 26, 2022).
Compliance with ATC clearances and instructions, 14 C.F.R. § 91.123 (2022).

[84] FAA. (2021, June 17). *Air Traffic Control* (FAA JO 7110.65Z). ¶4-8-11. Practice Approaches. USDOT. (January 26, 2022).

[85] FAA. (2021, June 17). *Air Traffic Control* (FAA JO 7110.65Z). ¶4-8-11(a)2. Practice Approaches. USDOT. (January 26, 2022).

[86] FAA. (2021, June 17). *AIM.* ¶4-4-10(d). Adherence to Clearance. USDOT. (January 26, 2022).

[87] FAA. (2021, June 17). *Air Traffic Control* (FAA JO 7110.65Z). ¶4-5-1(a). Vertical Separation Minima. USDOT. (January 26, 2022).

[88] FAA. (2021, June 17). *Air Traffic Control* (FAA JO 7110.65Z). ¶4-5-7(b). Altitude Information. USDOT. (January 26, 2022).

[89] Compliance with ATC clearances and instructions, 14 C.F.R. § 91.123(a) (2022).

[90] Finney, D. (2019, July 15). United Airlines Flight 232: What you need to know about 1989 plane crash in Iowa. *Des Moines Register*. https://www.desmoinesregister.com/story/news/2019/07/15/united-airlines-flight-232-july-19-1989-crash-sioux-city-iowa-airport-pilot-al-haynes-denver-chicago/1717687001/

NTSB. (1990, November 1). *Aircraft Accident Report* (Accident Number: AAR-90/06). (January 26, 2022).

[91] Aeronautical Experience, 14 C.F.R. § 61.129(a)4.(i) (2022).

[92] FAA. (2021, June 17). *AIM*. ¶4-2-3(a)3. Contact Procedures. USDOT. (January 26, 2022).

[93] FAA. (2021, June 17). *Pilot/Controller Glossary*. Traffic Advisories. USDOT. (January 26, 2022).

FAA. (2021, June 17). *AIM*. ¶3-2-1(e). Traffic Advisories. USDOT. (January 26, 2022).

[94] FAA. (2021, June 17). *Air Traffic Control* (FAA JO 7110.65Z). ¶7-8-4. Establishing Two-Way Communications. USDOT. (January 26, 2022).

[95] FAA. (2021, June 17). *Air Traffic Control* (FAA JO 7110.65Z). ¶7-9-3(b). Methods. USDOT. (January 26, 2022).

[96] FAA. (2021, June 17). *AIM*. ¶7-1-7(a)2. Categorical Outlooks. USDOT. (January 26, 2022).

[97] FAA. (2021, June 17). *Air Traffic Control* (FAA JO 7110.65Z). ¶5-9-1(e)1. Vectors to Final Approach Course. USDOT. (January 26, 2022).

[98] FAA. (2021, June 17). *Air Traffic Control* (FAA JO 7110.65Z). ¶5-9-1(a)2. Vectors to Final Approach Course. USDOT. (January 26, 2022).

[99] NTSB. (2017, December 12). *Aviation Accident Final Report* (Accident Number: CEN16FA211). (January 26, 2022).

[100] KPRC 2 Click2Houston. (2019, February 4). *Air traffic control* tapes reveal final moments before 2016 plane crash [Video]. YouTube. https://www.youtube.com/watch?v=M_BzNwCNiMA

[101] NTSB. (2016, June 9). *HOU Tower Accident Package* (Accident Number: CEN16FA211). (January 26, 2022).

[102] FAA. (2021, June 17). *Air Traffic Control* (FAA JO 7110.65Z). ¶2-1-14(b). Coordinate Use of Airspace. USDOT. (January 26, 2022).

[103] Eric Dey. (2016, June 27). *Crash Cirrus N4252G* [Video]. YouTube. https://youtu.be/HEVLqRIqd84

flyflyfly. (2016, June 11). *Cirrus SR20 N4252G crash at William P Hobby Airport (KHOU)* [Audio]. LiveATC.net. https://www.liveatc.net/recordings.php

NTSB. (2016, June 9). *HOU Tower Accident Package* (Accident Number: CEN16FA211). (January 26, 2022).

[104] FAA. (2021, June 17). *AIM.* ¶4-1-17(b). Radar Assistance to VFR Aircraft. USDOT. (January 26, 2022).

[105] Powered civil aircraft with standard category U.S. airworthiness certificates: Instrument and equipment requirements, 14 C.F.R. § 91.205(b)12 (2022).

[106] FAA. (2021, June 17). *Air Traffic Control* (FAA JO 7110.65Z). ¶2-1-4. Operational Priority. USDOT. (January 26, 2022).

[107] FAA. (2021, June 17). *Air Traffic Control* (FAA JO 7110.65Z). ¶2-1-1(b)1. ATC Service. USDOT. (January 26, 2022).

[108] Takeoff and landings under IFR, 14 C.F.R. § 91.175(f) (2022).

[109] NTSB. (2018, September 4). *Aviation Accident Final Report* (Accident Number: ERA17FA155). (January 26, 2022).

[110] National *Air Traffic Controllers Association* (NATCA). (2017, April 21). *Nate Enders and Family Remembered.* https://www.natca.org/2017/04/21/april-21-2017-nate-enders-and-family-remembered/

[111] FAA. (2021, June 17). *AIM.* ¶6-2-4(d)1. Inflight Monitoring and Reporting. USDOT. (January 26, 2022).

[112] Anderson, M. (2017, April 19). Family from plane crash identified. *Ocala StarBanner.* https://www.ocala.com/story/news/local/2017/04/19/family-from-williston-plane-crash-identified/21341223007/

[113] NTSB. (2018, August 23). *Investigative Photographs* (Accident Number: ERA17FA155). (January 26, 2022).

[114] Aircraft Owners and Pilots Association (AOPA). (2018, December 28). Emergency Locator Transmitter (ELT). (March 19, 2022). https://www.aopa.org/advocacy/aircraft/aircraft-operations/emergency-locator-transmitters

[115] FAA. (2021, June 17). *Air Traffic Control* (FAA JO 7110.65Z). ¶10-4-1. Traffic Restrictions. USDOT. (January 26, 2022).
FAA. (2021, June 17). *Air Traffic Control* (FAA JO 7110.65Z). ¶10-4-3. Traffic Resumption. USDOT. (January 26, 2022).

[116] FAA. (2021, June 17). *Air Traffic Control* (FAA JO 7110.65Z). ¶10-3-1. Overdue Aircraft/Other Situations. USDOT. (January 26, 2022).

[117] FAA. (2021, June 17). *Air Traffic Control* (FAA JO 7110.65Z). ¶10-3-4. ALNOT. USDOT. (January 26, 2022).

[118] FAA. (2022, January 31). *FAA Wildlife Strike Database* [Data Set]. USDOT. (March

9, 2022). wildlife.faa.gov

[119] FAA. (2021, June 17). *AIM*. ¶6-2-4. Emergency Locator Transmitter (ELT). USDOT. (January 26, 2022).

[120] FAA. (2021, June 17). *AIM*. ¶4-2-4(c). Student Pilot Radio Identification. USDOT. (January 26, 2022).

[121] FAA. (2021, June 17). *Air Traffic Control* (FAA JO 7110.65Z). ¶3-10-5(a). Landing Clearance. USDOT. (January 26, 2022).

[122] FAA. (2018, July 25). *Wrong Surface Landing* [Video]. YouTube. https://youtu. be/5II-s_j35cI

[123] NTSB. (2020, September 22). *Aviation Incident Final Report* (Accident Number: DCA14IA016). (January 26, 2022).

[124] CBS/AP. (2013, November 21). Boeing 747 car jet lands at wrong airport. *CBS News*. https://www.cbsnews.com/news/boeing-cargo-jet-lands-at-wrong-airport/

[125] NTSB. (2014, June 4). Operations - *Factual Report of Group Chairman* (Accident Number: DCA14IA037). (January 26, 2022).

[126] Bergqvist, P. (2013, January 25). Cause of C-17 Landing at Too-Small Airport Revealed. *Flying Magazine*. https://www.flyingmag.com/ news-cause-c-17-landing-too-small-airport-revealed/

[127] NTSB. (2014, January 15). *Air Traffic Control – FAA Memo Wrong Airport Arrival Briefing* (Accident Number: DCA14IA037). (January 26, 2022).

[128] NTSB. (2015, December). *Landing at the Wrong Airport* (NTSB Safety Alert [SA]-033). USDOT. (January 26,2022). https://www.ntsb.gov/Advocacy/safety-alerts/Documents/SA-033.pdf

[129] NTSB. (2018, September 25). *Aviation Incident Report* (Accident Number: DCA17IA148). (January 26, 2022).

[130] NTSB. (2018, April 24). *Air Traffic Control Factual Report* (Number: DCA17IA148). (January 26, 2022).

[131] FAA. (2018, May 3). *Air Canada Flight 759 Near Miss – San Francisco Airport* [Video]. YouTube. https://youtu.be/aGQlQFn0euI

[132] FAA. *Boeing 747-206B and Boeing 747-121, KLM Flight 4805, PH-BUF, Pan American Flight 1736, N735PA*. https://lessonslearned.faa.gov/ll_main. cfm?TabID=1&LLID=52

[133] Hendrickson, Bob. (2021). *Crossing*. (Page 222). Author. (January 26, 2022).

[134] Hendrickson, Bob. (2021). *Crossing*. (Page 222). Author. (January 26, 2022).

[135] Hendrickson, Bob. (2021). *Crossing*. (Page 221). Author. (January 26, 2022).

[136] FAA. (2017, August 18). *Incorrect Airport Surface Approaches and Landings* (SAFO 17010). USDOT. (January 26,2022). https://www.faa.gov/other_visit/aviation_industry/airline_operators/airline_safety/safo/all_safos/media/2017/safo17010.pdf

[137] FAA. (2018, July 25). *Wrong Surface Landing* [Video]. YouTube. https://youtu.be/5II-s_j35cI

[138] FAA. (2016, February 16). *Movement Areas on Houston George Bush Intercontinental Airport that are not Visible from the Airport Air Traffic Control Tower* (Letter to Airmen: LTA-IAH-2). USDOT. (January 26,2022).

[139] King, John. (2019, January 30). Why Notams are Garbage. *Flying Magazine*. https://www.flyingmag.com/why-notams-are-garbage/

[140] NTSB. (2018, September 25). *Aviation Incident Report* (Accident Number: DCA17IA148). Page 71. (January 26, 2022).

[141] FAA. (2021, June 17). *Air Traffic Control* (FAA JO 7110.65Z). ¶4-7-12(a)3. Airport Conditions. USDOT. (January 26, 2022).

[142] Wright, T. (2017, September 27). Army Blackhawk Collides With Drone Over NYC. *Smithsonian Magazine*. https://www.smithsonianmag.com/air-space-magazine/army-blackhawk-hits-drone-180965047/

[143] University of Dayton Research Institute. (2018, September 13). *Impact tests prove large aircraft won't always win in collision with small drones* [Press release]. https://udayton.edu/udri/news/18-09-13-risk-in-the-sky.php

[144] DJI. (2018, October 19). *DJI Demands Withdrawal Of Misleading Drone Collision Video* [Press release]. https://www.dji.com/newsroom/news/dji-demands-withdrawal-of-misleading-drone-collision-video

[145] Compliance with ATC clearances and instructions, 14 C.F.R. § 91.123(a) (2022).

[146] FAA. (2021, June 17). *AIM*. ¶4-2-2a. Radio Technique. USDOT. (January 26, 2022).

[147] FAA. (2021, June 17). *Air Traffic Control* (FAA JO 7110.65Z). ¶5-5-5(b). Vertical Application. USDOT. (January 26, 2022).

FAA. (2021, June 17). *Air Traffic Control* (FAA JO 7110.65Z). ¶2-7-2(c). Altimeter Setting Issuance Below Lowest Usable FL. USDOT. (January 26, 2022).

[149] FAA. (2021, June 17). *Air Traffic Control* (FAA JO 7110.65Z). ¶10-2-1. Information Requests. USDOT. (January 26, 2022).

[150] FAA. (2021, June 17). *Air Traffic Control* (FAA JO 7110.65Z). ¶2-1-4(b)1. Operational Priority. USDOT. (January 26, 2022).

FAA. (2021, June 17). *AIM*. ¶4-2-4(a)2. Aircraft Call Signs. USDOT. (January 26, 2022).

[151] FAA. (2021, June 17). *AIM*. ¶5-1-8(f)11.Note 2. Domestic IFR Flights. USDOT. (January 26, 2022).

[152] IFR cruising altitudes or flight level, 14 C.F.R. § 91.179 (2022).

[153] FAA. Laser Incidents. (March 8, 2022). https://www.faa.gov/about/initiatives/lasers/laws

[154] FAA. (2021, June 17). *Air Traffic Control* (FAA JO 7110.65Z). ¶5-2-18. Validation of Mode C Readout. USDOT. (January 26, 2022).

BIBLIOGRAPHY

Morgan, Robert K with Powers, Ron. (2002). *The Man Who Flew The Memphis Belle.* New American Library.

Hogan, Kevin. (2013). *Invisible Influence.* John Wiley & Sons, Inc.

Hendrickson, Bob. (2021). *Crossing.* Author.

Shankwitz, Frank. (2016). *Wishman.* Sherpa Press.

Klein, Arlene. (2014). *The Grandfather of Possibilities.* Author.

Federal Aviation Administration (FAA). (2021, June 17). *Air Traffic Control* (FAA JO 7110.65Z). United States Department of Transportation (USDOT).

FAA. (2021, June 17). *Facility Operation and Administration* (FAA JO 7210.3CC). USDOT.

FAA. (2021, June 17). *Aeronautical Information Manual.* USDOT.

INDEX

I

J

K

L

M

ABOUT THE AUTHOR

Andy has been flying airplanes since he was eight years old and has earned a Bachelor's of Science in Aviation from the University of North Dakota.

Working as an Air Traffic Control Specialist or Front-Line Manager, Andy has served throughout the eastern United States at several Federal Aviation Administration (FAA) facilities including Cleveland Air Route Traffic Control Center (ARTCC), Chicago ARTCC, Charleston Terminal Radar Approach Control (TRACON) and Washington ARTCC.

In addition, Andy was an ATC subject matter expert for the FAA's Air Traffic Safety Oversight (AOV) at FAA Headquarters in Washington, D.C.

As a member of Civil Air Patrol, Andy volunteers his time as a Search & Rescue / Disaster Relief Mission Pilot.

Outside of flying, Andy is a real estate investor and public speaker. Andy could be an excellent choice for your next event and is available internationally for keynote addresses and aviation presentations.

To contact Andy, or find out more information to have Andy as your next speaker, visit his website: atcAndy.com or email Andy@atcAndy.com.

Lightning Source UK Ltd.
Milton Keynes UK
UKHW020606090223
416722UK00016B/1002/J